DATE DUE

DE 9 06			

DEMCO 38-296

Does Training for the Disadvantaged Work?

LARRY L. ORR
HOWARD S. BLOOM
STEPHEN H. BELL
FRED DOOLITTLE
WINSTON LIN
GEORGE CAVE

With the assistance of:
Hans Bos
Neelima Grover
Michelle Wood
Robert Kornfeld, and
Aniruddha Bonnerjee

DOES TRAINING FOR THE DISADVANTAGED WORK?

Evidence from the National JTPA Study

An Abt Associates Study

THE URBAN INSTITUTE PRESS
Washington, D.C.

2100 M Street, N.W.
Washington, D.C. 20037

Library of Congress Cataloging in Publication Data

Does Training for the Disadvantaged Work? Evidence from the
National JTPA Study / [Larry L. Orr . . . et al.]

1. Occupational Training—Government Policy—United States—Evaluation.
2. Poor—Employment—Government Policy—United States.   3. United
States. Job Training Partnership Act.   I. Orr, Larry L.

HD5715.2.I558	1995	95-43052
331.25′92′0973—dc20		CIP

ISBN 0-87766-647-4 (paper, alk. paper)
ISBN 0-87766-646-6 (cloth, alk. paper)

Urban Institute books are printed on acid-free paper whenever possible.

Printed in the United States of America.

Distributed in North America by University Press of America:

4720 Boston Way
Lanham, MD 20706

Does Training for the Disadvantaged Work? Evidence from the National JTPA Study, by Larry L. Orr, Howard S. Bloom, Stephen H. Bell, Fred Doolittle, Winston Lin, and George Cave is an Abt Associates study.

The Urban Institute Press is a refereed press established and supported by the Urban Institute, a nonprofit policy research and educational organization established in Washington, D.C. in 1968. Through work that ranges from broad conceptual studies to administrative and technical assistance, the Institute's goals are to sharpen thinking about societal problems and efforts to solve them, improve government decisions, and performance, and increase citizen awareness of important policy choices. Its Press disseminates policy research on important social and economic problems by authors from both outside and inside the Institute. Publication decisions are made by the Press's Editorial Advisory Board on the basis of referee reports solicited from recognized experts in the field.

Conclusions are those of the authors and do not necessarily reflect the views of staff members, officers, trustees, advisory groups, or funders of the Urban Institute or Abt Associates.

*   *   *

The Urban Institute gratefully acknowledges the contribution from Sara Lee Corporation which made publication of this study possible.

Abt Associates is an employee-owned research firm, which performs program evaluation, policy analysis, and technical assistance for government agencies. It is built on the concept that sound information and empirical analysis are the best foundation for decision making. Founded in 1965, Abt has long been a leader in the design, implementation, and analysis of social experiments and program evaluation based on experimental designs.

Abt has offices in Cambridge and Amherst, Massachusetts; Bethesda, Maryland; Chicago, Illinois; and Moscow, Russia. Its clients include virtually every major U.S. government agency, a number of state governments, and foreign governments and international organizations of five continents.

ACKNOWLEDGMENTS

The National JTPA Study was conceived and recommended to the U.S. Department of Labor (DOL) by the Job Training Longitudinal Survey Advisory Panel chaired by Ernst Stromsdorfer; the panel also included Howard S. Bloom, Robert Boruch, Michael E. Borus, Judith M. Gueron, Alan Gustman, Peter Rossi, Fritz Scheuren, Marshall Smith, and Frank Stafford. The pathbreaking decision by DOL's Employment and Training Administration to implement a classical experimental evaluation of an ongoing national program was also influenced by the strong recommendation of the National Research Council Committee on Youth Employment Programs, chaired by Robinson G. Hollister, Jr., that random assignment designs be used to evaluate employment and training programs.

We are particularly grateful to Raymond J. Uhalde, Deputy Assistant Secretary for Employment and Training Administration, U.S. Department of Labor, who created the project and ensured that it was sustained throughout the lengthy period required to bring it to fruition. Other staff members of the Department of Labor who played a major role in formulating and implementing the project were David Lah, John Heinberg, Karen Greene, Dan Ryan, and Gerald Gundersen.

Thanks are also due for the insightful advice offered at key junctures by the Advisory Panel for the National JTPA Study: Isabel V. Sawhill, chair; John Bishop, Nancy Bross, Gary Burtless, Richard Hayes, Christopher King, Marilyn E. Manser, Ronald L. Oaxaca, Gary Reed, and Ernst Stromsdorfer.

The co-principal investigators for the National JTPA Study impact and benefit-cost analyses were Project Director Larry L. Orr, of Abt Associates Inc.; Howard S. Bloom, of New York University; and Judith M. Gueron, of the Manpower Demonstration Research Corporation (MDRC). Fred Doolittle, of MDRC, was Project Director for implementation of the study and process analysis. Stephen H. Bell, of Abt Associates, and George Cave, of MDRC, were the senior economists responsible for the impact analyses for adult women and youths, respectively. Winston Lin, of Abt Associates, made major contributions to the estimation methodology, performed all of the computations for the report, and drafted the appendixes.

Other members of the research team who made extensive contributions to the impact and benefit-cost analyses include Neelima Grover, Aniruddha Bonnerjee, and Robert Kornfeld, of Abt Associates; and Johannes (Hans) Bos and Cyril Toussaint, of MDRC. Major roles in crafting the analysis were played both by Judith M. Gueron, president of MDRC, and by Stephen Kennedy, Chief Social Scientist of Abt Associates and technical reviewer for the study. A number of helpful suggestions were also made by two anonymous reviewers for the Urban Institute Press.

Members of the research team who made major contributions to the development of the massive database compiled by the study include Michelle Wood, of Abt Associates, who supervised the collection and processing of the Background Information Forms and the collection and analysis of the cost data; Marjorie Morrissey, of the National Opinion Research Center, who served as survey director for the follow-up surveys; Robert Teitel, who supervised the preparation of the database, with the assistance of Kevin Ward, Peter Hurley, Aniruddha Bonnerjee, David Bell, Rhonda Byrnes, and Neelima Grover, all of Abt Associates; and Kirsten Alexander and Margie Washington, who produced the final report of the National JTPA Study. At MDRC, James Kemple and John Wallace served as liaisons between the impact analysis and the implementation analysis, and Robert Winthrop contributed to chapter 3.

This study owes its existence to the commitment and energies of the staff at the 16 JTPA service delivery areas who not only agreed to participate but also performed the many tasks necessary to implement the study. The following individuals served in the positions indicated during the course of the study:

Site	SDA/PIC Director	Study Coordinator
Butte, Montana	Sue Mohr	John Ilgenfritz Candi Watts
Cedar Rapids, Iowa	Robert Ballantyne	Bonnie Pisarik
Coosa Valley, Georgia	James H. Layton C. D. Rampley	Angeline Bedwell Gwen Dellinger
Corpus Christi, Texas	Irma Caballero Debra Seeger	Billie O'Dowdy

Site	SDA/PIC Director	Study Coordinator
Decatur, Illinois	John Roark	Jacque Matson
Fort Wayne, Indiana	Steve Corona	Betty Lou Nault
Heartland, Florida	Jack Lyons Clifton Thomas, Jr.	Alice Cobb
Jackson, Mississippi	Beneta Burt Archester Hampton	Archester Hampton
Jersey City, New Jersey	William Colon Anthony Corsi Jerry DelPiano	Keith Davis Judith Martin
Larimer County, Colorado	Neil Gluckman	Joni Friedman
Marion, Ohio	Samantha Carroll Jill Navarrette Patrick Powell	Steven Pyles
Northwest Minnesota	Gail Butenhoff	Ken Barborak
Oakland, California	Susan Caldwell Gay Plair Cobb	Paulette Cathey Edna David Ralph Zackheim
Omaha, Nebraska	Ola M. Anderson Fernando Lecouna III	Karen Benson
Providence, Rhode Island	William D. Fornicola Robert Palumbo Ronald Perillo	Ed Canner Bob Lonardo
Springfield, Missouri	Chet Dixon	Mary Schaeffer

CONTENTS

FOREWORD

Achieving economic self-sufficiency through work is a fundamental goal of our society. Among the policies necessary to reach this goal are training programs that enable the disadvantaged to become successful in the job market.

The federal government has sponsored job-training programs for unemployed and economically disadvantaged Americans over more than three decades, starting with the Manpower Development and Training Act (MDTA) of 1962. MDTA was replaced with the Comprehensive Employment and Training Act (CETA) of 1973. CETA was replaced, in turn, with the Job Training Partnership Act (JTPA) of 1982.

Researchers have tried to measure the impacts of all these programs, with widely varying and often inconsistent results. Definitive answers have been elusive because of the inherent difficulty of separating out what happened *as the result of* the program experience from what would have happened without the program.

The National JTPA Study is the first evaluation of a major ongoing national program that uses the classical experimental design of random assignment. This design solves the problem of measuring "what would have happened" by dividing the group of program eligibles into a group that is allowed to enter the program (treatment group) and a group that is not (control group). Only the program experience differentiates the two groups, ensuring that any systematic differences in job market success are the result of the program.

The JTPA impact analysis undertaken by Abt Associates—based on data covering over 20,000 JTPA applicants in 16 local programs across the country—provides definitive answers to three fundamental policy questions: What works among the array of program components currently used in employment and training policy? For whom? Is it worth the cost?

The Urban Institute Press is pleased to publish the results of this landmark study. It is our hope that the information it provides will contribute to the ongoing debate about how to improve the skills of the American people and make the dream of economic independence a reality for increasing numbers of disadvantaged Americans.

William Gorham

BACKGROUND: JTPA TITLE II YEAR-ROUND PROGRAMS, PREVIOUS RESEARCH, AND THE NATIONAL JTPA STUDY

The National JTPA Study was commissioned by the U.S. Department of Labor (DOL) in 1986, as part of the department's legislated mandate to study the effectiveness of programs funded by the Job Training Partnership Act of 1982 (JTPA). The original JTPA legislation specified that analysis be conducted of the "increase in employment and earnings for participants, reduced support costs, [and] increased tax revenues" (sec. 454 of JTPA).

The National JTPA Study employs a *randomized experiment* to estimate the impacts of JTPA Title II year-round programs operated by 16 local service delivery areas (SDAs) in the continental United States. Specifically, over the period November 1987 through September 1989, Title II eligible adults and out-of-school youths who applied to these 16 study sites and were judged by intake staff to be appropriate for enrollment in JTPA were randomly assigned to one of two groups: a *treatment group*, whose members were given access to program services, and a *control group*, whose members were not allowed to receive program services for a period of 18 months after their random assignment.[1] The study compares the subsequent earnings, employment, and welfare receipt of these two matched groups to estimate Title II impacts on the populations served at the sites.

The decision by the Department of Labor to sponsor this type of study was based both on a growing consensus among researchers that a randomized experiment was necessary to achieve valid and reliable evidence of the impacts of employment and training programs,[2] as well as on the unanimous recommendation to that effect by a research advisory panel convened by DOL to determine how best to evaluate JTPA programs (Stromsdorfer et al., 1985).

The 16 SDAs that participated in the study represent a broad range of programs, program participants, and labor markets. The study's findings—based on survey data, SDA administrative records, data from state unemployment insurance agencies, and data from state and local welfare agencies—provide the first valid and reliable evidence of the impacts of JTPA Title II year-round programs. The analysis focuses on a variety of different groups within the study sample of eligible program applicants. A first set comprises four main *target groups* of Title II: economically disadvantaged adult women and men, and female and male out-of-school youths.[3] A second set comprises groups defined by clusters of specific program services, or service strategies, recommended for participants by SDA intake staff. The study's analysis of these *service strategy subgroups* offers insight into the impacts of different combinations of specific program services on the groups of program participants deemed likely to benefit from them. Finally, the study also examines impacts on a number of *key subgroups* defined by individual characteristics—such as ethnicity, race, or such barriers to employment as welfare receipt, limited education, and limited recent work experience—that figure prominently in JTPA policy debates.

This report presents estimates of program impacts on the earnings of each of these groups over the first 30 months after random assignment. The report also presents estimates of program impacts on the attainment of a high school diploma or a general educational development (GED) certificate and on the receipt of Aid to Families with Dependent Children (AFDC) benefits and food stamps benefits. To provide a comprehensive framework for assessing the importance of those estimated impacts, the report concludes with a comparison of program costs and benefits. A companion volume to this report (Doolittle, 1993) describes how the 16 study sites (SDAs) operated their JTPA Title II year-round programs and how the randomized experiment was implemented.

The remainder of this chapter offers background on the JTPA program nationally, the results and limitations of previous research on employment and training program impacts, and the more specific goals and objectives of the National JTPA Study.

JTPA TITLE II PROGRAM NATIONALLY

The federal government has sponsored job-training programs for unemployed and economically disadvantaged Americans for almost three decades. These programs began with the Manpower Development and Training Act of 1962 (MDTA), which was replaced in 1973 by the Comprehensive Employment and Training Act (CETA), which, in turn, was replaced in 1982 by the Job Training Partnership Act (JTPA), the current federal program. Title II of JTPA—the focus of the present study—is designated to serve the employment and training needs of economically disadvantaged adults 22 years of age and older and youths 16 to 21 years old.[4] According to the statement of purpose in effect at the start of this study, Title II of JTPA was intended "to prepare youth and unskilled adults for entry into the labor force and to afford job training to those economically disadvantaged individuals and other individuals facing serious barriers to employment, who are in special need of such training, to obtain productive employment" (sec. 2 of JTPA). For adults, the program is intended to increase earnings and employment and reduce dependence on welfare. For youths, the program has somewhat broader objectives, which include fostering youths' attainment of educational credentials and occupational competencies, as well as increasing their earnings and employment.

JTPA was one of the first "New Federalism" programs, which sought to decentralize program planning and oversight. As such, it has stimulated wide variation in program content and administration. The ability to tailor programs to local needs and opportunities, rather than to implement a standard intervention, is fundamental to JTPA.

Administration

JTPA Title II year-round programs are funded by the federal government. At the time of this study, JTPA spent $1.6 billion annually to serve roughly 1 million participants (U.S. General Accounting Office, 1991). The states coordinate and regulate local JTPA activities, which are administered by county and city governments. Within this framework, the federal government allocates JTPA funds in two parts. The largest part, 77 percent of adult funding and 82 percent of youth funding, is allocated by a formula directly to the local SDAs administering the program.[5] The remaining funds are allocated to the states as set-asides to promote specific program objectives.[6]

Nationally, there are 649 SDAs, covering every part of the country. Formed by one or more local governments, the SDAs operate local JTPA programs with guidance from a Private Industry Council. These PICs comprise representatives of local businesses, unions, social service agencies, and employment and training organizations.

Services

SDAs provide *specific employment and training services* (often termed *program activities*) either directly through their own staffs or by contracting with other local service providers, such as public schools, community colleges, proprietary schools, and community-based organizations. The specific services offered come in many different forms, but they generally fall under one of six basic categories:

- *Classroom training in occupational skills (CTOS)*—in-class instruction in specific job skills such as word processing, electronics repair, and home health care;
- *On-the-job training (OJT)*—subsidized training that takes place as part of a paying job, often in a private-sector firm (JTPA usually pays half of the wages for up to six months, but the jobs are supposed to be permanent);
- *Job search assistance (JSA)*—assessment of participants' job skills and interests, along with training in job-finding techniques and help in locating job openings;
- *Basic education*—including adult basic education (ABE), high school or General Educational Development (GED, or high school equivalency) preparation, and English as a Second Language (ESL);
- *Work experience*—temporary entry-level jobs designed to provide basic employment skills and instill effective work habits (the jobs may be subsidized by JTPA if they are in the public sector); and
- *Miscellaneous services*—including assessment, job-readiness training, customized training, vocational exploration, job shadowing, and tryout employment, among a variety of other services.

For adult and out-of-school youth "terminees" who were enrolled in Title II programs nationwide during the sample intake period for the present study (November 1987 to September 1989), the most common *specific* services received were on-the-job training (28 percent of JTPA enrollees), classroom training in occupational skills (28 percent), and job search assistance (25 percent).[7]

Participants

Among the adults and out-of-school youths who were enrolled in Title II year-round programs during the sample intake period for the present study, 95 percent were classified as economically disadvantaged.[8] About 86 percent were identified as facing one or more barriers to employment, including limited education, limited recent work experience, and others.[9] The adults and out-of-school youths who enrolled in JTPA during this period were 54 percent female and 46 percent male. In terms of their ethnic backgrounds, 54 percent were white, 30 percent were black, and 12 percent were Hispanic. About 65 percent were high school graduates, 48 percent were receiving some form of public assistance when they applied to JTPA, and 29 percent were receiving Aid to Families with Dependent Children (AFDC).

Performance

One distinguishing feature of JTPA is its emphasis on program performance standards, especially with regard to the return on the program's investment in human capital, or the labor market skills and experience of program participants. For example, as stated in section 106(a) of the original JTPA legislation:

> The Congress recognizes that job training is an investment in human capital and not an expense. In order to determine whether that investment has been productive, the Congress finds that—
>
> (1) it is essential that criteria for measuring the return on this investment be developed; and
> (2) the basic return on the investment is to be measured by the increased employment and earnings of participants and the reductions in welfare dependency.

As a result of this emphasis, DOL has expended considerable effort to develop a system of performance standards by which to judge SDAs' achievement of program goals.[10] The standards for adults focus on employment and wage rates for participants in general and for welfare recipients in particular; those for youths focus on employment and attainment of one or more measures of skills enhancement. DOL also established standards for program costs, but less emphasis has been placed on those standards in the past several years.

Among the adults who entered Title II during the sample intake period for the present study, 69 percent had entered an unsubsidized job before leaving the program (that is, before their enrollment was terminated). The average hourly wage for those jobs was $5.86. Among out-of-school youths, 71 percent entered an unsubsidized job, began further training, or achieved another goal defined by DOL as a "positive termination."[11]

These JTPA performance indicators measure certain *outcomes* of participating in JTPA Title II programs, but they provide no indication of program impacts. For example, the fact that 69 percent of adult terminees found an unsubsidized job does not mean that JTPA caused their employment to occur. It is possible that all of these terminees who found a job might have done so without access to JTPA; if this were true, then we would have to say the program had no impact. On the other hand, if very few adult terminees would have found a job without JTPA, then the program could be judged to have had a large impact. In other words, a program outcome measure alone does not allow us to determine the impact of the program. To measure JTPA program *impacts*, the labor market outcomes of program participants must be compared with the outcomes participants would have experienced without the program, as measured by the experience of a control group whose members did not have access to the program.

Recent Policy Amendments

Because the Job Training Partnership Act was enacted as permanent legislation, it has not been subject to periodic reauthorizations, as CETA was. The JTPA program has therefore had a more stable history than its immediate predecessor, and was already well-established when this study began in 1986.

In 1986 Congress instituted minor changes in the program, and in 1988 DOL established new performance standards. On September 7, 1992, President George Bush signed the Job Training Reform Amendments of 1992 into law (PL 102-367). These amendments to JTPA address the following issues, among others:

- *Program targeting.* In response to concerns that JTPA's emphasis on performance standards discourages SDAs from serving clients who are most in need, the amendments require that at least 65 percent of the adults and youths in the year-round program be persons with identifiable barriers to employment.
- *Program services.* The amendments require a formal objective assessment and an individual service strategy for all program participants. Basic skills and occupational skills training must be provided if the assessment suggests they are needed, and work experience or job search assistance may not be provided alone unless the assessment indicates this is appropriate. Furthermore, enrollment in on-the-job training is limited to six months, and this period must vary in accordance with the skill level for which training is provided.
- *Program performance.* The amendments specify that incentive grants to SDAs be based in part on the extent to which they serve

persons with identifiable barriers to employment. In addition, performance standards must now reflect participants' acquisition of basic skills, achievement of specific occupational competencies, or attainment of a high school equivalency credential.

- *Programs for youths.* The amendments provide a separate title, II-C, for year-round programs for youths. At least 50 percent of the participants in this new title must be out-of-school youths. The Summer Youth Employment and Training program, Title II-B, is maintained as a separate program.
- *Other issues.* The new legislation also restructures current limitations on how SDAs can spend program funds, it modifies the basic formula for allocating JTPA funds to SDAs, it requires procedures to increase the fiscal accountability of SDAs, it specifies improvements to the data collected about local programs, and it includes provisions to enhance the coordination of JTPA programs with other human service programs.

PREVIOUS STUDIES OF EMPLOYMENT AND TRAINING PROGRAMS

Researchers have been trying to measure the impacts of employment and training programs for as long as the programs have been part of federal social policy. Since the passage of MDTA in 1962, literally scores of these studies have been conducted.

Central Methodological Problem

The central methodological problem in all these studies has been how to determine what the labor market experience of participants would have been without their access to the program in question. The most common approach has been to select a *comparison* group of persons who are as similar to program participants as possible, but who did not participate in the program. The labor market outcomes of this comparison group have then been used to estimate what the participants labor market outcomes would have been in the absence of the program. In addition, researchers have used statistical models to adjust their estimates for observed differences between participants (the *treatment group*) and the comparison group.

The problem stems from the fact that the only way to adjust for differences between these two groups is by using individual characteristics that can be measured. Thus, one cannot control directly for characteristics that affect labor market outcomes but that cannot be measured fully, such as motivation. Nevertheless, if these unmeasured or partially measured factors are the same for program participants and comparison group members, on average, or if they correlate in specific ways with factors that can be measured, they can be fully accounted for in estimates of program impacts.

For example, if the motivation level of participants and comparison group members were the same, the effect of this factor on the labor market outcomes of each group would be the same. In this case, the unmeasured characteristics of the two groups would balance out and would not bias the estimates of program impacts.[12] But if unmeasured characteristics that affect labor market outcomes are not well balanced between program participants and the comparison group, the impact estimates produced by comparison group methods will be biased. For example, if the motivation of program participants were higher than that of comparison group members, it would not be appropriate to attribute all of the subsequent difference between the earnings of these two groups to the program being studied. To do so would overstate the actual program impact, because even without the program, the participants would have earned more, on average, than the comparison group members. This problem of *selection bias* has been insurmountable for comparison group studies of the impacts of employment and training programs. Although a wide range of sophisticated statistical matching and modeling procedures have been used to address the problem, no acceptable solution has yet been found.

The basic limitation of the studies is simply that without perfect measures of the unmeasured variables, one cannot be certain whether the selection bias has been removed. In fact, that certainty is possible only when the problem does not exist. Comparison group studies therefore require an assumption that the problem has been resolved by the procedures used to adjust for selection bias. But different procedures have produced different results; and we cannot choose among the procedures with confidence because we cannot know which procedures most successfully removed the selection bias.

Random assignment is an alternative way to choose a group whose experience will reflect what program participants' labor market outcomes would have been without access to the program. Researchers are increasingly using this approach, which relies on a *control group* matched to the treatment group, because of its ability to eliminate selection bias. Basically, random assignment is like a lottery. Individuals first apply to a program and are screened to ensure their eligibility. Next, much like the flip of a coin, a computer randomly determines who can enter the program and who cannot. If there are more applicants than can be served by the program anyway, this procedure is a fair way to allocate the scarce resources involved. In addition, the laws of probability ensure that the applicants who are denied access to the program (the control group) do not differ systematically from the applicants who are offered access (the treatment group) in *any* way, measurable or not. Thus, the subsequent labor market outcomes of control group members serve as valid estimates of what these outcomes would have been for treatment group members if the latter had not had access to the program. And therefore, the difference between the labor market outcomes of the treatment and control groups represents a valid estimate of the true impact of the program.

Early Studies

The numerous studies of employment and training programs conducted in the 1960s and 1970s were generally limited to measuring short-term postprogram earnings and employment, as well as a few demographic characteristics, for program participants and members of a comparison group. Differences in demographic characteristics between the treatment group and comparison group were controlled for using standard statistical methods (ordinary least squares regressions). Because the data and statistical techniques used to control for selection bias in these studies were inadequate, little systematic knowledge emerged (see Perry et al., 1975).

Second-Generation Studies

Several studies conducted later in the 1970s and early 1980s were based on longitudinal earnings data for program participants and comparison group members (Ashenfelter, 1978; Kiefer, 1979; Cooley, McGuire, and Prescott, 1979; and Bloom, 1984b). These and subsequent studies applied relatively sophisticated statistical models to extensive data on large samples.[13]

The basic approach was to adjust for differences in the preprogram earnings patterns of participants and comparison group members when comparing the postprogram earnings of the two groups. Here the assumption was that because preprogram earnings predict participants' postprogram earnings without the program, controlling for the difference in preprogram earnings between participants and comparison group members would reduce selection bias to an acceptable level.

National CETA Evaluations

Optimism in the research community about the ability of longitudinal earnings data to control statistically for treatment-control group differences in preprogram earnings and thereby yield valid program impact estimates led to the adoption of this second-generation approach as the core strategy for the national CETA evaluations, which began in the 1970s. The evaluations were based on data from the Continuous Longitudinal Manpower Survey (CLMS), the Current Population Survey (CPS), and earnings records maintained by the Social Security Administration (SSA).

The CLMS was a large-scale survey of CETA participants. It collected detailed information on their individual characteristics and linked this information to annual earnings data on sample members in SSA records. The comparison group for the evaluations was drawn from the CPS. The CLMS and CPS data enabled researchers to combine statistical models of longitudinal earnings with a variety of procedures to match members of the comparison group to CETA participants, based on the detailed data on individual characteristics available for both groups.[14]

Several major studies were commissioned to estimate CETA impacts from the CLMS. Exhibit 1.1 draws from Barnow's (1987) detailed review of these studies.[15] Most striking are the results for male participants, which ranged from estimates of small earnings *gains* to large earnings *losses*, depending on the study. But the results for females also varied substantially; three of the four studies found that CETA markedly increased annual earnings, but the fourth found almost no effect. Thus, for both males and females, the estimates of CETA impacts depended critically on the statistical method used.[16] And according to Barnow (1987: 157): "Data limitations and the inability to adequately test the validity of the selection processes assumed make it impossible to determine which studies modeled the process correctly."

Randomized Experiments

In the mid-1970s researchers began to use an alternative approach, randomized experiments, to measure the impacts of employment and training programs. This approach, as noted earlier, employs a lottery

Exhibit 1.1 SUMMARY OF ESTIMATED CETA IMPACTS ON ANNUAL EARNINGS, FROM FOUR STUDIES USING CONTINUOUS LONGITUDINAL MANPOWER SURVEY (CLMS)

Study (year published)	Impact (in $)			
	Adult women:		Adult men:	
	White females	Minority females	White males	Minority males
Bloom and McLaughlin (1982)[a]	800** to 1,300**		200	
Dickinson, Johnson, and West (1984)[b]	13		−690**	
Bassi (1983)[c]	740** to 778**	426** to 671**	N.A.	117 to 211
Westat, Inc. (1984a)[d]	408** to 534**	336** to 762**	−4 to 500**	−104 to 658**

Source: Barnow (1987: 182–83, table 3).

a. Sample members were ages 25–60; impacts were for calendar years 1976–78, converted to 1980 dollars.

b. Sample members were ages 22–64; impacts were for calendar year 1978, reported in nominal dollars.

c. Sample members were ages 23–60; impacts were for calendar years 1977–78, reported in nominal dollars.

d. Sample members were ages 14–60; impacts were for calendar years 1977–78, reported in nominal dollars.

** Statistically significant at the .05 level (two-tailed test).

to choose which eligible applicants to a program are allowed to participate (the treatment group) and which are not (the control group). Again, the subsequent labor market outcomes of the control group serve as a valid estimate of what the outcomes of the treatment group would have been without the program; and thus, the treatment-control group *difference* in outcomes is a valid estimate of the program *impact*.

The first major employment and training study to use a randomized experiment was the National Supported Work Demonstration (Manpower Demonstration Research Corporation, 1980). Conducted between 1975 and 1979, the demonstration was a rigorous test of an intensive work experience program for four groups: long-term AFDC recipients, young high school dropouts, ex-addicts, and ex-offenders. The Supported Work Demonstration found large earnings impacts for AFDC recipients and small to negligible effects for the other three groups. But its successful use of a multisite, randomized experiment to measure the impacts of employment and training programs was an important finding in and of itself, one that would set a methodological precedent for later research.

As the desirability and feasibility of randomized experiments became more apparent, researchers began to use the approach more often. Several experimental studies of employment and training programs were initiated during the early and mid-1980s; some are now completed, whereas others are ongoing.

ADULTS

Most of the studies of employment and training programs for adults focused on programs for welfare recipients,[17] although several others examined programs for displaced workers, persons who permanently lost well-paying, stable jobs because of foreign competition or changing technology.[18]

The largest randomized experimental study of employment and training programs to date is the Demonstration of State Work/Welfare Initiatives (Gueron and Pauly, 1991). Begun in 1982, this project tested a wide range of programs for welfare applicants and recipients in eight states, with a total experimental sample of over 45,000 persons. Some of the programs studied covered a broad cross section of the AFDC caseload, were mandatory for AFDC recipients, and were operated as part of the existing Work Incentive program (WIN). Others covered only selected portions of the AFDC caseload, were voluntary, and were run as demonstrations to investigate the impacts of specific types of

Recommendations of National Academy of Sciences Committee on Youth Employment Programs

In 1985 the National Academy of Sciences convened a committee to review the existing research on employment and training programs for youths, especially those funded through the Youth Employment Demonstration Projects Act (YEDPA). The committee found that little could be said with confidence about the impacts of programs for youths, because the comparison group strategies that had been used to study the programs did not offer convincing evidence. The committee also concluded that

> control groups created by random assignment yield research findings about employment and training programs that are far less biased than results based on any other method. . . . Future advances in field research on the efficacy of employment and training programs will require a more conscious commitment to research strategies using random assignment. (Betsey et al., 1985)

Recommendations of JTLS Research Advisory Panel

Soon after JTPA was authorized in 1982, the Department of Labor began plans for a national evaluation of the program. This evaluation was to build on the longitudinal comparison group approach used in the CETA evaluations. It was to include a detailed survey for a national sample of JTPA participants, referred to as the Job Training Longitudinal Survey (JTLS), and a special national survey, the Survey of History of Work (SHOW), for constructing a comparison group (Westat, 1984a). But when the inconsistent findings from the various CETA studies began to emerge, and some of the early findings from the methodological studies of experimental and comparison group techniques were becoming available, DOL staff members began to rethink the department's plans. Seeking guidance on this issue, DOL convened a panel of experts; authors of the CETA studies were invited to present their findings and recommendations to the panel. The panel concluded (Stromsdorfer et al., 1985):

> The recommendations of the panel are strongly conditioned by the judgment that it will not be possible to solve the problem of selection bias within the context of a quasi-experimental design such as the JTLS/SHOW, at least not in a short enough time frame to meet Congress' needs for valid information to guide policy. Even though many authors studying employment and training programs have recognized the selection problem, no such study using a quasi-experimental de-

sign can be said to have controlled adequately for selection bias. The panel does not intend to set forth a counsel of despair. Rather, it is concerned that the past evaluations of CETA have consumed, and the contemplated evaluations of JTPA will continue to consume, millions of dollars and much valuable time. It would be extremely unfortunate if the analysis of the JTLS/SHOW design would yield the same ambiguous conclusions as has the analysis of the CLMS/CPS database for CETA.

There were also well-acknowledged trade-offs with the alternative: a randomized experiment. On the one hand, the panelists understood that the experimental approach represented the best chance to obtain valid and reliable impact estimates for the local programs to be studied. On the other hand, they recognized that not all local programs would agree to participate in such a study, and thus it would be difficult to obtain a probability sample of sites to ensure the generalizability of findings to the JTPA program nationally.

On balance, though, the advisory group decided that without valid estimates for the sites in the study, the issue of generalizability was not relevant. Its recommendation was therefore:

> The DOL should perform a selected set of classical experiments over the next several years that involve random assignment of program-eligible individuals to the treatment (experimental) group and to the non-treatment (control) group. This is the key recommendation of the panel. The intent is to use these experiments to:
> - evaluate the net impact of JTPA for selected target/treatment groups in a set of SDAs that volunteer to participate.
> - use these experimental results and the understanding of the selection process gained thereby to improve the effectiveness of quasi-experimental designs as a strategy for program evaluation. (Stromsdorfer et al., 1985: 22)

NATIONAL JTPA STUDY IN BRIEF

In June 1986 DOL awarded two separate contracts to conduct the National JTPA Study:

- A *Part A* contract with the Manpower Demonstration Research Corporation (MDRC) and its subcontractors, the National Governors' Association, the National Association of Counties, and the National Alliance of Business, to implement and monitor the experiment; and

- A *Part B* contract with Abt Associates and its subcontractors, New York University, MDRC, the National Opinion Research Center (NORC), Fu Associates, and ICF, to design the study, collect the required data, and conduct the analyses.

Following the recommendations of the JTLS Research Advisory Panel, the National JTPA Study consists of two parts:

- A *randomized experimental study* of JTPA Title II year-round programs, which is based on the experiences of eligible adults and out-of-school youths who applied to 16 local SDAs in the continental United States between November 1987 and September 1989; and
- A *nonexperimental methods study* to analyze the JTPA selection process and develop and evaluate comparison group procedures for estimating program impacts.

The core of the study is the randomized experiment, in which eligible program applicants were randomly assigned to either a treatment group, whose members were offered access to Title II services, or a control group, whose members could not obtain those services for a period of 18 months. (The control group could, however, obtain employment and training services from other local programs.) As demonstrated in Bloom (1991), the treatment and control groups were indeed well matched, as one would expect from a strictly applied random assignment procedure. As noted early in this chapter, because of the large sample size, the study is able to make valid treatment–control group comparisons for a variety of different subgroups, including four main target groups, groups recommended for different clusters of services, and selected key subgroups of interest to policymakers and program planners.

The nonexperimental methods study was designed to assess the reliability of existing nonexperimental evaluation techniques and, if necessary, develop new ones. To support the study, extensive baseline and follow-up data were collected on a sample of JTPA-eligible non-applicants in four of the study sites; comparable data were collected on the experimental control group in those sites. These data were to be used to analyze the process whereby individuals select themselves and/or are selected by program staff to participate in JTPA, as well as to assess the performance of alternative comparison groups and statistical selection adjustment procedures against that of a true control group.[22] These data are available as part of the National JTPA Study public use files.

The primary goal of the National JTPA Study, to estimate the effectiveness of Title II programs as they normally operate, called for certain key decisions regarding the study's design.[23] First was the challenge of recruiting and selecting SDAs to serve as sites. Because the study did not have a legislative mandate requiring SDA participation, it had to rely on SDAs that were willing to volunteer. But SDAs were reluctant to participate in the study for a number of reasons. For one thing, the experimental design required to address the key research questions of the study was complex, and SDAs were concerned about its possible effects on their programs. In addition, SDAs were concerned about the potential political fallout that random assignment might generate. Further complicating matters was the fact that in order for an SDA to participate, all local organizations and key individuals involved (the SDA, its Private Industry Council, the vendors, and local government officials) had to agree. This requirement of unanimity greatly reduced the chances that a prospective site would volunteer. For these reasons, it was not possible to draw a strict probability sample of sites.[24] Instead, a range of SDAs from across the country were recruited to participate. From among them, the 16 SDAs that were willing and able to participate became sites for the study (see Doolittle and Traeger, 1990).

A second major design decision was that, because JTPA program staff often recommend more than one program service for an applicant, the study was constructed to measure the impacts of clusters of program services—what we term *service strategies*—not single services in isolation, such as classroom training in occupational skills, or on-the-job training, or job search assistance. Isolating the impacts of single services would have required comparing the experiences of treatment and control group members for each. To construct such treatment and control groups would have required a special demonstration that would have had to have been run quite differently from regular JTPA programs.

Instead, this study was designed to estimate the impacts of three distinct service strategies: one that recommended sample members for classroom training in occupational skills (and in some cases other, secondary services); a second that recommended sample members for on-the-job training (and in some cases other, secondary services); and a third that recommended sample members mainly for other services besides classroom training in occupational skills and on-the-job training. The mix of services a sample member actually received was distinctly different for each services strategy and reflected in part (but not entirely) the main service for which the sample members were recommended.

The third key design decision was that, because control group members would be able to receive employment and training services from other, non-JTPA providers, the study was designed to estimate the effect of JTPA as an *incremental source* of these services. This is probably the most relevant comparison to make, because JTPA expenditures add services to the existing landscape of employment and training programs. Thus, to assess the program in this regard requires examining the extent to which JTPA adds services to the local community and, in turn, the extent to which this increment in services resulted in an impact on labor market outcomes for the treatment group. We also compare the incremental *costs* of adding JTPA services with the incremental impacts of the program, to determine the cost-effectiveness of the local programs studied.

Finally, because local JTPA program staff can only offer program services to applicants, not force them to enroll, the study is designed to provide estimates of the impact of offering *access* to JTPA services, not the impact of receiving them. From these estimates it is also possible, however, to infer what the likely impact of receiving program services was. The study provides these inferred estimates as an additional perspective from which to judge the program's effectiveness.

SUMMARY

The National JTPA Study offers important substantive and methodological contributions to the literature, especially in light of how little is known about the effectiveness of employment and training programs, and about how to measure their effectiveness. The study provides valid and reliable evidence on the effectiveness of JTPA Title II year-round programs in a diverse group of sites. It thereby helps to identify those for whom the programs are working (or not) and which service strategies are working (or not) for each target group. By identifying program successes, the study can help guide future efforts to study the factors that promote success. And by identifying situations in which the program is not working, the study can help target efforts for change.

The study findings by themselves cannot provide a blueprint for action. Rather, they can only identify issues to be addressed in the future, which must, in turn, be based on the development and rigorous testing of new approaches to serving the labor market needs of disadvantaged persons.

Notes

1. The period of random assignment was different for each SDA, but the first sample member entered the study in November 1987 and the last one entered in September 1989.

2. See Fraker and Maynard (1984); LaLonde (1986); Betsey, Hollister, and Papageorgiou (1985); and Burtless and Orr (1986).

3. The study excluded in-school youths, for reasons discussed in chapter 2.

4. Some local Title II-A programs also serve 14- and 15-year-olds.

5. The formula allocates funds in two steps: first to each state and then to the SDAs within each state. The states, however, have no direct role in this allocation.

6. For adults, these state set-asides comprise 5 percent for services to older workers, 8 percent to coordinate JTPA programs with educational programs, 5 percent for SDA performance incentives, and 5 percent for state auditing and administrative costs. For youths, the set-asides comprise 8 percent for educational coordination, 5 percent for performance incentives, and 5 percent for state administration.

7. Job Training Quarterly Survey (JTQS) data. The JTQS is conducted by the U.S. Bureau of the Census, under contract to DOL, and reported by Westat.

8. JTPA defines *economically disadvantaged* as having a family income equal to or below either the poverty guideline set by the U.S. Office of Management and Budget or 70 percent of the lower living standard set by the U.S. Department of Labor. Findings presented in this and the following paragraph were computed from Job Training Quarterly Survey (JTQS) data for the relevant months.

9. Ten types of barriers to employment were included: (1) having been employed 15 or fewer weeks during the 26 weeks before application to JTPA (67 percent of the enrollees); (2) lack of a high school diploma (35 percent); (3) having reading skills below the seventh grade level (22 percent); (4) being an ex-offender (9 percent); (5) having a physical handicap (9 percent); (6) being a war veteran (9 percent); (7) being a long-term AFDC recipient (9 percent); (8) being over 55 years old (6 percent); (9) having a limited English speaking ability (4 percent); and (10) being a displaced homemaker (3 percent).

10. The original Title II performance standards measured only immediate postprogram outcomes. DOL added several measures of subsequent labor market outcomes in program year 1988.

11. The findings in this paragraph were computed from JTQS data for a sample of JTPA terminees who were enrolled in the program during the sample intake period for the present study.

12. In addition, if the motivation level were different for program participants and comparison group members, but correlated in certain ways with characteristics that were measured (such as past earnings, age, gender, and race), then by controlling statistically for differences in measured variables, one could simultaneously control for

differences in unmeasured factors. Once again, the effect of unmeasured characteristics would be "neutralized."

13. Ashenfelter (1978) used an autoregressive model; Kiefer (1979), a fixed-effect model; and Bloom (1984b), a time-varying, fixed-effect model.

14. To select comparison group members, Westat (1984b) used discrete cell-matching, and Dickinson, Johnson, and West (1984), a continuous Mahalanobis nearest-neighbor matching procedure. Bassi (1983) and Bloom and McLaughlin (1982) used a simple screening criterion.

15. These authors also produced other reports on their CETA evaluations, which were reviewed in Barnow (1987).

16. The ranges of impact estimates presented in Exhibit 1.1 for *a given study* (row) reflect findings for different subgroups and thus are not shown here as evidence of a method-specific variation in impact findings. That evidence lies across the *different studies*, that is, in each column in the exhibit.

17. See Gueron and Pauly (1991) for a comprehensive review of these studies.

18. See Bloom (1990) and Corson et al. (1989).

19. Exceptions are the findings for ex-addicts and ex-convicts in the Supported Work Demonstration, almost all of whom were men, and the findings on several work/welfare programs that served men receiving AFDC-UP.

20. The Buffalo Dislocated Worker Demonstration Program (Corson, Long, and Maynard, 1985) is another example. Although conducted as a randomized experiment, the study estimated program impacts using nonexperimental comparison group methods. Thus, its findings are not directly comparable to those of the Texas and New Jersey demonstrations.

21. See Cave et al. (1993) for a discussion of these findings and corresponding findings for key subgroups within the JOBSTART study sample.

22. The nonexperimental analysis was conducted by the National Opinion Research Center, under subcontract to Abt Associates. As of this writing, the analysis of the JTPA selection process has been completed, but the report on nonexperimental evaluation methods has not been submitted to Abt Associates.

23. See Bloom et al. (1990) and Doolittle and Traeger (1990).

24. Original plans called for a probability sample of sites, although the difficulty of achieving this objective was acknowledged from the outset. When it became clear that this approach was not feasible owing to the constraints of the present study, the process was modified to focus on recruiting the most diverse group possible of SDAs that were willing and able to participate.

Chapter Two

THE 30-MONTH IMPACT AND BENEFIT-COST ANALYSES

This chapter describes the 30-month impact and benefit-cost analyses of the National JTPA Study. The first main section outlines the implementation of the experimental design, indicating how the 16 study sites were selected and how client intake and random assignment were conducted. This section also defines the target groups and service strategy subgroups for which program impacts were estimated.

The second main section describes the types of program impacts estimated in the 30-month analysis. The section begins by defining the 30-month earnings sample and then distinguishes between impacts on the treatment group overall (impacts per JTPA assignee), which were estimated directly from the experimental data, and impacts on those treatment group members who were actually enrolled in the program (impacts per JTPA enrollee), which were inferred using a simple extension of the experimental data. We then explain how the impact estimates represent the impact of the increment in employment and training services that Title II provides, beyond those otherwise available to low-income Americans. The section ends by defining the educational attainment and welfare outcomes also used as the basis for measuring program impacts in this report.

The third section describes how we compare the costs with the benefits of JTPA Title II programs at the 16 study sites. The last section describes the main sources of data used in this report: a Background Information Form completed by sample members when they applied to JTPA; two follow-up surveys; enrollment and tracking data from the 16 sites; quarterly earnings data from state unemployment insurance agencies; AFDC and food stamp data from state and local agencies; and program cost data from several key sources.

IMPLEMENTATION OF STUDY DESIGN

The main goal of the National JTPA Study was to produce valid and reliable estimates of program impacts on the future earnings, educational attainment, and welfare receipt of adults and out-of-school youths that reflect:

- The *incremental* employment and training services received by persons allowed to enter JTPA, beyond what they would have received without JTPA;[1]
- The effects of JTPA programs operating under conditions that were as close to normal as possible; and
- The experience of a diverse group of SDAs from around the country.

To attain that goal, Title II applicants in 16 SDAs across the country were randomly assigned to either a treatment group (that was given access to JTPA services) or a control group (that was not) during the period from November 1987 through September 1989.[2] Because of the large size of the experimental sample for this 30-month analysis (15,981) and the nature of the random assignment, we have in essence separate experiments for each of these main subgroups, as well as for smaller key subgroups defined by such characteristics as ethnicity and the barriers to employment sample members were facing when they applied to JTPA.

Site Selection

As noted in chapter 1, the 16 study sites were recruited from among service delivery areas (SDAs) in the continental United States.[3] As described in chapter 3, and in Doolittle (1993), these SDAs represent a broad range of different administrative arrangements, program services, participant characteristics, and labor market conditions. The program impacts reported here, therefore, reflect much of the diversity that exists within JTPA nationwide.

The sites do not, however, represent a probability sample of SDAs that would allow us to generalize the study findings to the Title II program nationwide. For reasons detailed in the final design report (Bloom et al., 1990) and in the first implementation report (Doolittle and Traeger, 1990), it was not possible to recruit such a sample. Instead, we recruited SDAs based on their diversity, their willingness to participate, their ability to implement the experimental design, the size of the experimental sample they could provide, and the likely composition of this sample.

Diversity was a key criterion because of our desire to provide estimates of program impacts under as broad a range of conditions as possible. We did not want to base the study on a few isolated SDAs that were similar to one another and different from most others. And we particularly did not want a sample of SDAs that were unusually successful or unusually unsuccessful in terms of the JTPA standards used to assess their performance.

As indicated in chapter 1, the SDAs' willingness to participate was essential because no legislative mandate required them to do so. Moreover, administrators' concerns about problems that might arise if they did participate were a major obstacle to overcome. One problem that was especially acute was that *all* of the parties affiliated with the SDA (the SDA director and staff, members of the Private Industry Council, local service providers, and local government officials) had to agree before the SDA could participate in the study and properly implement study procedures. The SDAs' ability to implement the fairly complex experimental design, without unduly disrupting their normal operations, was also essential. We therefore did not recruit some SDAs that might have been willing to join the study but were experiencing administrative difficulties.

The size of the experimental sample each SDA could provide was another important consideration. Not only did we need a large total experimental sample, but we also had to limit the number of sites for logistical reasons. We therefore did not recruit sites with fewer than 500 Title II year-round program terminees in program year 1984 (the most recent year for which data were available at the time).

The preceding criteria were not embodied in formal site selection rules. Instead, they served as an informal guide to help direct the marketing and outreach efforts of the implementation team. Exhibit 2.1 shows the names and locations of the 16 SDAs that ultimately participated in the study. In each SDA the experiment included virtually all of the eligible adults and out-of-school youths who applied to JTPA Title II during the sample intake period for that SDA and who were judged by SDA staff to be appropriate for program services.[4] That period differed for each SDA, but the first sample member entered the study in November 1987 and the last one entered in September 1989.

Client Intake and Random Assignment

Exhibit 2.2 illustrates the client intake and random assignment process used to create the treatment and control groups. Although specific details of the process varied from site to site, to accommodate existing local institutional arrangements and operating practices, the same basic procedure was followed at all sites.

Exhibit 2.1 LOCATION OF THE 16 STUDY SITES

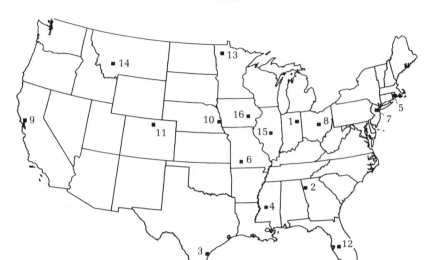

1. Fort Wayne, Indiana	9. Oakland, California
2. Coosa Valley, Georgia	10. Omaha, Nebraska
3. Corpus Christi, Texas	11. Larimer County, Colorado
4. Jackson, Mississippi	12. Heartland, Florida
5. Providence, Rhode Island	13. Northwest, Minnesota
6. Springfield, Missouri	14. Butte, Montana
7. Jersey City, New Jersey	15. Decatur, Illinois
8. Marion, Ohio	16. Cedar Rapids, Iowa

The process began with normal JTPA procedures for recruiting applicants and determining their program eligibility.[5] Those applicants judged eligible were then assessed by local SDA staff members to determine which JTPA services would be most appropriate to meet their individual needs. At that point the staff members recommended applicants for one or more specific program services.[6] Those recommendations, in turn, formed the basis for assigning all sample members to one of three service strategy subgroups: classroom training, on-the-job training (OJT)/job search assistance (JSA), and other services (defined in a later subsection).

During this process, staff members explained to applicants that not all of them could be served, and that because the SDA was participating in a special study, a lottery would be used to select those who would be allowed to participate in JTPA and those who would not over the next 18 months. Applicants then signed a consent form in-

Exhibit 2.2 RANDOM ASSIGNMENT MODEL FOR NATIONAL JTPA STUDY

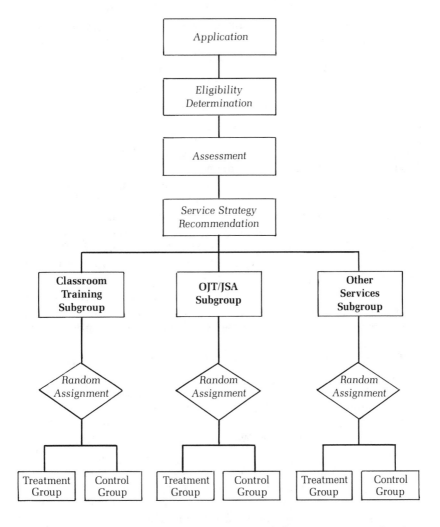

dicating that they understood the nature of the participant selection process and giving permission to the research contractor to obtain information on their earnings, employment, and welfare receipt from the administrative records of governmental agencies.

At that point an SDA staff member telephoned a random assignment clerk from the study team, who randomly assigned each applicant to treatment or control status *within* each service strategy subgroup, as shown in Exhibit 2.2. Specifically, two-thirds of the experimental sample was assigned to the treatment group (whose members were allowed to receive JTPA Title II services), and one-third was assigned to the control group (whose members were not allowed to receive those services for 18 months).[7] The SDA staff then telephoned or wrote treatment group members to schedule their participation in JTPA; control group members usually were informed of their status by letter, although some were informed by telephone or in person.

Four Target Groups

The 30-month analysis focuses on four main *target groups:* adult women and adult men, and female and male out-of-school youths. Because members of each target group were randomly assigned to treatment or control status independently of one another, the random assignment process produced an independent randomized experiment for each of these target groups. The distinction between adult women and men is based on the accumulated evidence of differences between the impacts of employment and training programs estimated for the two groups (for example, Ashenfelter, 1978; Kiefer, 1979; Bloom and McLaughlin, 1982; Bassi, 1983; Dickinson et al., 1984; and Westat, 1984b). Out-of-school youths were separated from adults in the analysis because of the major differences between their positions in the labor market.

The study was limited to out-of-school youths in Title II rather than all Title II youths, because the evaluation team expected that programs and relevant outcomes for in-school youths and out-of-school youths would differ too much for them to be analyzed together and because the samples for in-school youths were expected to be too small for separate analyses. We also anticipated that it would be difficult to obtain consent to implement random assignment in public schools, where some JTPA services for in-school youths are provided.

Findings for out-of-school youths are reported separately by gender because of the major differences in the impact estimates for female youths and male youths and because other major studies of programs for youths maintain this precedent. In addition, for reasons discussed later, impact estimates are reported separately for the roughly 20 percent of the male youths who reported having been arrested before they applied to JTPA (referred to as male youth arrestees) and the remaining 80 percent who did not (male youth non-arrestees).

At the time of the study, 30 percent of the participants in the JTPA Title II year-round program nationwide were adult women, 25 percent were adult men, 23 percent were out-of-school youths, and 22 percent were in-school youths. The National JTPA Study therefore focuses on target groups that comprise about three-quarters of the population currently being served by JTPA.

Three Service Strategies

The program services that JTPA applicants ultimately receive depend on a number of factors, including the types of services that the applicants want, judgments by program staff about the suitability of specific services for particular applicants, and the availability of services at the time an individual applies to the program. Sometimes the services provided to an applicant are determined by deliberate planning (for example, a basic education course followed by occupational skills training). At other times, however, they are determined by trial and error, producing an evolving sequence of efforts to find one or more suitable services.

In short, it is difficult to predict which service or services an applicant will receive. In addition, JTPA often provides more than one service to an applicant. As a result, it was not possible both to achieve our mandate to examine the impact of JTPA programs as they were being operated at the time (Bloom et al., 1990) and to isolate the effect of receiving a particular program service, because to isolate the effect of a *single* specific program service would require restricting certain sample members to that service and thus substantially altering the normal decision-making process of JTPA.

To examine the impacts of the different types of services offered by JTPA programs, we therefore grouped treatment and control group members into three *service strategy subgroups* defined in terms of the specific program services *recommended* for them before random assignment.[8] We based our definitions on service recommendations because (1) doing so enabled us to match treatment group members and their control group counterparts (which would not have been possible using program services *received*); (2) we judged that service recommendations were the best available predictors of services received and therefore the best available way to distinguish among sample members according to the services they subsequently received; (3) this approach had a minimal effect on the normal JTPA decision-making process, and (4) it enabled us to account for the combinations and sequences of services received by many JTPA participants.

Exhibit 2.3 shows the services allowed in the definition of each service strategy. The definitions are based on the initial staff recommendation for each sample member, with modest restrictions on the

Exhibit 2.3 SPECIFIC PROGRAM SERVICES ALLOWED BY EACH OF THREE
SERVICE STRATEGY DEFINITIONS

	Service strategy		
Specific program service	Classroom training	OJT/ JSA	Other services
Classroom training in occupational skills	Yes	No	Yes
On-the-job training (OJT)	No	Yes	Yes
Job search assistance (JSA)	Yes	Yes	Yes
Basic education	Yes	Yes	Yes
Work experience	Yes	Yes	Yes
Miscellaneous	Yes	Yes	Yes

specific program services that participants could subsequently receive. Specifically:[9]

- The *classroom training strategy* was defined to include sample members who were recommended for classroom occupational skills training but *not* for on-the-job training (OJT). Any other service—such as job search assistance, basic education, and work experience (but not OJT)—could be recommended in addition to the defining service for this strategy. Most sample members recommended for this service strategy who were subsequently enrolled in JTPA received classroom training in occupational skills or basic education or both (see Exhibit 3.18 in chapter 3).
- The *OJT/JSA strategy* was defined to include sample members who were recommended for OJT but *not* classroom occupational skills training. All secondary services (but not classroom occupational skills training) could be recommended in addition to the defining service for this strategy. Most sample members recommended for this service strategy who were later enrolled in JTPA received OJT or JSA, or both (see Exhibit 3.18 in chapter 3).
- The *other services strategy* was defined to include sample members who were recommended for neither classroom occupational skills training nor OJT.[10] This strategy produced a substantially different mix of services for adults than for youths. Adults recommended for this strategy who were later enrolled in JTPA received mainly job search assistance and miscellaneous services, such as customized combinations of classroom occupational skills training and OJT. Youths recommended for the strategy who became enrolled in JTPA received mainly basic education or miscellaneous services, such as tryout employment (in which participants are hired on a probationary basis to learn a job and prove themselves qualified for per-

manent employment) and job shadowing (in which participants accompany and observe a regular employee to learn what is required to hold a job). Hence, for adults this strategy focused more on immediate employment, whereas for youths it focused more on education and entry-level job skills (see Exhibit 3.18 in chapter 3).

As chapter 3 demonstrates, these definitions produced subgroups that in fact, reflected distinctly different service strategies. Note, however, that each service strategy subgroup ultimately received predominantly two key services. Hence, the study findings reflect more than the impact of the single defining service for each strategy.

IMPACT ESTIMATES IN 30-MONTH ANALYSIS

This section briefly describes how we obtained the program impact estimates presented in this report.

Thirty-Month Earnings Sample

The random assignment process described previously produced a total experimental sample of 20,601 treatment and control group members from the 16 study sites. Bloom (1991) described the baseline characteristics of this full experimental sample.[11] Estimates of program impacts on earnings presented in this report were based on data for a subsample of the full experimental sample containing 15,981 members, with each sample member weighted equally. This subsample was selected to provide 30 months of continuous earnings information from the same data source for each sample member; we refer to it as the *30-month earnings sample.*

The 30-month earnings sample was selected from the full experimental sample through a process that left almost no margin for systematic differences to arise between the treatment group and control group members who remained in the analysis (see appendix B). Exhibit 2.4 lists the number of sample members who remained at each stage of the process, by target group. First, a total of 473 treatment group members from 5 sites were deleted randomly to ensure a 2/1 treatment/control group ratio in all sites.[12] Exhibit 2.4 refers to this deleted group as the "extra treatment group members." It was deleted from the sample to simplify the impact analysis. Also dropped at this stage were the 5 sample members from Oakland, California, who were

Exhibit 2.4 DERIVING 30-MONTH EARNINGS SAMPLE FROM FULL EXPERIMENTAL SAMPLE

	All target groups	Adult women	Adult men	Female youths	Male youth non-arrestees	Male youth arrestees
Full experimental sample	20,601	8,058	6,853	3,132	2,041	517
Sample after exogenous deletions for:						
Extra treatment group members[a]	20,123	7,936	6,724	3,015	1,949	499
Late cohorts[b]	19,019	7,497	6,303	2,864	1,871	484
Persons in non-UI sites randomly excluded from Second Follow-up survey[c]	16,347	6,191	5,223	2,712	1,755	466
Male youth arrestees in non-UI sites[d]	16,304	6,191	5,223	2,712	1,755	423
Sample after deletions for missing data:						
30-month earnings sample	15,981	6,102	5,102	2,657	1,704	416
Potentially nonrandom attrition rate	2.0%	1.4%	2.3%	2.0%	2.9%	1.7%

a. A total of 473 treatment group members in 5 sites were randomly excluded to ensure a 2/1 treatment/control group ratio in all sites. Also, the 5 sample members under 22 years of age from Oakland, Calif., were deleted because youths were excluded from the experimental design in Oakland.

b. Deleted were all treatment and control group members randomly assigned after December 1988 in Jackson, Miss.; after April 1989 in Butte, Mont., Jersey City, N.J., and Marion, Ohio; and after June 1989 in Omaha, Neb.

c. The "non-UI" sites (where UI earnings data were not available) are Butte, Jersey City, Marion, and Oakland.

d. The remaining sample at this stage has the statistical properties of a randomized experiment.

under 22 years old, because youths were excluded from the experimental design in Oakland.

Then, in five sites, all remaining sample members randomly assigned to treatment or control status after specific cutoff dates were deleted from the sample.[13] This additional group of 1,104 sample members, referred to in Exhibit 2.4 as the "late cohorts," was deleted because given the project data collection schedule, the late date of their random assignment made it impossible to collect 30 months of follow-up data for them.

Next, in the 4 sites where usable earnings data could not be obtained from unemployment insurance (UI) wage records, a total of 2,672 treatment and control group members were deleted *randomly.* This was done because follow-up surveys to provide the earnings data required for the impact analysis were only fielded for a random subsample of the full experimental sample.[14] In these 4 sites we also excluded the 43 male youths who reported having been arrested before random assignment. This was done because, as we discuss in chapter 4, the survey and UI earnings data gave contradictory results for male youth arrestees in the other 12 sites. To compare the two data sources over a common sample, we excluded the male youth arrestees in the four sites without UI earnings data. Finally, in the 4 sites where UI data were not available, 312 sample members (2 percent of the remaining subsample) were dropped, due to survey nonresponse.[15] In the 12 sites where UI data were available, there was virtually no further sample loss at this stage because UI earnings records were used for survey nonrespondents; only 11 sample members in these sites were dropped because of missing data.

At each stage but the last, members of the full experimental sample were deleted in ways that were *random* with respect to treatment or control status. Hence, only through the deletion of the final small group (2 percent of the subsample that remained prior to the last step), was it possible for systematic differences to arise between the final treatment group and control group. Therefore, the margin for selection bias due to preexisting differences between the treatment group and the control group was extremely limited.

The main difference between the 30-month earnings sample and the full experimental sample was the mix of JTPA enrollment cohorts over time and the mix of sites they represented. The 30-month earnings sample also differed somewhat in these regards from the subsample used for the 18-month impact report (Bloom et al., 1993). Nevertheless, estimates of program impacts on the earnings of each target group in the first 18 months after random assignment obtained from the 30-month subsample were quite similar to those obtained from the 18-month subsample.

Impacts per JTPA Assignee

Because the random assignment process outlined in Exhibit 2.2 produced treatment and control groups with no systematic differences at random assignment, the subsequent labor market experience of the control group provides a valid estimate of what the experience of the treatment group would have been if JTPA had not been available to its members. For example, if the mean earnings of the control group were $7,000 during the first year after random assignment, one could infer that the treatment group would have earned this amount (plus or minus a margin to reflect random sampling error) in that same year without assistance from JTPA. Moreover, if the *actual* mean earnings of the treatment group were $7,500 during that year, one could infer that JTPA increased treatment group earnings by $7,500 minus $7,000, or $500, on average (plus or minus a margin to reflect random sampling error). Similar logic can be used to estimate program impacts on dichotomous outcomes that are naturally expressed in percentage terms. For example, if 80 percent of the treatment group were employed at some time during the first year after random assignment, and 70 percent of the control group were employed during that time, the best estimate would be that JTPA increased employment by 10 percentage points.

These impact estimates rely exclusively on *direct* comparisons of outcomes for all treatment group members (whether they were subsequently enrolled in JTPA or not) and all control group members. Hence, they represent the average impact of the program on all sample members who were randomly assigned to the group having access to the program—the treatment group. We refer to these findings as estimates of *impacts per assignee*, and they represent the effect of providing treatment group members with *access* to JTPA Title II services, relative to what they could have accomplished without access to those services.

This comparison of treatment and control group outcomes can be conducted separately for many different subgroups within the experimental sample, thereby providing separate program impact estimates for each subgroup. In effect, the experimental design allows for a separate experimental treatment-control group comparison for any sample subgroup that can be defined in terms of common factors measured before or at random assignment. For example, the design can yield separate experimental estimates for women, men, whites, blacks, Hispanics, welfare recipients, high school dropouts, and so on.

The experimental analysis for the study follows standard statistical practice and uses multiple regression analysis to increase the statistical precision of the program impact estimates. Regression analysis controls for chance differences between the treatment group and control group in a wide range of baseline characteristics, which are included in the regression model as covariates. Appendix B describes the procedures employed in each case.

Not all treatment group members ultimately became enrolled in JTPA. The estimated impacts per JTPA assignee therefore do not measure the effect of actually participating in JTPA. Instead, they measure the average effect on eligible applicants of making JTPA Title II services available to economically disadvantaged members of the community. Note, however, that because control group members could and did obtain employment and training services from non-JTPA providers, the comparison of outcomes for treatment group and control group members represents the *incremental* effect of JTPA services relative to the services that could have been received elsewhere in the area (discussed in the next section).

Impacts per JTPA Enrollee

As just noted, the estimated JTPA impact per assignee represents the average effect of the program on all treatment group members, whether they became enrolled in JTPA or not. This result can be expressed as a weighted average of the impact on those who were enrolled plus the impact on those who were not enrolled, where the weights are the proportion who were enrolled and the proportion who were not. If the program had *no* effect on those who did not become enrolled, the impact per assignee understates the impact per enrollee because the impact per assignee is the weighted average of a zero impact per nonenrollee and the average impact per enrollee. In this case, to *infer* the average *impact per JTPA enrollee*, one need only divide the impact per assignee by the proportion of assignees who were enrolled (see Bloom, 1984a).[16]

For example, if the average impact per assignee were $500, and 60 percent of the treatment group were enrolled in JTPA after random assignment, the estimated impact per JTPA enrollee would be $500/.6, or $833. Thus, estimated impacts per enrollee are proportional to estimated impacts per assignee. In this example, the 60 per-

cent enrollment rate implies an estimated impact per enrollee that is
1/.6 or 1.67 times the estimated impact per assignee.

For each outcome analyzed, we present estimated impacts per enrollee, as well as impacts per assignee. To the extent that treatment
group members who did not become enrolled in JTPA were not affected by the program, one can interpret our estimates of the impact
per JTPA enrollee as the average effect of enrolling in a JTPA Title II
program relative to what the enrollees could have accomplished if
they had not enrolled in the program. To the extent that nonenrolled
treatment group members experienced program impacts similar to
those of enrollees, our estimates will systematically overstate the true
impacts per enrollee. Indeed, when interpreting the estimated impacts
per enrollee, it should be noted that some members of the treatment
group who were not enrolled in JTPA did receive limited JTPA services. This occurrence reflects a practice by some SDAs of not enrolling applicants immediately after they are judged eligible for the
program.

To investigate the extent to which these treatment group nonenrollees received JTPA services, we conducted a separate analysis based
on checks of SDA administrative records for a small subsample of
treatment group members and on discussions with SDA staff members about what happened to nonenrollees in this subsample (see
Bloom et al., 1993, Appendix F). The administrative records indicated
that about 40 percent of the subsample were not later enrolled in Title
II. Discussions with SDA staff about those nonenrollees indicated that
about half received no JTPA service and half received some service.
The specific program services received were usually limited, however,
mainly constituting attempts to *arrange* services for applicants by
referring them to potential employers for on-the-job training; by providing some job search assistance; or by attempting to arrange classroom training. The fact that these applicants were not formally enrolled in JTPA probably means that these placement attempts were
unsuccessful; under the JTPA performance standards, SDAs have a
strong incentive to enroll individuals who can be placed in jobs. Thus,
with few exceptions, it is unlikely that the services treatment group
nonenrollees received appreciably affected their future labor market
experience, although we cannot be sure about the effect.

We therefore consider our inferred estimates of impacts per JTPA
enrollee to be reasonable estimates of the impact of enrollment in the
program. If, however, one believes that the services received by nonenrollees had a nonnegligible impact on their future earnings, these
estimates can be viewed as likely upper bounds on the magnitude of

the true impact of enrolling in the program, and our estimates of impacts per JTPA assignee can be viewed as likely lower bounds on the magnitude of program impacts on enrollees.[17]

Incremental Impact of JTPA

Whether the impacts are reported per JTPA assignee or per JTPA enrollee, they reflect the *incremental* effect of JTPA services beyond what sample members could have accomplished without access to JTPA, but *with* access to services from non-JTPA providers. In other words, they reflect the effect of adding JTPA services to the existing landscape of employment and training programs in the community.

The effect of those non-JTPA services is embodied in the labor market outcomes of the control group members. The difference between the outcomes of the treatment group and the control group therefore reflects the effect of the increment in services made available to treatment group members by JTPA. Hence, our impact estimates do not reflect what would happen in the absence of any employment and training services, but, rather, what would happen without JTPA services.

To measure this increment in services, we measured the employment and training services received by treatment and control group members from JTPA and from other providers. In chapters 3 and 4 we report the difference in service receipt between the treatment group and the control group to illustrate the size of the increment that produced the program impacts estimated. We also include a detailed analysis of the costs of these services, and compare the added costs of additional services received by the treatment group to the estimates of program impacts. This forms the basis for our benefit-cost analysis of the program.

Impacts on Attainment of High School Diploma or GED Certificate

Helping dropouts obtain a high school diploma or a General Educational Development (GED) certificate is a key goal of JTPA. We estimated the incremental impacts of JTPA on this outcome for sample members who were school dropouts when they applied to JTPA, because only school dropouts can experience such an impact. To estimate this impact per assignee on dropouts, we compared the percentage of treatment group dropouts who attained a high school credential during their 30-month follow-up period with the percentage of control group dropouts who did so.[18] Separate impact estimates were obtained for dropouts in each target group, based on follow-up survey data for a subsample of 1,751 treatment and control group members from the 30-month earnings sample.[19] To estimate impacts on educational attainment *per enrollee* for school dropouts in each target group, we adjusted the estimates of impacts per assignee to account for the JTPA enrollment rate of the dropouts in the target group (as was done to estimate impacts on earnings per enrollee). Finally, to *infer* the impact on the attainment of a high school credential by each target group overall, the estimated impact on school dropouts (per assignee or per enrollee) was multiplied by the proportion of the treatment group members who were school dropouts when they applied to JTPA. Because only a minority of the treatment group members in each target group were school dropouts (especially among adults), the margin for JTPA to have a large impact on the educational attainment of any target group overall was limited.[20]

Impacts on AFDC and Food Stamp Benefits

Reducing welfare dependence is another central goal of JTPA. We estimated program impacts on this outcome in terms of the extent to which JTPA reduced the average AFDC benefits and food stamp benefits received in each target group, using the same estimation procedures described previously for impacts on earnings. Data for the analysis (discussed later) were obtained from a mix of follow-up surveys and administrative records obtained from state welfare offices. Usable data on AFDC benefits were obtained for a subsample of 6,206 persons from six sites, and usable data on food stamp benefits were obtained for a subsample of 5,141 persons from five sites.[21] Although usable data for these estimates were obtained only for a subset of sites, the estimated earnings impacts for these sites yielded approximately the same conclusions as those for all 16 sites. Thus, there is no obvious reason to expect estimates of impacts on AFDC benefits or food stamp benefits to differ appreciably either.[22]

Impacts on Arrest Rates of Youths

We also present estimates of JTPA impacts on the arrest rates of youths. Data on arrests were obtained from responses to follow-up surveys. Arrest rates were measured and analyzed for youths because past evaluations of employment and training programs have focused considerable attention on this issue. This information was not collected for adults in order to reduce data collection costs and because past studies of employment and training programs generally have not focused on this outcome for adults.

Increase in Employment and Training Services Due to JTPA: Measuring the Service Increment

As noted earlier, the National JTPA Study was designed to measure the impacts of the incremental services provided by JTPA, beyond those that would have been available outside of JTPA. The services that would have been available without JTPA are represented by the services received by the control group. Because JTPA is not the only employment and training service provider in most communities, a number of control group members received employment and training services from non-JTPA sources, as anticipated.

Providing treatment group members with access to JTPA did, however, increase the services they received beyond those received by control group members. In other words, random assignment produced a treatment group and a control group that were the same in all regards except one—treatment group members received more employment and training services. It is this *difference* in services that produced the observed impacts. We refer to these impacts as *incremental* impacts, because they represent the change in earnings produced by the incremental services provided by JTPA.

To measure the size of this service increment, data on the JTPA services received by treatment and control group members were obtained from the SDA administrative records in our 16 sites, and data on services received from any source (JTPA or otherwise) were obtained from responses to our two waves of follow-up surveys. In addition, data on the costs of services received by sample members were obtained from a variety of sources. From these data, we constructed three different measures of the service increment and reported both the increment per assignee and the increment per enrollee. The first measure was the percentage of sample members who received any employment service after random assignment. The second measure was the average number of hours of service received by all sample members, including zero hours for those receiving no service. The third measure was the average cost of the services received, including a cost of zero for sample members receiving no service.

ANALYSIS OF BENEFITS AND COSTS OF JTPA

Chapters 4 and 5 of this report present estimates of the impacts of JTPA on the earnings, educational attainment, welfare benefits, and arrest rates of members of the study sample. Although beneficial impacts on these outcomes would be evidence that the program is achieving its objectives, for the program to be worthwhile to society its beneficial effects must outweigh its costs. Therefore, chapter 6 compares the estimated benefits of JTPA with its costs.

Because the benefits and costs of the program may accrue to different groups within society, it is important to examine the redistributional consequences of the program, as well as its overall net benefits to society. Therefore, our benefit-cost analysis is conducted from the perspective of participants, nonparticipants (including taxpayers), and society as a whole. The principal expected benefit of the program is increased participant earnings.[23] We distinguish between increased earnings from private employers, which represent added output and therefore are not a cost to anyone else in society, and on-the-job training (OJT) wage subsidies, which are a benefit to participants at the cost of nonparticipants. Gains in earnings from private employers are the net of any postprogram earnings gains less any earnings forgone while in the program.

The principal expected cost of the program is the cost of the incremental employment and training services received by enrollees. As noted earlier, program impacts on earnings and other outcomes reflect the incremental services received by enrollees beyond those they would have received had they been excluded from JTPA. Therefore, in assessing program benefits and costs, impacts on earnings should be compared with the cost of these *incremental* services, not with the total cost of services received by enrollees. The incremental costs of employment and training services are measured by the treatment-control difference in cost per enrollee of total JTPA and non-JTPA services received.

Reductions in welfare benefits as a result of enrollment in JTPA represent a cost (loss of income) to participants and a benefit (reduction in taxes) to nonparticipants. Although it is important to measure this redistributional effect, from the standpoint of society as a whole these effects are offsetting.[24] Net benefits to society are calculated as the sum of all social benefits and costs. Similarly, net benefits to participants or nonparticipants are calculated as the sum of all benefits and costs to that group.

DATA FOR THIS REPORT

The data used to produce the impact estimates in this report come from seven main sources:

- A Background Information Form completed by sample members (with assistance from local SDA staff members if necessary) when they applied to JTPA;
- First and Second Follow-up Survey interviews that asked sample members about their earnings, employment, and receipt of employment and training services;
- Enrollment and tracking data from the 16 SDAs, which include information on enrollment, service receipt, and termination status;
- State unemployment insurance records on the quarterly wages paid to sample members by local employers;
- State welfare agency records on AFDC and food stamp benefits received;
- SDA administrative records on the cost of services provided through the program; and,
- Published sources and a telephone survey of selected education and training organizations in the study sites to measure the costs of the services they provided.

The Background Information Form is the primary source of baseline information on sample members. Administered as part of the program application process at each site over the course of the sample intake period, the form obtained data on applicants' demographic characteristics, education and training, employment history, living situation, and public assistance experience, as well as contact information for the follow-up interviews. Data from the Background Information Form were used in this report for three main purposes: to describe the 30-month earnings sample; to define the sample subgroups for which separate impact estimates were calculated; and to construct variables to control for individual differences in the multiple regression models.

The First Follow-up Survey, as noted earlier, was scheduled for the full experimental sample for periods that varied across sample members from 13 to 22 months after random assignment. This survey comprised a 30-minute interview that asked sample members about their earnings, employment, and receipt of employment and training services during the period from random assignment to the date of the interview. It also asked questions about current family composition and related issues. The survey was conducted by telephone, with in-person interviews for sample members who could not be reached by telephone. The response rate for the First Follow-up Survey was 84 percent, which is unusually high, especially for low-income persons.

The Second Follow-up Survey collected the same information as the First Follow-up Survey, for the period between the two surveys. Second Follow-up Survey interviews were scheduled 24–43 months after random assignment, and were also administered by telephone, with in-person follow-up for sample members who could not be reached by telephone. Interviews were attempted with a random sub-sample of the full experimental sample (22 percent of adult women, 26 percent of adult men, and 62 percent of female and male youths). The response rate on the Second Follow-up Survey was 78 percent.

In the 12 study sites where usable data on earnings were obtained from UI wage records, these data were used to measure earnings during the 30-month follow-up period for all sample members for whom 30 consecutive months of follow-up earnings data were not available from the follow-up surveys. Appendix B describes how the survey and UI data were combined to produce the database for the earnings impact estimates presented in this report.

Collection of UI earnings records allowed us to measure the earnings of survey nonrespondents and sample members who were not included in the Second Follow-up Survey, in addition to providing independent verification of the earnings data collected from survey respondents. At the same time, the survey data provided more detailed information about the employment and earnings of respondents—e.g., hours of employment and earnings by job, as well as exact dates of employment, in contrast to the simple aggregate quarterly earnings measures provided by UI.

Computerized administrative records from the 16 SDAs in the study provided information on JTPA enrollment rates for sample members, the amount of time JTPA enrollees spent in the program, and the specific program services they received. These enrollment and tracking data were used to describe the JTPA program services received by sample members, to compare the specific program services received by persons recommended for the three service strategies, and to identify control group members who entered JTPA during their 18-month embargo period (less than 2 percent did so).

Computerized data were obtained from the state welfare agencies of 4 sites on the dollar amount of AFDC benefits received by sample members during the follow-up period and the number of months for which they received AFDC benefits. These data were combined with survey data on AFDC benefits for 2 additional sites; this outcome was included in the follow-up surveys in these sites because it was judged from the outset that administrative data on AFDC would not be available for these sites. Attempts were made to obtain data on AFDC benefits from administrative records from the remaining 10 sites. All but one of those sites provided at least some data, but in each case the data were incomplete (i.e., missing either sample members or months) and, despite repeated requests, the state was unable to provide complete data.[25] In the remaining case, state law prohibited release of benefit data. For similar reasons, data on food stamp benefits received by sample members were obtained from state administrative records for 2 sites, from follow-up surveys for 3 sites, and were not available for 11 sites.

To measure the cost of employment and training services received by treatment and control group members, a variety of different data sources were used. Appendixes A and B describe how these data were obtained and how they were used for the analysis in this report. Data on the cost of JTPA services were obtained from the administrative records of the 16 SDAs that participated in the study. The costs of other employment and training services were obtained from published sources, in many cases for the specific training institutions identified by sample members in their response to the follow-up surveys. In addition, a telephone survey was conducted to obtain data on the cost of services provided by selected institutions in each site that were identified by sample members in the surveys. These data were combined to provide a basis for estimating the cost of services received by sample members for each of a number of major service categories, which in turn were used to compute the average cost of services received by treatment and control group members.

Notes

1. As explained later, study findings should not be interpreted as the total impact of JTPA versus no employment and training services.

2. The period of random assignment varied across sites.

3. In JTPA parlance *service delivery area* refers to both the local administrative agency for the program and the geographic area it serves.

4. The Oakland, Calif., SDA excluded youths from the study because of recruitment problems. Formal agreements with some of the SDAs excluded certain small groups of applicants from the study (and therefore from random assignment) for one of three main reasons: (1) logistical problems, such as widely dispersed groups that would have

required many different intake locations; (2) recruitment problems for particular groups, such as older workers; and (3) the nonvoluntary nature of certain applications, namely, among groups required to apply to JTPA either by the courts (usually as a condition for parole) or as a condition for receiving public assistance. Doolittle and Traeger (1990) described the groups that were excluded from the experiment, if any, at each site.

5. Sites were given a limited amount of technical assistance to improve their client recruitment procedures, so that enough eligible people would apply to JTPA to provide for a control group without reducing the number of persons served by the SDA. To the extent that this additional recruitment changed the mix of clients in the programs, and to the extent that any such change in client mix produced a change in average impacts, the additional recruitment may have altered the nature of the population for which the impact findings can be generalized. There is no empirical evidence with which to assess this possibility, however.

6. Throughout this report we refer to classroom training in occupational skills, basic education, on-the-job training (OJT), job search assistance (JSA), work experience, and miscellaneous services as *specific program services*. They are often referred to as *program activities* in the employment and training literature.

7. This 2/1 ratio of treatment group members to control group members represents an explicit trade-off between the need for statistical precision in program impact estimates (the optimum ratio for which is 1/1) and a practical need to minimize the size of the control group in order to minimize the number of persons that had to be turned away by local program staff and the number of additional applicants that had to be recruited to provide for a control group.

8. Previous reports for this project (Bloom et al., 1990; Doolittle and Traeger, 1990; and Bloom, 1991) termed the service strategies "treatment streams" and termed the three strategies as classroom training, on-the-job training, and other activities. The names and characterizations of these service strategies evolved over time as we learned more about the actual services received by each service strategy subgroup.

9. Two infrequent exceptions to the service strategy definitions presented here were limited classroom training provided to some members of the OJT/JSA subgroup before they received on-the-job training, and limited on-the-job training provided after some members of the classroom training subgroup received classroom training in occupational skills. A small number of applicants for whom intake staff recommended substantial amounts of both OJT and classroom training in occupational skills were included in the "other services" subgroup.

10. Formal agreements were made with each SDA to specify a maximum allowable percentage of experimental sample members recommended for the other services strategy. This limit was based on the previous experience of each site, and no site reached its limit.

11. Bloom (1991) described a full experimental sample containing 20,602 cases. Subsequently, two of these cases were discovered to represent the same person.

12. In five sites that experienced recruitment problems, the treatment-control group ratio was increased temporarily from 2/1 to 3/1 or 6/1, in order to reduce the number of eligible applicants lost to the program because they were assigned to control group status. Consequently, the overall treatment-control group ratio for the full experimental sample is slightly greater than 2/1. When constructing the 30-month study sample, however, we randomly deleted these "extra" treatment group members, thus producing an analysis sample with a constant 2/1 ratio for all sites and subgroups.

13. Deleted at this stage were all treatment and control group members randomly assigned after December 1988, in Jackson, Miss.; after April 1989, in Butte, Mont.,

Jersey City, N.J., and Marion, Ohio; and after June 1989 in Omaha, Neb. This was analytically equivalent to stopping random assignment on these dates in these sites.

14. The Second Follow-up Survey, which extended the follow-up period beyond that for the 18-month report, was only fielded for a random subsample of the full experimental sample. Subsampling was required because of limited project resources. A greater proportion of youths than adults was subsampled because the overall samples of youths were appreciably smaller than those for adults.

15. More precisely, 292 sample members were dropped due to survey nonresponse (no survey response was available), and 20 sample members were dropped due to survey item nonresponse (the interview was obtained but usable earnings data were not available).

16. An additional adjustment was made for the fact that 1.6 percent of the control group enrolled in JTPA, despite the experiment's embargo on their participation. This adjustment had almost no effect on the resulting estimates. For simplicity, then, we ignore this adjustment in the following discussion.

17. Our inferred impacts per enrollee would understate the impact of enrollment only in the unlikely event that the impact of JTPA services on nonenrollees was opposite in sign to the impact on enrollees. This might happen if, for example, the experience of unsuccessful referrals discouraged nonenrollees in ways that would not have occurred in the absence of the evaluation.

18. The measure of educational attainment was obtained from answers to a question on a Second Follow-up Survey (discussed later) that asked sample members if they had a high school diploma or a GED certificate at the time of the interview and, if so, the date they received it. This information was used to determine whether the respondent had the credential 30 months after random assignment. School dropouts were defined as sample members who indicated at baseline on their Background Information Form (also discussed later) that they had neither a high school diploma nor a GED certificate when they applied to JTPA.

19. Estimates of impacts on educational attainment presented in this report are similar to those in the 18-month impact report (Bloom et al., 1993) for all target groups except male youths. Findings from the two reports are not directly comparable, however, because they are based on two different samples and two different measures of educational attainment. The analysis in the 18-month report was based on all respondents to the First Follow-up Survey, which attempted interviews with the entire experimental sample; the 30-month analysis is based on respondents to the Second Follow-up Survey, which included only a random subset of the experimental sample. Moreover, the 18-month analysis used a more restrictive measure of education attainment, based on whether the sample member had received a high school diploma or GED *through participation in an education or training program.*

20. The percentage of treatment group members in the educational impact sample who were school dropouts when they applied to JTPA was 24 percent for adult women, 32 percent for adult men, 47 percent for female youths, 58 percent for male youth non-arrestees, and 65 percent for male youth arrestees.

21. As detailed later, data on AFDC benefits were obtained from the administrative records of state welfare agencies for 4 sites. Data on AFDC benefits were obtained from follow-up surveys for 2 sites because it was judged from the outset of the project that this information could not be obtained from administrative records for these sites. Attempts were made to obtain these data from administrative records for the remaining 10 sites, but usable data could not be obtained. For the same reasons, data on food stamp benefits were obtained from follow-up surveys for 3 sites, from administrative records for 2 sites, and were not available for 11 sites.

22. The relationship between changes in earnings and changes in welfare benefits is, however, a complex one, involving the level of benefits, local reporting procedures, and the initial level of earnings, among other factors. This relationship is being further explored in follow-up studies by Abt Associates, using the National JTPA Study database.

23. In evaluating an employment and training program, impacts on educational attainment, such as receipt of a GED, are treated as intermediate outcomes whose value to society is in raising the future earnings of participants. Any such benefits of increased educational attainment should be captured in the program's impacts on earnings. To avoid double-counting, we therefore do not include impacts on educational attainment separately in the benefit-cost analysis.

24. Reductions in welfare receipt may also result in reductions in the costs of program administration for AFDC and food stamps. Such savings would not be offset by costs to participants. However, because we found no significant impacts on months of receipt of AFDC and food stamps, we did not attempt to measure impacts on the administrative costs of these programs.

25. In some cases, the omissions were not discovered until after the relevant months of data had been taken off the state system and archived. States were generally unwilling to retreive data from archives.

Chapter Three

STUDY SITES, 30-MONTH EARNINGS SAMPLE, AND PATTERNS OF JTPA ENROLLMENT AND SERVICE RECEIPT

This chapter describes the study sites and sample discussed in this report. The first section catalogs characteristics of the 16 service delivery areas (SDAs)[1] that agreed to participate in the national JTPA study and compares those characteristics—of the local population and economy, the JTPA programs in place, program participants, and program services—with averages for the broader national group of 649 SDAs during the years the study sample was selected. The second section of the chapter presents a more detailed examination of the 15,981 members of the 30-month earnings sample and the composition of the main subgroups analyzed in this report. Finally, the last section details patterns of JTPA enrollment and service receipt among these subgroups. These topics are analyzed in more depth in other study reports.

SIXTEEN STUDY SITES

As noted in chapter 2, the 16 study sites were recruited from among those SDAs in the continental United States with at least 500 terminees (persons ending their enrollment in Title II-funded services) in program year 1984.[2] Exhibit 2.1 shows the site locations and abbreviated site names used in this report. The formal name, census region, and largest city of each SDA are shown in Exhibit 3.1. These 16 sites are spread throughout the nation, with 2 in the Northeast, 4 in the South, 7 in the Midwest, and 3 in the West. They include sites located in large metropolitan areas with large minority populations (Jersey City, N.J., and Oakland, Calif.), others located in predominately rural areas or small towns (e.g., Coosa Valley, Ga.; Marion, Ohio; Northwest Minnesota; Butte, Mont.), and still others with a mixture of urban,

Exhibit 3.1 KEY FACTS ABOUT 16 STUDY SITES

Site	SDA name	Census region	Largest city
Fort Wayne, Ind.	Northeast Indiana	Midwest	Fort Wayne
Coosa Valley, Ga.	Coosa Valley, Ga.	South	Rome
Corpus Christi, Tex.	Corpus Christi/Nueces County, Tex.	South	Corpus Christi
Jackson, Miss.	Capital Area, Miss.	South	Jackson
Providence, R.I.	Providence/Cranston, R.I.	Northeast	Providence
Springfield, Mo.	Job Council of the Ozarks, Mo.	Midwest	Springfield
Jersey City, N.J.	Jersey City, N.J.	Northeast	Jersey City
Marion, Ohio	Crawford/Hancock/ Marion/Wyandot Counties, Ohio	Midwest	Marion
Oakland, Calif.	Oakland, Calif.	West	Oakland
Omaha, Neb.	Greater Omaha, Neb.	Midwest	Omaha
Larimer County, Colo.	Larimer County, Colo.	West	Fort Collins
Heartland, Fla.	Heartland, Fla.	South	Lakeland
Northwest Minnesota	Northwest, Minnesota (Crookston and Thief River Falls)	Midwest	Thief River Falls
Butte, Mont.	Concentrated Employment Program, Mont.	West	Butte
Decatur, Ill.	Macon/De Witt Counties, Ill.	Midwest	Decatur
Cedar Rapids, Iowa	East Central Iowa	Midwest	Cedar Rapids

suburban, and rural areas (Fort Wayne, Ind.; Omaha, Neb.; Decatur, Ill.). According to 1990 U.S. census data, the size of the largest city within each of these SDAs ranges from 372,000 in Oakland and 336,000 in Omaha to under 10,000 in Northwest Minnesota's Thief River Falls.

No large central cities are included among the study sites. JTPA operations in many central cities are decentralized, with service providers playing an important role in intake and assessment. In Los Angeles, for example, at the time of site selection over 50 organizations were involved in client intake for the program. Because the research design involved coordinating random assignment with client intake and assessment, the research team was unable to develop workable study procedures for SDAs with such decentralized intake. Nevertheless, two smaller SDAs in large metropolitan areas (Jersey City and Oakland) did participate in the study, and they have many of the same characteristics (in terms of clients, economic conditions, and service availability) as large central cities.

Population Characteristics

As shown in Exhibit 3.2, the sites were also quite diverse in population densities and poverty rates.[3] Three entirely urban SDAs stand out in population density (Providence, Jersey City, and Oakland), while Northwest Minnesota and Butte, fall at the other extreme. Fort Wayne's relatively low population density is an average of the city of Fort Wayne and the eight surrounding predominately rural counties that are also part of this SDA. The average population density for the 16 sites is above that for the nation as a whole, at least in part because rural SDAs with only a small number of participants were not recruited to participate in the study.[4]

The poverty rates, shown in the right-hand column of the exhibit, show similar variety.[5] The sites containing large metropolitan areas with large minority populations—Jersey City and Oakland—had the highest poverty rates, but other sites with prominent minority populations such as Corpus Christi, Tex. (Hispanic), Jackson, Miss. (black),

Exhibit 3.2 SELECTED POPULATION CHARACTERISTICS OF
             16 STUDY SITES

Site	Residents per square mile,[a] 1989	Percentage of residents in poverty, 1979
Fort Wayne, Ind.	160	5.9
Coosa Valley, Ga.	110	10.7
Corpus Christi, Tex.	360	13.4
Jackson, Miss.	360	12.8
Providence, R.I.	4,680	12.1
Springfield, Mo.	80	10.1
Jersey City, N.J.	7,000	18.9
Marion, Ohio	120	7.2
Oakland, Calif.	6,620	16.0
Omaha, Neb.	550	6.7
Larimer County, Colo.	70	5.9
Heartland, Fla.	100	11.3
Northwest Minnesota	10	11.1
Butte, Mont.	10	7.5
Decatur, Ill.	150	7.8
Cedar Rapids, Iowa	90	6.0
16-site average	1,279	10.2
National average, all SDAs	733	9.7

Source: Unweighted annual averages calculated from JTPA Annual Status Report computer files produced by U.S. Department of Labor.
a. Of service delivery area (SDA).

and Providence (black and Hispanic) also had higher-than-average poverty rates. Two predominately rural sites (Coosa Valley and Northwest Minnesota) and one with a mix of urban and rural areas (Heartland, Fla.) had poverty rates slightly above the 16-site and national averages.

Economic Conditions

Economic conditions at the sites, summarized in Exhibit 3.3, reflect differences in both regional economic conditions and the local economic base. Corpus Christi's residents, for example, experienced persistently high unemployment (column 1) during the late 1980s, as the oil industry suffered an extended slump.[6] At the other extreme, Providence's low unemployment rate was the result of the New England

Exhibit 3.3 SELECTED ECONOMIC CONDITIONS AT 16 STUDY SITES

Site	Mean unemployment rate, 1987–89 (1)	Mean earnings, 1987 (2)	Percentage employed in manufacturing, mining, or agriculture, 1988 (3)	Annual growth in retail and wholesale earnings, 1989 (4)
Fort Wayne, Ind.	4.7%	$18,700	33.3%	−0.1%
Coosa Valley, Ga.	6.5	16,000	42.8	2.1
Corpus Christi, Tex.	10.2	18,700	16.8	−15.5
Jackson, Miss.	6.1	17,600	12.8	−2.4
Providence, R.I.	3.8	17,900	28.0	9.7
Springfield, Mo.	5.5	15,800	19.4	−1.8
Jersey City, N.J.	7.3	21,400	20.9	9.9
Marion, Ohio	7.0	18,600	37.7	1.7
Oakland, Calif.	6.8	23,000	14.6	3.0
Omaha, Neb.	4.3	18,400	11.8	1.8
Larimer County, Colo.	6.5	17,800	21.2	−3.1
Heartland, Fla.	8.5	15,700	23.8	−0.3
Northwest Minnesota	8.0	14,100	23.0	2.4
Butte, Mont.	6.8	16,900	9.6	−5.7
Decatur, Ill.	9.2	21,100	27.1	−1.1
Cedar Rapids, Iowa	3.6	17,900	21.9	−0.5
16-site average	6.6	18,100	22.8	0.0
National average, all SDAs	6.6	18,167	23.4	1.5

Source: Unweighted annual averages calculated from JTPA Annual Status Report computer files produced by U.S. Department of Labor.
Note: Missing data for certain measures precluded using same year across columns.

region's high technology boom of the same period, while the low rates in Fort Wayne, Omaha, and Cedar Rapids, Iowa, reflect the economic resurgence some mid-sized metropolitan areas in the Midwest were enjoying at the time. Decatur's high unemployment, however, illustrates that the recovery was not ubiquitous; in this manufacturing and food processing center, the recovery of the mid- to late 1980s was weak.

The variation in the average earnings of the population in each site (Exhibit 3.3, column 2) reflects in part the wage disparities between urban areas (for example, Oakland versus Northwest Minnesota) and in part the concentration of high-wage industries in some sites (petroleum in Corpus Christi and heavy manufacturing in Fort Wayne and Decatur).[7] These differences in the local economic base are further illustrated in column 3 of Exhibit 3.3, which displays the percentage of workers employed in the goods-producing industries of manufacturing, mining, and agriculture.

The last column of Exhibit 3.3, annual growth in retail and wholesale earnings during 1989, captures the effects of economic conditions in that year on each SDA. Corpus Christi's economic downturn is starkly visible (a decline of − 15.5 percent), as is the economic boom in the Northeast during the late 1980s (see Jersey City with a growth rate of 9.9 percent and Providence with 9.7 percent). Nevertheless, on all of these measures, the 16-site average is quite similar to the national average for all SDAs.

Participant Characteristics

The sites also exhibited diversity in their program participants. Exhibits 3.4 and 3.5 display selected characteristics of program terminees during the sample intake period.[8] The large differences in ethnic distribution across the sites reflect differences both in the local population generally and in the populations eligible for JTPA. In particular, the SDAs with large metropolitan areas have a much higher proportion of black and Hispanic terminees than do SDAs in rural areas because of the overall ethnic composition of those areas. The highest minority percentages are in Corpus Christi (71 percent Hispanic and 8 percent black), Jackson (85 percent black), Jersey City (68 percent black and 21 percent Hispanic), and Oakland (68 percent black, 6 percent Hispanic, and 19 percent other minorities, mostly Asian). On average, though, the ethnic composition of the sites practically mirrored that of SDAs nationally.

Exhibit 3.4 SELECTED CHARACTERISTICS OF TITLE II TERMINEES AT
16 STUDY SITES, PROGRAM YEARS 1987–89

	Percentage of all terminees			
Site	Youths, ages 14–21[a] (1)	White, non-Hispanic (2)	Black, non-Hispanic (3)	Hispanic (4)
Fort Wayne, Ind.	46	74	22	3
Coosa Valley, Ga.	43	80	20	0
Corpus Christi, Tex.	45	21	8	71
Jackson, Miss.	58	14	85	0
Providence, R.I.	45	34	38	21
Springfield, Mo.	39	95	3	1
Jersey City, N.J.	55	5	68	21
Marion, Ohio	41	95	3	2
Oakland, Calif.	44	7	68	6
Omaha, Neb.	37	42	51	4
Larimer County, Colo.	20	78	2	17
Heartland, Fla.	42	57	37	5
Northwest Minnesota	47	95	0	3
Butte, Mont.	39	90	0	3
Decatur, Ill.	44	60	39	0
Cedar Rapids, Iowa	50	87	9	1
16-site average	44	58	28	10
National average, all SDAs	44	61	26	10

Source: Unweighted annual averages calculated from JTPA Annual Status Report computer files produced by U.S. Department of Labor.
a. Includes both out-of-school and in-school youths. Experimental sample does not include in-school youths or youths under age 16.

Exhibit 3.5 shows the proportion of all terminees who faced one of seven selected barriers to employment. Again, the averages for the 16 study SDAs are very close to the averages for all SDAs. Furthermore, in both the study sites as a group and all SDAs nationally, the proportion of terminees facing any one of these barriers was relatively low. The only exception was the barrier of limited recent work experience (column 3), which affected 43 percent of terminees in the typical study site and 40 percent in the average SDA nationally.

The site rankings on these employment barriers varied substantially across the measures. For example, terminees in Coosa Valley, Corpus Christi, and Providence had the highest incidence of educational barriers (Exhibit 3.5, columns 2 and 6), whereas terminees in Marion, Butte, and Cedar Rapids were the most likely to have limited recent work experience and a physical or mental disability (columns 3 and 5).

Exhibit 3.5 SELECTED BARRIERS TO EMPLOYMENT FACED BY TITLE II TERMINEES AT 16 STUDY SITES, PROGRAM YEARS 1987–89

Site	Long-term AFDC recipients[b] (1)	High school dropouts[c] (2)	Unemployed 15+ weeks in past 26 (3)	Limited English (4)	Physical or mental disability (5)	Reading < 7th grade level (6)	Ever arrested (7)
			Percentage of all terminees[a]				
Fort Wayne, Ind.	2	25	33	0	15	17	7
Coosa Valley, Ga.	4	42	8	0	14	31	2
Corpus Christi, Tex.	8	41	49	1	4	33	8
Jackson, Miss.	21	25	42	0	11	21	3
Providence, R.I.	7	37	45	12	4	29	7
Springfield, Mo.	3	28	34	1	3	7	4
Jersey City, N.J.	7	27	43	3	4	4	3
Marion, Ohio	9	25	43	0	23	23	7
Oakland, Calif.	25	17	73	17	11	25	5
Omaha, Neb.	16	18	25	0	10	9	4
Larimer County, Colo.	3	21	49	1	14	12	5
Heartland, Fla.	6	30	57	1	13	17	13
Northwest Minnesota	13	12	7	0	17	10	4
Butte, Mont.	1	15	41	0	19	5	10
Decatur, Ill.	16	11	64	0	10	26	10
Cedar Rapids, Iowa	11	18	74	2	23	11	6
16-site average	10	25	43	3	12	18	6
National average, all SDAs	9	25	40	3	14	21	8

Source: Unweighted annual averages calculated from JTPA Annual Status Report computer files produced by U.S. Department of Labor.
a. Includes adults and both out-of-school and in-school youths ages 14 to 21. Experimental sample does not include in-school youths or youths under age 16.
b. Family receiving AFDC for any 24 or more of the 30 months preceding determination of eligiblity for JTPA.
c. No high school diploma or general equivalency diploma (GED).

Program Characteristics

Title II year-round program operations differed widely across the sites in terms of the size of the program, the average duration of program services, and program costs. As shown in Exhibit 3.6, the programs ranged in size from 354 terminees annually in Larimer County, Colorado, to 1,793 in Heartland, Florida, over the three-year period 1987–89.[9] The range for the average length of time that terminees spent in the program was also large: for adults the average number of weeks enrolled ranged from a low of 7 in Providence to a high of 34 in Corpus Christi, whereas the range for youths was from 5 to 33, in the same two cities. Average annual federal costs per adult terminee reflected both the differences in the lengths of enrollment and the higher

Exhibit 3.6 SELECTED CHARACTERISTICS OF JTPA TITLE II PROGRAMS AT 16 STUDY SITES, PROGRAM YEARS 1987–89

Site	Mean number of adult and youth terminees[a] (1)	Mean number of weeks enrolled		Mean federal program cost per adult terminee (4)
		Adults (2)	Youths[a] (3)	
Fort Wayne, Ind.	1,195	16	31	$1,561
Coosa Valley, Ga.	1,063	12	15	2,481
Corpus Christi, Tex.	1,049	34	33	2,570
Jackson, Miss.	1,227	8	15	1,897
Providence, R.I.	503	7	5	2,841
Springfield, Mo.	938	17	17	1,898
Jersey City, N.J.	853	16	14	3,637
Marion, Ohio	714	27	26	2,199
Oakland, Calif.	1,396	16	17	2,539
Omaha, Neb.	1,111	11	12	2,404
Larimer County, Colo.	354	32	26	1,937
Heartland, Fla.	1,793	15	24	1,782
Northwest Minnesota	430	29	28	2,371
Butte, Mont.	576	21	19	2,665
Decatur, Ill.	525	29	25	3,039
Cedar Rapids, Iowa	658	31	23	2,212
16-site average	899	20	21	2,377
National average, all SDAs	1,177	20	22	2,241

Source: Unweighted annual averages calculated from JTPA Annual Status Report computer files produced by U.S. Department of Labor.
a. Includes adults and both out-of-school and in-school youths ages 14 to 21. Experimental sample does not include in-school youths or youths under age 16.

service costs (based on higher office rental and salary rates) in large metropolitan areas such as Jersey City and Oakland. The sites as a group differed somewhat from the national average in program size (number of terminees), because the study did not include the very largest SDAs.

SDAs have responsibility for selecting and defining the roles of other organizations that will provide JTPA-funded services. These providers range from other public agencies to community-based and other nonprofit organizations to proprietary schools and private-sector firms. Exhibit 3.7 displays the variety of service providers that contracted with the 16 SDAs to supply employment and training services during the sample intake period.

Public educational institutions—vocational-technical schools, community colleges, and universities—provided classroom training in 15 sites, and proprietary schools were providers in half of the 16 sites. Arranging for subsidized on-the-job training (OJT) positions in the private sector was done by SDA staff members themselves at 7 SDAs or with the assistance of the state job service, which played a role in 3 of the SDAs; in another, a community-based organization was also involved. The job service alone arranged for OJT in another 2 SDAs, and a community college arranged for the service in 1 SDA. In 2 SDAs, private-sector firms arranged for some OJT positions. A wide variety of organizations provided JTPA-funded job search assistance, although the SDA, the job service, or both were the most common providers.[10] Basic education was provided by public schools or community colleges in 9 of the 12 sites offering it. The remaining 4 SDAs did not offer basic education as a discrete, identifiable service.

A further important choice facing SDAs was whether to provide classroom training in occupational skills by referring individual clients to training providers; by purchasing a class for a group of clients through a contract with a service provider; or by pursuing both approaches. On the one hand, if an adequate service provider network existed, individual referrals allowed SDA staff to match the training to the interests and needs of specific clients (rather than recruit to fill a class); referrals also avoided the possibility of flooding specialized labor markets with numerous program completers at once. On the other hand, purchasing a class allowed the SDA to exert more control over course offerings and curriculum and—if staff members were able to identify occupations in demand—to pinpoint JTPA training resources where there would be a strong demand for graduates.

Exhibit 3.7 MOST COMMON SERVICE PROVIDERS USED BY JTPA TITLE II PROGRAMS AT 16 STUDY SITES, BY SPECIFIC PROGRAM SERVICE

Site	Specific Program Service			
	Classroom training in occupational skills (1)	On-the-job training (2)	Job search assistance (3)	Basic education (4)
Fort Wayne, Ind.	Proprietary school Vocational-technical school	SDA	Community-based organization SDA	Not provided as separate service
Coosa Valley, Ga.	Community college Vocational-technical school	Community-based organization Private-sector firm	Community-based organization	Community college
Corpus Christi, Tex.	Community-based organization Community college Proprietary school	Private-sector firm State job service	Community-based organization	Community college
Jackson, Miss.	Community-based organization Community college Proprietary school	State job service SDA	Community-based organization State university	Public school
Providence, R.I.	Community-based organization Proprietary school Vocational-technical school	SDA	Not provided as separate service	Not provided as separate service
Springfield, Mo.	Vocational-technical school	SDA	SDA	Public school Vocational-technical school

Jersey City, N.J.	Community-based organization Proprietary school Vocational-technical school	SDA	Community-based organization SDA	Proprietary school
Marion, Ohio	Community College Vocational-technical school	SDA	SDA	SDA
Oakland, Calif.	Community-based organization Proprietary school SDA	Community-based organization SDA	Community-based organization Proprietary school SDA	Community-based organization
Omaha, Neb.	Community-based organization Community college Proprietary school	SDA	Community-based organization SDA	Not provided as separate service
Larimer County, Colo.	Vocational-technical school/ community college[a]	SDA	State job service SDA	Public school Vocational-technical school/ community college
Heartland, Fla.	Community-based organization Proprietary school Vocational-technical school	State job service SDA	State job service	Community college
Northwest Minnesota	Community college State university Vocational-technical school	State job service	State job service	Not provided as separate service

(continued)

Exhibit 3.7 MOST COMMON SERVICE PROVIDERS USED BY JTPA TITLE II PROGRAMS AT 16 STUDY SITES, BY SPECIFIC PROGRAM SERVICE (continued)

Site	Specific Program Service			
	Classroom training in occupational skills (1)	On-the-job training (2)	Job search assistance (3)	Basic education (4)
Butte, Mont.	Community-based organization Community college Public school	State job service	State job service	Public school
Decatur, Ill.	Community college	Community college	Community college	Public school
Cedar Rapids, Iowa	Community college Vocational-technical school	State job service SDA	Not provided as separate service	Community college

Source: Information collected by study team during SDA visits.
Note: Information on last two categories of program services—work experience and miscellaneous services—examined in this report is not shown because the former was rarely offered and the latter were too numerous to represent here.
a. In Larimer County the vocational-technical school became a community college during the course of the study.

The 16 SDAs in the study showed considerable diversity in how they made this strategic choice:

- *Six SDAs relied exclusively on individual referrals to training providers.* These included three rural sites (Marion, Northwest Minnesota, and Butte) and three mixed urban-rural sites (Fort Wayne, Decatur, and Cedar Rapids), which relied primarily on public vocational-technical institutes or other public technical or community colleges. These sites tended to emphasize classroom training in occupational skills less than other sites.[11]
- *Four SDAs relied exclusively on contracts to purchase classes.* The four (Jackson, Providence, Omaha, and Heartland) were in urban or mixed urban-rural areas and wrote from five to nine contracts each within a program year. The training was for occupations including truck driving, security guard, retail sales, automotive maintenance, food preparation, marketing, clerical, photocopy machine repair, and home health aide.
- *The remaining six SDAs used a mixture of individual referrals and class contracts.*[12] Three of these SDAs, which were in larger, urban areas (Corpus Christi, Jersey City, and Oakland), relied on community-based organizations for training contracts in addition to public vocational-technical institutes, colleges, or proprietary schools. The other three, which included medium-sized towns and rural areas (Coosa Valley, Springfield, and Larimer County) relied primarily on public vocational-technical schools and colleges.

Agency Standards and Program Performance

As noted in chapter 1, the U.S. Department of Labor has set certain standards for the performance of JTPA service delivery areas. Exhibit 3.8 lists the employment standard set for adults in each of the 16 SDAs studied (termed "predicted" performance) and their actual performance on that standard in program year 1988; Exhibit 3.9 does the same for two standards for youths: the "positive termination rate" and the "entered employment rate."[13] The columns labeled "difference" in the two exhibits indicate the difference between expected and actual performance on these three indicators.[14] On all three measures, the study sites include some that performed much better than the standard set for them, others that slightly exceeded the standard, and still others that failed to meet the standard. On average, though, the 16 study sites exceeded their predicted rate by an amount that was quite close to that for SDAs nationally.

Exhibit 3.8 AGENCY PERFORMANCE STANDARDS AND JTPA TITLE II
PERFORMANCE AT 16 STUDY SITES: ENTERED EMPLOYMENT
RATES OF ADULT TERMINEES, PROGRAM YEAR 1988

| | Entered employment rate | | |
Site	Actual (1)	Predicted (2)	Difference, in percentage points (3)
Fort Wayne, Ind.	84.0%	72.4%	11.6%
Coosa Valley, Ga.	83.5	68.2	15.3
Corpus Christi, Tex.	72.0	67.1	4.9
Jackson, Miss.	67.6	69.2	− 1.6
Providence, R.I.	74.3	70.2	4.1
Springfield, Mo.	89.0	76.4	12.6
Jersey City, N.J.	86.5	64.2	22.3
Marion, Ohio	55.5	59.4	− 3.9
Oakland, Calif.	67.4	66.1	1.3
Omaha, Neb.	65.0	65.7	− 0.7
Larimer County, Colo.	68.0	69.5	− 1.5
Heartland, Fla.	74.5	68.7	5.8
Northwest Minnesota	73.5	69.1	4.4
Butte, Mont.	74.0	67.1	6.9
Decatur, Ill.	79.4	65.1	14.3
Cedar Rapids, Iowa	76.9	73.1	3.8
16-site average	74.5	68.2	6.2
National average, all SDAs	74.2	67.3	6.9

Source: Unweighted annual averages calculated from JTPA Annual Status Report
(JASR) computer files produced by U.S. Department of Labor.
Notes: "Entered employment rate" is percentage of all adult terminees who had found
a job before terminating their enrollment in JTPA. "Predicted" entered employment rate
is based on JTPA performance standard reported in JASR, program year 1988.

Services Received at Study Sites

Although the study sites are similar to SDAs nationally in many ways,
they exhibit one important difference from their counterparts nationally: they emphasized classroom training and job search assistance
more, and on-the-job training and miscellaneous services less. Our
report on program impacts at 18 months presents detailed comparisons of the services received by JTPA enrollees in the study sample
and those received by JTPA terminees nationally (Bloom et al. 1993,
Appendix B).[15] The pattern of more classroom training and job search
assistance in the study sites than was the case nationally, and less
OJT and miscellaneous services, was apparent for all four target
groups.

Exhibit 3.9 AGENCY PERFORMANCE STANDARDS AND JTPA TITLE II PERFORMANCE AT 16 STUDY SITES: POSITIVE TERMINATION RATES AND ENTERED EMPLOYMENT RATES OF YOUTH TERMINEES, PROGRAM YEAR 1988

	Positive termination rate[a]			Entered employment rate[a]		
Site	Actual (1)	Predicted (2)	Difference, in percentage points (3)	Actual (4)	Predicted (5)	Difference, in percentage points (6)
Fort Wayne, Ind.	77%	75%	2%	50%	38%	12%
Coosa Valley, Ga.	N.A.	N.A.	N.A.	48	41	7
Corpus Christi, Tex.	78	72	6	48	48	0
Jackson, Miss.	76	72	4	34	44	−10
Providence, R.I.	75	78	−3	54	46	8
Springfield, Mo.	94	76	18	70	56	14
Jersey City, N.J.	85	80	5	N.A.	N.A.	N.A.
Marion, Ohio	74	75	−1	44	38	6
Oakland, Calif.	73	78	−5	50	45	5
Omaha, Neb.	81	73	8	N.A.	N.A.	N.A.
Larimer County, Colo.	72	74	−2	N.A.	N.A.	N.A.
Heartland, Fla.	77	74	3	49	35	14
Northwest Minnesota	76	78	−2	38	44	−6
Butte, Mont.	86	76	10	56	45	11
Decatur, Ill.	74	74	0	25	10	15
Cedar Rapids, Iowa	66	78	−12	60	50	10
16-site average[b]	78	76	2	48	41	7
National average, all SDAs[b]	81	75	6	50	41	9

Source: Unweighted averages calculated from JTPA Annual Status Report (JASR) computer files produced by U.S. Department of Labor.
Notes: "Positive termination rate" is percentage of all youth terminees who, before terminating their JTPA enrollment, had found a job, attained recognized employment competencies established by the Private Industry Council (PIC), completed elementary, secondary, or postsecondary school, enrolled in another training program or an apprenticeship, enlisted in the armed forces, or returned to school full-time. "Entered employment rate" is percentage who had found a job. "Predicted" rate of each of these is based on JTPA performance standard reported in JASR, program year 1988. N.A.: Not applicable; SDA does not use this standard.
a. Includes both out-of-school and in-school youths ages 14–21. Experimental sample does not include in-school youths or youths under age 16.
b. Average excludes SDAs not using standard in question.

The analysis of program impacts presented in this report controls for these differences between services received by the study sample and those received nationally by JTPA participants by presenting separate impact findings for sample subgroups who were recommended for different service strategies and consequently received different clusters of JTPA services.

MESHING STUDY PROCEDURES WITH CLIENT FLOW IN JTPA

Implementation of the evaluation in the study sites involved integrating random assignment and baseline data collection procedures into the intake process of an ongoing program. This section describes the normal JTPA application and intake process and shows how the study procedures were incorporated into that process.

Exhibit 3.10 presents the basic steps common to all SDAs in the study by which an individual eligible for JTPA could apply for the program, be randomly assigned, and (if assigned to the treatment group) enroll in the program. Normally, many more people contact the SDA or a service provider to learn about the program and inquire about eligibility rules than actually apply. Consequently, as Exhibit 3.10 shows, individuals may "exit" from the intake process at each step. This could occur because they find other opportunities, decide JTPA is unlikely to provide what they want, or are discouraged by what staff tell them about their prospects in the program. This section groups the major steps in the client flow process into three stages.

Stage 1. Connecting with Those Eligible for and Interested in JTPA: Recruitment, Application, Eligibility Determination, and Background Information Form (BIF) Completion

Recruitment. The study made no change in the eligibility rules for the program. In each local area served through a single SDA, the size of the eligible population will vary with the characteristics of the population and local labor market conditions. However, JTPA is not a legal entitlement for all who satisfy the eligibility requirements, and JTPA funding is usually sufficient to serve fewer than 10 percent of those eligible. Nevertheless, recruitment of program applicants takes substantial effort in many (though not all) SDAs and can involve both the local administrative entity running the program and agencies under contract to provide various training and employment services.

Exhibit 3.10 FLOW OF SAMPLE MEMBERS IN THE NATIONAL JTPA STUDY SITES

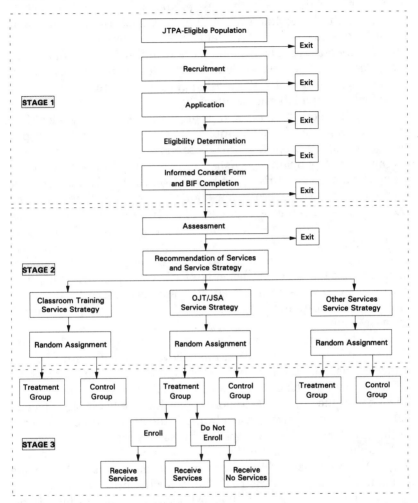

Note: Because of limited space, the stage 3 sample flow has been fully depicted only for the OJT/JSA service strategy, although it would be the same for the other two strategies.

Recruitment is a special challenge because SDAs must identify eligible individuals who are interested in the types of training and employment services that JTPA provides and are able to participate without receiving stipends or other program-related income support. For those without other sources of support, the program must offer income-generating services such as OJT or job search.

The experience of program operators indicates that the level of unemployment in the area is the best predictor of the difficulty of recruitment: the lower the level of unemployment, the harder it is to recruit applicants for JTPA. Because JTPA does not provide in-program income, as jobs become more plentiful JTPA becomes relatively less attractive. As evidence of this, even though low-income workers are eligible for JTPA, most applicants are unemployed or had previously left the labor force altogether.

During the period of random assignment, sites had to identify a large enough pool of eligible applicants who were interested in participating and "appropriate for JTPA services" to be able both to serve the number of people they wished to enroll and to create a control group. In most sites, this could be achieved in two ways. First, site staff could increase recruitment efforts and expand their applicant pool, because the eligible population for JTPA remained much larger than the number of people recruited in the study SDAs. Second, staff could reduce the "exit" of individuals from the applicant process prior to random assignment by streamlining application procedures or marketing the potential benefits of JTPA more clearly. Sites that chose to increase recruitment efforts were encouraged by the study team to seek additional applicants who fulfilled existing SDA enrollment priorities.

Because labor market conditions changed during the period of random assignment (in most sites, unemployment rates declined), it is difficult to isolate the effect of this "study-induced" expansion of the applicant pool on the characteristics of applicants. However, program operators in the study sites reported that the combination of factors led them to recruit fewer job-ready applicants than had been the case in the mid-1980s, when unemployment was higher.[16]

Application and Eligibility Determination.   Those who applied for JTPA during the study period completed the normal SDA or state forms used to establish their eligibility for the program. They were also required to provide the standard documentation (usually information about recent family income or receipt of public assistance), the extent of which varied from state to state. SDA staff then had to determine if applicants were eligible for the program. The study made no change in the eligibility determination process, and staff were told to complete this process as they normally would. Those found eligible would continue through to assessment; ineligibles were normally told they could not be served.[17]

Completion of Background Information Form (BIF).   By this point in the process, applicants in the study sites typically had completed the study Background Information Form (BIF), with assistance from the program staff. The study design allowed some local flexibility as to the precise point when the form was to be completed, in order to lessen the burden on local staff who assisted applicants in filling it out. In most sites, staff and applicants filled out the BIF when the usual SDA application materials were completed, but in some instances completion of the BIF occurred as part of the assessment interviews. The BIF provided basic data on preprogram characteristics of those randomly assigned—information that was used to identify members of subgroups analyzed separately in the study, as well as to control for baseline characteristics of the sample in estimating impacts. At the time the BIF was completed, applicants also signed an informed consent form, acknowledging that they understood that, because of the study, admission to the program would be based partly on a "lottery" and giving the evaluators permission to use data pertaining them.

Stage 2. Identifying the Research Sample: Assessment, Recommendation for Services, Designation of Service Strategy, and Random Assignment

Assessment. Following eligibility determination (or possibly simultaneously for those very likely to be eligible), SDA and/or service provider staff assessed the current interests, skills, and service needs of applicants. The extent and complexity of this assessment varied greatly among the study SDAs; in some it consisted of several days of testing and interviews, whereas in others service recommendations were based on a short interview at the time the application was completed. Rural areas with limited service offerings, in which applicants may have had to travel long distances to the program office, were most likely to have combined the application with an abbreviated assessment. During the study, local staff were told to follow past practices as closely as possible, and in most SDAs assessment practices were not changed by the study.[18]

Recommendation for Services. Based on their assessment of clients, local staff developed recommendations for services reflecting client needs, interests, and preferences. For about three-quarters of the sample, staff recommended a single service—most commonly classroom training in occupational skills (CTOS) or on-the-job training—but for the remaining one-quarter, staff recommended a combination of services. For some applicants, staff decided that no JTPA services would be appropriate and—as would normally be the case—

these individuals did not continue through the remaining steps of the JTPA intake process and were not part of the research sample.

Designation of Service Strategy. The service strategy subgroups defined for evaluation purposes distinguished between these two emphases or primary services, but also accommodated combinations of services. Individuals recommended by local staff for CTOS but not OJT were part of the service strategy subgroup labeled classroom training. Those recommended for OJT but not CTOS were part of the service strategy labeled on-the-job training/job search assistance (OJT/JSA). Those recommended for neither CTOS nor OJT, or for both services, were part of the third strategy labeled other services. Over the course of working with clients, site staff could provide individual services different from those originally recommended, but the services they did provide were expected to be consistent with the service strategy originally chosen.

Random Assignment to Treatment or Control Group. The random assignment procedure was straightforward. Site staff telephoned evaluation staff (using a toll-free number), provided background information on each individual to allow tracking of sample build up by target group, and listed the service recommendation and service strategy designation. Evaluation staff gave site staff the person's assignment (treatment or control). Site staff were then to follow their service recommendations for those randomly assigned to the treatment group. Evaluation staff kept a roster of those randomly assigned and their assignment, to ensure that if a person in the sample reapplied to the program, he or she would be treated consistently during the follow-up period.

Those in the control group were excluded from JTPA-funded services in the SDA for the following 18 months, but were provided a list of alternative service providers in the community whom they could contact independently.[19] Sites were successful in enforcing the "control embargo" rule; only about 3 percent of the controls were enrolled in any JTPA services at any point during the follow-up period.

Essentially, as shown in Exhibit 3.10, this process created a separate control group for each service strategy, permitting separate impact estimates for how each service strategy "worked" for the people recommended for it. It is important to recognize that, whereas treatment and control groups were well-matched within each service strategy subgroup, local staff recommended people with different characteristics for the three service strategies, so that the samples in the three service strategy subgroups differed in important ways.

Stage 3. Efforts to Arrange Services for Treatment Group: Enrollment in JTPA and Involvement of the Nonenrolled with JTPA

Individuals randomly assigned to the treatment group were offered access to JTPA services. This offer and the resulting services provided were the "treatment" being tested through the random assignment experiment. As discussed in the following paragraphs, many factors affected whether an individual actually enrolled in JTPA.

The impact analysis in the National JTPA Study presents impact estimates for all persons assigned to the treatment group and—alternatively—for all those in the treatment group who enrolled in JTPA. Enrollment in JTPA is generally equivalent to receiving JTPA services. However, as this section explains, the two concepts are not always identical.

Enrollment in JTPA Services. Enrollment in JTPA occurs when SDA staff enter a person's name and application data into the local JTPA management information system (MIS) and enroll him or her in one or more specific JTPA-funded services. This step makes the person an official JTPA participant, whose service receipt and progress are tracked and whose termination and postprogram status (e.g., employment and wages) are noted as part of the JTPA performance standard system. By enrolling clients, SDA staff are held accountable through the JTPA performance standard system for the costs that JTPA incurred in serving them and for their success when they left the program. As discussed in more detail later in this chapter, 65 percent of the sample were enrolled in JTPA at some point in the follow-up period. Thus, Exhibit 3.10 shows individuals who enrolled in JTPA as a subset of each of the three treatment groups.

Nonenrolled Treatment Group Members. Three factors help explain why some members of the treatment group would never be enrolled in JTPA:

- Despite the initial assessment that a client is appropriate for JTPA, staff may be unable to find a service provider willing to accept the person.
- Applicants may change their minds about JTPA as they continue to seek other opportunities or learn more about the program.
- The design of the JTPA performance measurement system encourages local staff to ensure that applicants will participate and do well in a service before they are enrolled and counted as a JTPA participant. Many SDAs have believed that they have discretion in defining the point at which individuals "count" in their perfor-

mance measures and have responded to the system's incentives by delaying enrollment.

Most of the study sites enrolled individuals in classroom training when they attended their first class or in OJT when they worked their first day, although one site did enroll people during assessment. In a few sites, local staff could refer people to job search assistance or job club without enrolling them, in order to observe how they acted in this setting as part of an "extended assessment." The applicants may never have been enrolled in JTPA unless they found a job or, because their behavior in the job club showed motivation and promise of employability, were referred to another service.

These factors suggest that nonenrolled members (as well as enrolled members) of the treatment group could have had some postrandom assignment involvement with the JTPA system. To understand the extent to which this occurred, the research team drew a sample of nonenrolled treatment group members in 12 sites[20] and talked with local staff about their efforts to work with these individuals after random assignment. The local staff had no contact with 15 percent of this sample of nonenrollees after random assignment, because they were unable to locate them again. Another 11 percent reported that they were no longer interested in JTPA, for a variety of reasons. Another 20 percent of these nonenrollees were recontacted, but staff never arranged service for them. One percent of the nonenrollees were found to be ineligible upon recontact. The remaining 53 percent of the sample of nonenrolled treatment group members had some postrandom assignment involvement with JTPA without being enrolled. The most common service, provided for 36 percent of the nonenrollee sample, was one or more referrals to employers for a possible OJT position. Twenty percent participated in job club or other job search assistance. This small study suggests that local staff worked with about half of the treatment group members who never enrolled in JTPA, though in many cases little service was provided. The fact that these individuals were never enrolled in JTPA suggests that whatever services were provided were unsuccessful in obtaining employment for the individual and that, therefore, the program had little or no impact on the earnings of these nonenrolled applicants.

PROFILE OF 30-MONTH EARNINGS SAMPLE

As described in chapter 2, the 30-month earnings sample contained 15,981 persons for whom continuous data on earnings were available for at least 30 months after random assignment. Two-thirds of the sample were treatment group members and one-third were control group members. The sites' contributions to the sample ranged from 3,605 in Fort Wayne to 133 in Butte, as shown in the first column of Exhibit 3.11. Target group composition varied by site (columns 2 through 6), because of differences in both the eligible populations and the recruiting and service emphases across sites, as well as certain exclusions from the study. Most notably, youths in Oakland were excluded from the study at the request of the site. The size of the youth target groups at the other study sites also reflects differing emphases on serving in-school versus out-of-school youths. Because in-school youths were not included in the study, those sites that targeted much of their youth program on this group have a lower percentage of youths in their study sample.

Exhibit 3.12 shows sample sizes for the final study target groups— adult women, adult men, female youths, male youth non-arrestees, and male youth arrestees—and three service strategy subgroups: classroom training, OJT/JSA, and other services. Adult women formed about 38 percent of the sample (6,102 out of 15,981); adult men, a third of the sample; and out-of-school youths about 30 percent (with 17 percent female and 13 percent male). Within the full sample, SDA staff recommended about 32 percent for the classroom training strategy, 39 percent for the OJT/JSA strategy, and 29 percent for the other services strategy.

Exhibit 3.13 presents selected baseline characteristics for each target group. For reasons explained in chapter 4, the impact analysis subdivides male youths according to whether they reported having been arrested prior to random assignment. The two groups did not differ substantially on other baseline characteristics. As shown in the top panel of the exhibit, non-Hispanic whites made up over half of the sample in all target groups. Blacks comprised about a quarter of the sample and Hispanics 10 to 15 percent. Other ethnic groups comprised 3 percent or less of the sample.

To determine whether JTPA impacts varied with the degree of labor market disadvantagedness, this report includes separate estimates for subgroups facing selected barriers to employment. Following a framework developed for several studies of JTPA by the U.S. General Accounting Office (1991), this analysis focuses on the following barriers:

- *Welfare receipt,* measured as receiving Aid to Families with Dependent Children (AFDC), General Assistance, or other cash welfare upon application to JTPA;

Exhibit 3.11 SIZE OF 30-MONTH EARNINGS SAMPLE: FULL SAMPLE AND TARGET GROUPS, BY STUDY SITE

Site	Full sample (1)	Adult women (2)	Adult men (3)	Female youths[a] (4)	Male youth non-arrestees[a] (5)	Male youth arrestees[a] (6)
Fort Wayne, Ind.	3,605	1,392	1,321	432	336	124
Coosa Valley, Ga.	1,806	788	407	410	169	32
Providence, R.I.	1,554	463	485	267	282	57
Corpus Christi, Tex.	1,497	524	412	335	185	41
Springfield, Mo.	1,201	401	427	191	134	48
Omaha, Neb.	1,189	636	283	180	77	13
Jackson, Miss.	1,137	353	315	272	174	23
Larimer County, Colo.	1,024	485	362	109	51	17
Heartland, Fla.	596	234	202	93	41	26
Northwest Minnesota	559	179	254	61	55	10
Cedar Rapids, Iowa	498	190	163	79	52	14
Decatur, Ill.	470	177	219	30	33	11
Jersey City, N.J.	295	81	52	107	55	0
Marion, Ohio	250	74	100	49	27	0
Oakland, Calif.	167	87	80	0	0	0
Butte, Mont.	133	38	20	42	33	0
All sizes	15,981	6,102	5,102	2,657	1,704	416

Source: Unadjusted frequencies based on Background Information Form data.
a. Out-of-school youths only.

Exhibit 3.12   SAMPLE SIZES IN 18-MONTH STUDY: FULL SAMPLE AND TARGET GROUPS, BY SERVICE STRATEGY SUBGROUP

Service strategy subgroup	Full sample (1)	Adult women (2)	Adult men (3)	Female youths[a] (4)	Male youth non-arrestees[a] (5)	Male youth arrestees[a] (6)
Classroom training	5,110	2,343	1,034	1,150	489	94
OJT/JSA	6,180	2,284	2,571	614	554	157
Other services	4,691	1,475	1,497	893	661	165
All subgroups	15,981	6,102	5,102	2,657	1,704	416

Source: Unadjusted frequencies based on Background Information Form data.
a. Out-of-school youths only.

Exhibit 3.13 SELECTED BASELINE CHARACTERISTICS OF EACH TARGET GROUP

Characteristic	Adult women	Adult men	Female youths[a]	Male youth non-arrestees[a]	Male youth arrestees[a]
Ethnicity					
White, non-Hispanic	59.6%	61.6%	51.5%	54.1%	62.7%
Black, non-Hispanic	26.4	25.4	31.2	28.4	26.0
Hispanic	11.9	9.7	15.7	15.0	10.3
Other	2.1	3.2	1.6	2.5	1.0
Barriers to employment					
Receiving cash welfare	34.7	11.2	29.8	9.5	6.8
No high school diploma or GED	27.9	30.7	48.4	57.2	63.0
Worked less than 13 weeks in past 12 months	51.6	40.0	58.2	46.6	48.0
Number of barriers					
None of the above	30.8	40.6	22.1	24.6	21.5
One of the above	35.0	40.4	33.3	41.0	43.8
Two of the above	26.0	16.3	31.1	30.1	31.0
Three of the above	8.2	2.7	13.5	4.3	3.8
Work and training histories					
Ever employed	82.9%	91.6%	78.8%	84.5%	87.7%
Mean individual earnings in past 12 months	$2,489	$4,057	$1,373	$2,228	$1,956
Previously received occupational training	44.8%	46.0%	25.4%	30.7%	26.8%

Source: Unadjusted frequencies based on Background Information Form data.
a. Out-of-school youths only.

- *Limited education,* measured as a lack of a high school diploma or general educational development (GED) certificate upon application; and
- *Limited recent work experience,* measured as having worked less than 13 weeks in the 12 months preceding the application.

The incidence of each of these specific barriers among target group members is shown in the second main panel of Exhibit 3.13. The bottom panel of the exhibit shows several related measures of prior work and training experience: whether the sample member had ever been employed for pay; earnings in the 12 months before random assignment; and whether the person had ever received occupational training.

Adult women and female out-of-school youths were considerably more likely than their male counterparts to be receiving cash welfare and to have limited recent work experience. Adult men tended to be the most employable and to have the most extensive work experience. In particular, nearly 70 percent of the adult men had a high school diploma or GED; and adult men had by far the highest average earnings of the four groups in the year preceding application to JTPA. The youth target groups were the most disadvantaged. Only about half of all female youths and 40 percent of the male youths had a high school credential. Youths' average earnings in the year before their application were only about half the earnings level of their adult counterparts.

Exhibit 3.13 also shows the proportion of each target group facing none, one, two, or all three of these barriers to employment. Almost 70 percent of the full sample was facing at least one barrier, but only 6.8 percent was facing all three. There were important differences among the target groups, however. As noted earlier, the out-of-school youths in the sample were the most disadvantaged; here they exhibit the highest incidence of barriers, with 44.6 percent of female youths facing two or three barriers. Adult men were at the other extreme, with 81.0 percent facing none or only one of the barriers.

PATTERNS OF JTPA ENROLLMENT AND SERVICE RECEIPT

This section provides a context for understanding the impacts estimated in the later chapters, by describing the service strategies JTPA staff recommended for the sample, the rates at which treatment group

youths and 34 percent of female youths, but for only 29 percent of adult men and 24 percent of adult women.

Differences in Employability across Service Strategy Subgroups

Throughout the later discussions of impacts on the three service strategy subgroups within each target group, it is important to bear in mind that the three subgroups differed from one another in important ways. SDA staff made their service strategy recommendations for more- or less-intensive employment and training services based in large part on each applicant's job skills, experience, and needs. One clear way to summarize the differences among the subgroups is to use the control group's earnings over the 30-month follow-up period as a measure of employability.[21] Throughout this report the earnings of the control group serve as our estimate of what the treatment group would have earned in the absence of the program. Thus, they also indicate the treatment group's employability without access to the program.

Exhibit 3.15 displays the total 30-month earnings of control group members in various target group–service strategy subgroup combinations. Differences in employability across subgroups are readily apparent. In every target group, those control group members recommended for the OJT/JSA strategy had the highest average earnings over the 30 months following random assignment. The most striking finding in the table is the high earnings level of male youth non-arrestee control group members recommended for OJT/JSA—which surpassed even that of adult men in the OJT/JSA subgroup. This estimate suggests that local staff routed a very job-ready group of male youths to OJT/JSA.

JTPA Enrollment Rates by Target Group and Service Strategy Subgroup

As explained in chapter 2, this report presents two sets of impact estimates: impacts per JTPA assignee (treatment group member) and inferred impacts per JTPA enrollee (treatment group member who became enrolled in JTPA after random assignment). Exhibit 3.16 shows that 65 percent of the treatment group became enrolled in JTPA during the first 18 months after random assignment. Enrollment rates across the five target groups varied by only a few percentage points, but differed more substantially among the service strategy subgroups. In every target group the highest enrollment was among those recommended for the classroom training strategy.

Exhibit 3.15 MEAN EARNINGS OF CONTROL GROUP OVER 30-MONTH FOLLOW-UP PERIOD: TARGET GROUPS, BY SERVICE STRATEGY SUBGROUP

Service strategy subgroup	Mean earnings of control group			
	Adult women (1)	Adult men (2)	Female youths[a] (3)	Male youth non-arrestees[a] (4)
Classroom training	$11,021	$17,713	$9,208	$16,039
OJT/JSA	13,967	19,192	13,559	20,430
Other services	11,362	17,873	8,798	13,373
All subgroups	12,241	18,496	10,106	16,375
Sample size	2,014	1,703	850	583

Source: Estimates based on First and Second Follow-up Survey responses and earnings data from state unemployment insurance (UI) agencies.
Note: Estimates for male youth arrestees are not shown in this exhibit because of small sample sizes.
a. Out-of-school youths only.

Exhibit 3.16 TREATMENT GROUP ENROLLMENT IN JTPA: FULL SAMPLE AND TARGET GROUPS, BY SERVICE STRATEGY SUBGROUP

Service strategy subgroup	Full sample (1)	Adult women (2)	Adult men (3)	Female youths[a] (4)	Male youth non-arrestees[a] (5)	Male youth arrestees[a] (6)
Classroom training	77.1%	77.2%	77.1%	76.1%	78.5%	81.5%
OJT/JSA	58.2	57.4	57.4	58.9	62.9	62.4
Other services	61.2	60.5	60.0	60.0	68.2	56.8
All subgroups	65.1	65.7	62.3	66.6	69.5	64.3
Sample size	10,706	4,088	3,399	1,807	1,121	291

Source: Enrollment and tracking data from 16 service delivery areas (SDAs).
a. Out-of-school youths only.

This variation in enrollment across the three service strategy subgroups is not surprising. As discussed in more detail in the National JTPA Study implementation report (Doolittle, 1993), the enrollment process was far from automatic. In the case of classroom training, for example, SDA staff had to link program applicants with a training provider that would accept them. For on-the-job training, the staff had to find an employer willing and able to offer the desired training in exchange for a subsidy. In some cases, the applicant found a job or became discouraged and withdrew before services could be arranged. In other cases, applicants were enrolled in other services, such as job search assistance or basic education, while more intensive services were being arranged. Enrollment ultimately occurred when staff entered an applicant's name into the local JTPA management information system, at which point the *enrollee* was counted among program participants for the purposes of meeting JTPA performance standards.

Differences in JTPA Service Receipt across Target Groups and Service Strategy Subgroups

As noted in chapter 2, the impact of JTPA depends on the difference between the services received by those with access to the program and the services they would have received had they been excluded from the program. Here we simply summarize the JTPA services received by the treatment group overall (including both those who did and those who did not enroll) and by enrollees only.

Exhibit 3.17 details the specific program services received by *treatment group members* in each service strategy subgroup within the full sample and target groups. Recall that the classroom training subgroup includes all sample members for whom classroom training in occupational skills was recommended, and the OJT/JSA subgroup includes all those for whom OJT was recommended. The other services strategy subgroup includes all sample members for whom neither classroom training in occupational skills nor OJT was recommended or both were recommended.

The patterns of service receipt differed markedly for the three subgroups. In every target group, over 50 percent of the classroom training subgroup received the primary service—occupational skills training. Members of the OJT/JSA subgroup, however, were apt to receive one of two services: on-the-job training or job search assistance. Only a small percentage of the classroom training subgroup received on-the-job training, and only a small percentage of the OJT/

Exhibit 3.17 PERCENTAGE OF TREATMENT GROUP RECEIVING SPECIFIC JTPA SERVICES: FULL SAMPLE AND TARGET GROUPS, BY SERVICE STRATEGY SUBGROUP

Specific program service	Full sample (1)	Adult women (2)	Adult men (3)	Female youths[a] (4)	Male youth non-arrestees[a] (5)	Male youth arrestees[a] (6)
Classroom training subgroup						
Never enrolled	22.9	22.8	22.9	23.9	21.5	18.5
Classroom training in occupational skills	60.4	61.7	60.0	59.5	56.8	61.5
Basic education[b]	11.9	8.3	6.6	18.7	20.6	30.8
On-the-job training	5.0	4.4	8.2	3.2	4.3	6.2
Job search assistance	22.9	21.4	13.2	28.9	33.4	40.0
Work experience	4.9	5.8	2.1	6.0	4.3	3.1
Miscellaneous[c]	11.1	12.2	11.9	9.5	8.9	6.2
OJT/JSA subgroup						
Never enrolled	41.8	42.6	42.6	41.1	37.1	37.6
Classroom training in occupational skills	4.1	5.6	2.5	5.4	3.3	5.0
Basic education[b]	1.6	1.4	1.2	2.8	3.0	1.0
On-the-job training	30.1	30.2	28.4	32.7	34.6	29.7
Job search assistance	20.3	18.4	20.9	19.6	25.3	23.8
Work experience	2.4	2.4	2.4	2.6	1.9	5.0
Miscellaneous[c]	5.3	4.8	5.8	5.1	6.6	3.0

			Other services subgroup			
Never enrolled	38.8	39.5	40.0	40.0	31.8	43.2
Classroom training in occupational skills	10.5	17.5	4.9	10.9	7.7	5.6
Basic education[b]	12.7	7.1	5.5	23.9	24.8	16.8
On-the-job training	5.3	6.2	5.9	4.0	4.9	0.8
Job search assistance	13.7	15.3	15.6	11.2	10.2	11.2
Work experience	1.7	2.4	0.6	2.6	1.6	0.8
Miscellaneous[c]	33.5	32.5	34.6	30.1	37.8	34.4
Sample size	10,706	4,088	3,399	1,807	1,121	291

Source: Enrollment and tracking data from 16 SDAs.

Note: Percentages may not add to 100 because sample members may receive multiple services.

a. Out-of-school youths only.

b. "Basic education" includes Adult Basic Education (ABE), high school or General Educational Development (GED) preparation, and English as a Second Language (ESL).

c. "Miscellaneous" includes assessment, job-readiness training, customized training, vocational exploration, job shadowing, and tryout employment, among other services.

JSA subgroup received classroom training in occupational skills. Thus, although not all sample members received the services recommended for them, the service recommendations did define three subgroups receiving distinctly different service mixes, as intended.

Exhibit 3.18 focuses on JTPA *enrollees only* and highlights the two key services received in each target group—service strategy subgroup combination. This breakdown provides further insight into the services received by the first two service strategy subgroups and helps to clarify the more complex patterns of receipt for the other services subgroup. Specifically:

- Most of the treatment group members recommended for the classroom training service strategy (79 to 86 percent) received either classroom training in occupational skills (the defining service for that strategy), basic education, or both. Hence, in terms of the services actually received, it is most appropriate to characterize this service strategy as one focused on classroom instruction.

- Most of the treatment group members recommended for the OJT/JSA service strategy (62 to 74 percent) received either on-the-job training (the defining service for that strategy), job search assistance, or both. Hence, it is most appropriate to characterize this service strategy as one focused mainly on immediate employment, with or without subsidized training.

- Most of the adult treatment group members recommended for the other services strategy (72 to 79 percent) received either job search assistance or miscellaneous services, or both. Most of the youth treatment group members recommended for the other services strategy (76 to 83 percent) received either basic education, miscellaneous services, or both. Thus, adults in this subgroup were more likely to receive services that focused on immediate employment, whereas youths were more likely to receive services that focused on basic education and other preemployment services.

The findings for classroom training are straightforward, but those for the OJT/JSA and other services strategies require some background on program operations and the research design to be understood.

The OJT/JSA service strategy was intended for applicants seeking employment who, in the judgment of local staff, appeared to need on-the-job training and a wage subsidy to develop the skills necessary to be hired as unsubsidized workers. The initial actions taken to arrange on-the-job training, however, were often very similar to what staff members would do to help an applicant find unsubsidized employment; the first step in both cases was to find an employer interested

Exhibit 3.18 KEY JTPA SERVICES RECEIVED BY TREATMENT GROUP MEMBERS ENROLLED IN PROGRAM: TARGET GROUPS, BY SERVICE STRATEGY SUBGROUP

Key services in each service strategy subgroup	Percentage of enrollees receiving one or both services				
	Adult women (1)	Adult men (2)	Female youths[a] (3)	Male youths non-arrestees[a] (4)	Male youths arrestees[a] (5)
Classroom training subgroup					
Classroom training in occupational skills/basic education[b]	85.2	82.0	85.5	79.7	79.2
OJT/JSA subgroup					
On-the-job training/job search assistance	73.6	70.8	70.2	72.9	61.9
Other services subgroup					
Job search assistance/miscellaneous[c]	72.3	79.3	—	—	—
Basic education[b]/miscellaneous[c]	—	—	75.6	83.0	78.9
Sample size	2,687	2,117	1,024	779	187

Source: Enrollment and tracking data from 16 SDAs.
Note: As shown in bottom panel, key services received by "other services" subgroup differed between adults and out-of-school youths.
a. Out-of-school youths only.
b. "Basic education" includes Adult Basic Education (ABE), high school or General Educational Development (GED) preparation, and English as a Second Language (ESL).
c. "Miscellaneous" includes assessment, job-readiness training, customized training, vocational exploration, job shadowing, and tryout employment, among other services.

in hiring a new employee. Furthermore, the applicant might also be seeking an unsubsidized job, often with help from SDA staff in the form of job search assistance. As shown in Exhibit 3.17, across all target groups roughly equal proportions of treatment group members (18 to 25 percent) who had been recommended for the OJT/JSA strategy enrolled in job search assistance.

The other services strategy, by definition, involved a diverse group of clients. SDA staff recommended this strategy for applicants facing serious employment barriers, who needed basic education or preemployment skills enhancement before they could benefit from classroom training in occupational skills or on-the-job training, or before they could be expected to obtain a job. At the same time, the other services strategy was appropriate for those who were so obviously employable that they needed only job search assistance or for those needing preemployment skills training services, such as vocational exploration, job shadowing, and tryout employment, among a large number of other services that varied across sites. These specialized preemployment services are grouped together as "miscellaneous services" in the exhibits of this report.

Although job search assistance was a common activity in all three service strategies, it was only in the other services strategy that an applicant could be recommended for this service alone. Thus, as shown in Exhibit 3.18, within the other services subgroup the difference in the service pattern between adults (who received primarily job search assistance or miscellaneous services) and youths (who received primarily basic education or miscellaneous services) suggests that those very job-ready applicants recommended for this strategy were primarily adults, whereas the youths recommended for this strategy tended to have more serious skill deficits that had to be addressed through basic education or preemployment skills training.

Enrollment Patterns over Time among Enrollees and Treatment Group Overall

There were also clear differences among the service strategy subgroups and, to a lesser extent, target groups in the duration of their enrollment in Title II. As shown in Exhibit 3.19, among treatment group members who were enrolled in JTPA, those recommended for the OJT/JSA strategy tended to have the shortest periods of enrollment, whereas those recommended for the classroom training strategy had the longest. The relatively short average enrollments among members of the OJT/JSA subgroup reflect their high rate of receiving job search

Exhibit 3.19 MEDIAN NUMBER OF MONTHS ENROLLED IN JTPA AMONG TREATMENT GROUP MEMBERS ENROLLED IN PROGRAM: FULL SAMPLE AND TARGET GROUPS, BY SERVICE STRATEGY SUBGROUP

Service strategy subgroup	Full Sample (1)	Adult women (2)	Adult men (3)	Female youths[a] (4)	Male youth non-arrestees[a] (5)	Male youth arrestees[a] (6)
Classroom training	5.5	5.9	4.2	5.9	5.1	5.8
OJT/JSA	2.4	2.3	2.5	2.3	2.5	2.4
Other services	3.1	3.7	2.4	3.5	2.9	3.2
All subgroups	3.5	3.8	2.8	4.3	3.2	3.7
Sample size	6,974	2,687	2,117	1,204	779	187

Source: Enrollment and tracking data from 16 SDAs.

a. Out-of-school youths only.

SDA based on the success of its program terminees, as measured by their employment rates, wage rates, and—for youths—a broader measure called positive termination. But only those individuals who formally enroll in JTPA are counted in this performance standards system, and so the SDAs have an incentive to wait until an applicant actually begins receiving a service designed to increase employability before enrolling him or her. In many SDAs, initial assessment, counseling, development of an employability plan, and referrals to potential service providers all typically happen before applicants are formally enrolled in JTPA.

Second, this pattern of services provided to nonenrollees does not bias the estimates of program impacts per *assignee* presented in this report, since these measure the impact of access to JTPA on *all* members of the treatment group, whether they become enrolled or not. Furthermore, the benefit-cost analysis presented in this report includes estimates of the JTPA costs of serving all those in the treatment group; thus, the comparison of impacts per assignee with costs per assignee necessary for that analysis will also be valid. The finding that some JTPA services were provided to treatment group nonenrollees is cause for caution, however, in interpreting the alternative impact estimates—impacts per enrollee—presented in the following chapters. As explained in chapter 2, impacts per assignee should be interpreted as a lower bound, and impacts per enrollee as an upper bound, on the true impact of JTPA on those treatment group members who actually received some program service.

SUMMARY

The most basic conclusion of this chapter is that the study sites and the 15,981 members of the 30-month earnings sample resemble SDAs and their participants nationally and also include much of their diversity. The sites, although not chosen randomly, include several with very strong economies during the late 1980s, others experiencing modest growth, and still others slowly recovering from job losses in the recession of the early 1980s. Furthermore, the sites' performance on key Department of Labor standards for Title II year-round programs showed similar diversity, with both strong and weak performers, and average performance close to the mean for all SDAs. As with the sites, the members of the study sample are themselves a diverse group, allowing an analysis of program impacts on numerous subgroups of interest to policymakers and program planners.

In addition, the study's definition of three main service strategies recommended by SDA staff produced distinct subgroups that differed systematically not only in the types of JTPA services they ultimately received but also in their baseline characteristics. As a result, the estimates of program impacts presented in later chapters offer an assessment of how well these clusters of services—classroom training, on-the-job training/job search assistance (OJT/JSA), and other less-intensive services—were working for the particular types of individuals they were designed to serve, rather than measures of the effects of these different service mixes for the same group of individuals.

This chapter has also provided a context for understanding the JTPA services both recommended for and received by treatment group members—the source of the program impact. Just under two-thirds (65 percent) of the treatment group was enrolled in JTPA. In general, the services enrollees received were of a relatively short duration, reflecting JTPA's national emphasis during the 1980s on job placement and low service costs.

Those treatment group members recommended for the classroom training strategy were the most likely of the three service strategy subgroups to be enrolled in JTPA, to stay enrolled for a relatively long time, and to receive some form of classroom instruction. Those recommended for the OJT/JSA strategy had the lowest overall enrollment rates, but they were also the most employable of the three groups; these enrollees tended to receive on-the-job training, job search assistance, or both. As intended, the other services subgroup included individuals with diverse backgrounds and service needs. Some adults in this group were also among the most employable, and so a substantial number of them were enrolled in job search assistance only, whereas youths in this group tended to be among the least job-ready, and so they were more apt to be enrolled in basic education and other services designed to address their lack of work experience.

Notes

1. As noted in chapter 2, "service delivery area" refers here to both the local administrative agency for the program and the geographical area it serves. Most SDAs provide

some specific program service themselves, but many also contract with other providers of employment and training services.

2. Program year 1984 (July 1984 through June 1985) was the most recent year for which data were available at the time site selection for the study began.

3. In this and the following exhibits, the site and national averages are unweighted.

4. The averages shown in Exhibits 3.2–3.9 are unweighted averages of SDA characteristics, both for the study sites and for all SDAs in the nation. They therefore represent the *typical SDA* in the study or in the nation, not the SDA in which the *typical participant* resides.

5. The poverty rates reported in the JTPA Annual Status Report file are based on information from the 1980 Census, which collected data on annual income in 1979.

6. The unemployment rates presented are for the labor force living in the geographic area included in each SDA.

7. Average earnings are calculated by dividing the total payroll reported by employers in the SDA to federal and state unemployment insurance agencies by the number of employees in the SDA.

8. The frequencies shown in Exhibits 3.4 and 3.5 are for all JTPA Title II terminees during the program years listed, and are based on data in the JTPA Annual Status Reports (JASR) compiled by the Department of Labor. These JASR data are the best source of information on individual SDAs and the people they serve, but they do not allow for separate breakdowns of out-of-school and in-school youths. The latter group was excluded from the National JTPA Study (as explained in chapter 2).

9. The average number of terminees annually during the period of the study's random assignment is not related to the sample size in each SDA in any simple way, because the duration of random assignment varied across sites.

10. Two SDAs (Providence and Cedar Rapids) did not offer job search assistance as a discrete service, but instead offered it only as an integrated part of other services.

11. Unfortunately, the enrollment and tracking data collected from most sites did not include information on the occupation for which people were trained, and the multiplicity of individual referrals prevented the research team from examining contracts for each training placement that would identify the occupation.

12. As for the first group, data limitations precluded a complete examination of the occupations involved. But the available information on class contracts at these sites suggests the training was for occupations similar to those noted for the second group.

13. The predicted performance levels are set by DOL regression models that control for the characteristics of both the SDA's labor market and its Title II terminees. In most, but not all, of the sites these adjusted standards were the level against which states assessed local performance for the purpose of allocating incentive grants. In some cases, the state agency made further adjustments to the standard produced by the regression model, to reflect special circumstances not taken into account by that model.

14. The state of Georgia chose not to use the youth positive termination rate as a standard in program year 1988, and so the standard is not reported for Coosa Valley. Similarly, Jersey City, Omaha, and Larimer County, Colorado, were in states not using the youth entered employment rate. In calculating the 16-site and national averages in these exhibits, we excluded any sites not using the standard in question.

15. Bloom et al. (1993, Appendix B) compares enrollment and tracking data from the 16 study SDAs on the services received by treatment group members who were enrolled in JTPA during the follow-up period with Job Training Quarterly Survey data on the services received by JTPA terminees nationally who were enrolled in the program during the sample intake period for this study.

16. Data on the applicant pool in most study sites were not available, and there were no data nationally on applicants for JTPA. The JTPA Annual Status Report (JASR) data do include information on the characteristics of program "terminees" in each SDA (e.g., the percentage from various racial groups, the percentage who were school dropouts, etc.). Analysis using these data suggests that there were clear changes in the characteristics of terminees in individual study sites from year to year before and during the study. One important finding was the extent of year-to-year changes in terminee characteristics in SDAs during "normal" (i.e., nonstudy) years. These were likely to be linked to important programmatic changes such as a shift in contractors (e.g., closing out a contractor who drew applicants from one group in the community and beginning another contract with a service provider drawing applicants primarily from another group) or because of important changes in the applicant pool (e.g., because of a plant closing or an influx of new residents).

17. Under JTPA rules, up to 10 percent of enrollees can have incomes above the normal eligibility cutoff if they have other barriers to employment. Most SDAs in the study rarely used this exemption, choosing instead to use it as a "safety valve" for cases in which auditors found some enrollees ineligible.

18. In some SDAs, modifications were made during the study period because of locally initiated changes in program design. For example, in the late 1980s throughout the JTPA system, there was a gradual trend away from multistep, multivisit application procedures commonly used in the early 1980s (when unemployment rates had been much higher) to "screen out" the "less motivated" applicants. During the final period of the study, sites also began to test reading levels of applicants, under new federal rules requiring reporting of basic skills.

19. After 18 months, members of the control group could receive JTPA services if they returned to the SDA or service provider on their own. However, SDA staff agreed not to make any speicial effort to recruit members of the control group at the end of their exclusion from JTPA.

20. The samples were drawn in two time periods: November 1988–January 1989 and March–June 1989, and included most of the SDAs where random assignment was occurring at those times.

21. Control group earnings are based on the follow-up survey data and UI wage records used in the analysis of program impacts as discussed in later chapters.

Chapter Four

PROGRAM IMPACTS ON
THE TARGET GROUPS

This chapter presents estimates of JTPA impacts on the earnings, educational attainment, and welfare receipt of adult women, adult men, female youths, male youth non-arrestees, and where possible, male youth arrestees.[1] As indicated in earlier chapters, these impacts represent the *incremental effect* of the additional employment and training services received by JTPA assignees or enrollees beyond what they would have received without JTPA. To help interpret the estimates of incremental impacts, we also present measures of the *service increments* that produced these impacts.

The first part of this chapter presents findings for adults, and the second presents findings for youths. Each part: (1) describes the pattern of JTPA enrollment rates over time among treatment group members; (2) presents measures of the increment in employment and training services produced by JTPA; (3) describes the treatment and control group patterns of earnings throughout the 30-month follow-up period; and (4) presents estimates of program impacts on earnings, attainment of a high school credential, receipt of AFDC, receipt of food stamps, and, for youths, arrest rates during the 30-month follow-up period.

FINDINGS FOR ADULTS

This section presents the main study findings for adult men and women.

JTPA Enrollment Patterns Over Time: Adult Treatment Groups

In the early part of the follow-up period, treatment group earnings may have been affected by participation in JTPA in several different ways. On the one hand, enrollment in occupational skills training or basic education may have actually delayed employment for some treatment group members early in the follow-up period, causing their earnings to be lower than those of their control group counterparts. On the other hand, enrollment in job search assistance or on-the-job training may have led to faster job placements for other treatment group members, causing their earnings to surpass those of their control group counterparts in the early months of the follow-up period.

Any difference between treatment group and control group earnings later in the follow-up period, however, should be relatively free of these conflicting effects of program participation and should therefore reflect the postprogram effects of JTPA. Exhibit 4.1 helps to establish this distinction between *in-program* and *postprogram* periods, by showing the percentage of all those assigned to the treatment group who were enrolled in JTPA in each month of the follow-up period.

Among adult women in the treatment group, 52 percent were enrolled in JTPA during the first month after random assignment.[2] By the 7th month after random assignment, their enrollment rate had declined to 26 percent, and by the 18th month it was only 6 percent. Among adult men in the treatment group, 51 percent were enrolled in JTPA during the 1st month after random assignment, 15 percent were enrolled during the 7th month, and 3 percent were enrolled during the 18th month. Throughout this report, we refer to the first 6 months after random assignment (months 1–6) as the in-program period; we refer to the next 12 months (months 7–18) as the first postprogram year, and the next 12 months (months 19–30) as the second postprogram year.[3] The pattern of JTPA enrollment rates for adults in Exhibit 4.1 indicates that this convention is a reasonable approximation. Similar findings presented for youths later in this chapter (Exhibit 4.12) are consistent with this interpretation.

Increase in Employment and Training Services due to JTPA: Measuring the Service Increment

As noted earlier, the National JTPA Study was designed to measure the impacts of the *incremental* services provided by JTPA, *beyond those that the assignee would have obtained if excluded from JTPA.* The services that would have been available to individuals excluded from JTPA are represented by the services received by the control group.[4] Because JTPA is not the only employment and training service provider in most communities, it was expected that a number of control group members would receive employment and training services from non-JTPA sources. Therefore, the impact estimates presented

Exhibit 4.1 PERCENTAGE ENROLLED DURING EACH OF THE FIRST 18 MONTHS
AFTER RANDOM ASSIGNMENT: ADULT TREATMENT GROUP
MEMBERS

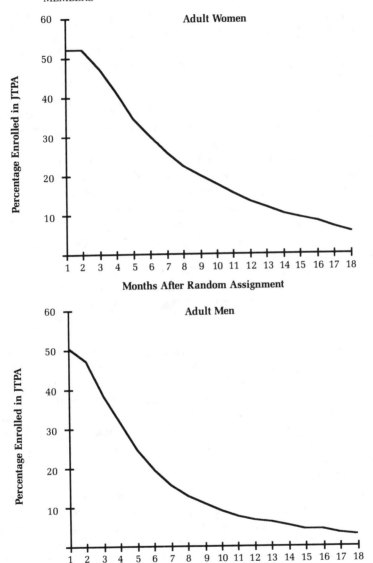

Sources: Unadjusted frequencies based on enrollment and tracking data from the 16
service delivery areas (SDAs).
Sample sizes: adult women, treatment group = 4,088; adult men, treatment group =
3,399.

earlier should not be interpreted as the total effect of JTPA relative to no services at all, but only the effect relative to the non-JTPA services received by the control group.[5]

Providing treatment group members with access to JTPA did, however, increase the services they received beyond those received by control group members. In other words, random assignment produced a treatment group and a control group that were the same in all regards except that treatment group members received *more* employment and training services. It is this difference in services that produced any impacts that were observed. We refer to these impacts as *incremental* impacts, because they represent the change in earnings produced by the incremental service provided by JTPA.

Exhibit 4.2 presents three measures of the service increment for each target group. The top panel shows the percentage of sample members who received any employment and training service after random assignment. The middle panel contains the average number of hours of service received by all sample members, including zero hours for those receiving no service. The bottom panel shows the average cost of services received, including a cost of zero for sample members receiving no service. The service receipt measures presented in Exhibit 4.2 summarize detailed information on the receipt of specific services: classroom training in occupational skills, basic education, on-the-job training, work experience, job search assistance, and miscellaneous other services. For most services, receipt rates and hours of service were measured with data from the follow-up surveys, rather than SDA records, in order to capture both JTPA and non-JTPA services. On-the-job training and work experience were measured using data from the SDA management information system at each site, however, because in most communities these services are provided only by JTPA and because survey respondents were unlikely to be able to distinguish on-the-job training and work experience from regular jobs.

Receipt rates and hours of classroom training in occupational skills, basic education, job search assistance, and other services were measured using data from the follow-up surveys. Survey data may understate the receipt of these services, especially job search assistance, because of respondent recall error. Nevertheless, the follow-up surveys are the best existing source of comparable information on these services for both the treatment and control groups. In the benefit-cost analysis presented in chapter 6, we perform a sensitivity analysis to determine the potential effect of survey underreporting on the estimated net benefits of the program.

Exhibit 4.2 EMPLOYMENT AND TRAINING SERVICES RECEIVED BY ADULT TREATMENT AND CONTROL GROUP MEMBERS

| | Treatment group | Control group | Difference per | | | |
			Assignee	(Standard error)	Enrollee	(Standard error)
			Percentage receiving a service			
Adult women	59.5	33.1	26.4***	(1.4)	40.7***	(2.2)
Adult men	49.6	23.4	26.2***	(1.5)	42.1***	(2.4)
			Mean hours of services received			
Adult women	359	190	169***	(16)	260***	(25)
Adult men	267	131	136***	(15)	219***	(24)
			Mean cost of services received			
Adult women	$2,147	$1,286	$861***	(124)	$1,324***	(191)
Adult men	1,571	902	669***	(117)	1,076***	(188)

Sources: Estimates based on First Follow-up Survey responses, published school expenditure data, SDA enrollment and expenditure records, and a telephone survey of vocational/technical schools.

Sample sizes: adult women, 5,253; adult men, 4,026.

*Statistically significant at .10 level, **at .05 level, ***at .01 level (two-tailed test).

Similarly, only the costs of on-the-job training, work experience, and job search assistance were measured with data from SDA records. The costs of classroom training in occupational skills, basic education, and other services were measured with data from other sources, because JTPA does not always pay the full resource cost of these services. For example, JTPA enrollees often receive classroom training at community colleges, which are heavily subsidized by local taxpayers. In the benefit-cost analysis, it will be important to include all social costs of the program. To obtain the full resource cost of services received, we used data from several sources. In the follow-up survey, respondents were asked to name the specific institutions where they received training. For training provided at high schools and two- and four-year colleges, we used institution-specific data on the full cost of instruction collected by the U.S. Department of Education and the U.S. Bureau of the Census. To obtain institution-specific data on the cost of training at private vocational and technical schools, we conducted a survey of schools named by follow-up survey respondents. Data from these sources were used to calculate the full cost per hour or day of each type of training; these unit costs were then used to estimate the cost of services received by each sample member.[6]

The first column in Exhibit 4.2 presents each of the three service measures for treatment group members, and the second column presents these measures for controls. The third column reports the treatment-control difference for each service measure—i.e., the average service increment per *assignee*. The fourth column reports the average service increment per JTPA *enrollee*, obtained by adjusting the increment per assignee in accord with the JTPA enrollment rate of sample members (as is done to produce the estimates of program impacts per enrollee presented later).[7] Estimates of impacts per assignee should be compared to the estimated service increment per assignee; estimates of program impacts per enrollee should be compared to the estimated service increment per enrollee.

As expected, not all members of the treatment group received employment and training services, and many members of the control group did receive services. Nevertheless, access to JTPA approximately doubled the incidence of service receipt for adult assignees—from 33 percent of adult women to 60 percent, and from 23 percent of adult men to 50 percent. These differences were statistically significant (see Exhibit 4.2).

The average number of hours of service received by treatment group members was also about twice that received by controls for both adult women and adult men, a difference that was also statistically significant (Exhibit 4.2). This implies that the average number of hours of service for recipients in the treatment group was about the same as that for recipients in the control group. So the difference between the average number of hours of service for all treatment group members and all control group members was due mainly to the fact that a higher proportion of the treatment group received service, not to the receipt of more intensive services by treatment group members.

Likewise, the average cost of services received by adult treatment group members was 67 to 75 percent greater than the average cost of services received by adult control group members, once again representing statistically significant differences (Exhibit 4.2).[8] This implies that, although the average cost of services per recipient among treatment group members was somewhat less than that per recipient among control group members, the difference in the average service cost for treatment group and control group members was due mainly to the difference in the percentage of each group that actually received services, not to differences in their cost per recipient.

It is easier to assess the absolute magnitude of the service increment produced by JTPA when these measures are expressed on a per enrollee basis. Exhibit 4.2 indicates that enrollment in JTPA increased the likelihood of receiving an employment or training service by just over 40 percentage points for both adult women and adult men. Enrolling in JTPA increased the average amount of services that adult women received by 260 hours per enrollee. This is equivalent to adding about six or seven weeks of full-time training for each woman in the treatment group who enrolled in JTPA. The corresponding service increment for men was 219 hours per enrollee, which is roughly equivalent to adding five or six weeks of full-time training. On balance then, *JTPA produced a modest increase in the amount of services received by enrollees beyond what they would have received had they been excluded from the program.*

This modest service increment produced a correspondingly modest increase in the cost of services received by JTPA enrollees. Adult women who enrolled in JTPA received about $1,300 more in services then they would have otherwise, and adult men who enrolled received roughly $1,100 more in services than they would have otherwise. As detailed later, the modest service increment produced by JTPA for adults also produced a modest increase in their future earnings.

Quarterly Earnings Trends:
Adult Treatment Groups and Control Groups

Exhibit 4.3 shows the earnings experience of adult treatment group and control group members over the 10 quarters after random assignment.[9] Separate data are presented for adult women and adult men. We consider the experience of adult women first. The estimates underlying the earnings curve for the treatment group represent an *outcome* of JTPA—what the treatment group earned after its members gained access to JTPA: from $892 in the 1st follow-up quarter to $1,491 in the 10th.[10] This information does not indicate what the treatment group would have earned without access to JTPA, however, which is what one must know to calculate estimates of program impacts. It is the control group curve that provides this information.

Average earnings of women in the control group ranged from $871 in the first follow-up quarter to $1,327 in the tenth. The control group earnings trend provides two crucial pieces of information. First, in representing what the treatment group would have earned, on average, without access to JTPA, it serves as the basis for the treatment-control group comparisons of the experimental impact analysis. Second, the control earnings trend demonstrates the importance of making these comparisons in evaluating employment and training programs, since it indicates that, even without access to JTPA, treatment group members would have increased their average earnings substantially over the course of the follow-up period.

Exhibit 4.3 indicates that the average earnings of adult women in the treatment group also rose after random assignment and, indeed, rose more quickly than the earnings of control group members. Treatment group earnings continued to rise gradually over time and remained above the average earnings of control group members throughout the entire follow-up period.

The earnings experience for adult men is similar to that for adult women. The average quarterly earnings of both the treatment group and the control group rose sharply immediately after random assignment and then continued to increase slowly thereafter. But the earnings of treatment group members were consistently higher than those of control group members throughout the follow-up period (see Exhibit 4.3). Hence, the quarterly earnings patterns of treatment group and control group members for both women and men suggest that JTPA increased the average earnings of adults who were allowed to participate in the program. We turn now to direct estimates of these program impacts.

Incremental Impacts on Earnings:
Adult JTPA Assignees and Enrollees

In the simplest terms, our estimates of average program impacts on earnings equal the difference between the average earnings of treat-

Exhibit 4.3 QUARTERLY EARNINGS: ADULT WOMEN AND MEN

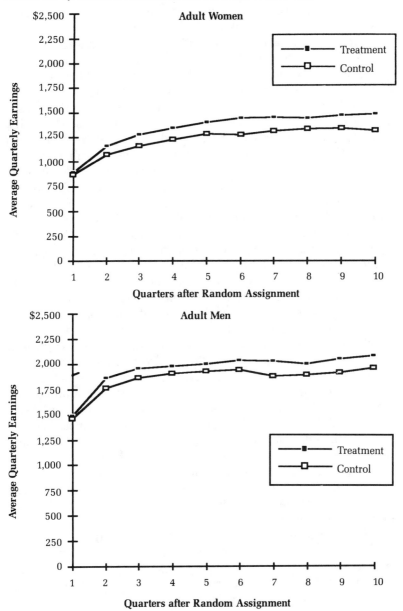

Sources: Estimates based on First and Second Follow-up Survey responses and earnings data from state unemployment insurance (UI) agencies.
Sample sizes: Adult women: treatment group = 4,088, control group = 2,014. Adult men: treatment group = 3,399, control group = 1,703.

ment group members and the average earnings of control group members. Exhibit 4.4 presents these estimates for adult women and men. The first column of the exhibit lists the mean earnings of treatment group members during months 1–6 after random assignment (the "in-program period"), months 7–18 (the first postprogram year), months 19–30 (the second postprogram year), and the entire follow-up period (months 1–30). Column 2 of the exhibit lists the mean earnings of control group members during each of the same time periods. Estimates of impacts per assignee in each time period are shown in the third column. These estimates equal the difference between the mean earnings of treatment group members and the mean earnings of control group members.[11] For example, the estimated impact on the total earnings of adult women in the treatment group (assignees) during follow-up months 1–6 was a statistically significant $109. This impact was obtained by taking the difference between the average earnings of treatment group members during the period ($2,060) and the corresponding average earnings of control group members ($1,951).

Column 4 of Exhibit 4.4 presents the standard error of each impact estimate, to provide a measure of the uncertainty about the estimate due to random sampling error. For example, the standard error of the $109 estimate of the program impact per adult female assignee during follow-up months 1–6 was $60. Based on the standard error of an impact estimate, one can represent the margin of sampling error of the estimate by computing a confidence interval around it. For example, a 90 percent confidence interval for an impact estimate can be computed by taking the value of the estimate itself, plus or minus 1.65 times the standard error of the estimate. The 90 percent confidence interval for the in-program impact on adult female assignees is therefore $109 (the estimate itself) plus or minus 1.65 times $60 (the standard error of the estimate), or $109 plus or minus $99.[12]

When presented as confidence intervals, the margin of error of the impact estimate is readily apparent. As shown later, even though most of the impact estimates in this report are based on data for large samples, their margins of error are quite large. For estimates of subgroup impacts based on smaller samples, the margins of error are even larger. Because of the inherent variability or unpredictability of the outcomes for which impacts were estimated (earnings, educational attainment, and welfare receipt), all impact estimates in this report are subject to considerable sampling error.

Substantial margins of error are endemic to virtually any study of the impacts of an employment and training program. Thus, it is important not to interpret the impact estimates of the present study or

Exhibit 4.4 IMPACTS ON EARNINGS PER ADULT ASSIGNEE, BY FOLLOW-UP PERIOD

	Mean earnings		Impact per assignee		
	Treatment group (1)	Control group (2)	In dollars (3)	(Standard error) (4)	As percent of (2) (5)
Adult women					
Months 1–6	$ 2,060	$ 1,951	$ 109*	($60)	5.6%
Months 7–18	5,485	4,961	525***	(149)	10.6
Months 19–30	5,872	5,330	542***	(175)	10.2
Total	13,417	12,241	1,176***	(336)	9.6
Adult men					
Months 1–6	3,351	3,226	125	(98)	3.9%
Months 7–18	7,964	7,635	329	(236)	4.3
Months 19–30	8,159	7,635	524**	(267)	6.9
Total	19,474	18,496	978*	(529)	5.3

Sources: Estimates based on First and Second Follow-up Survey responses and earnings data from state unemployment insurance (UI) agencies.

Sample sizes: adult women, 6,102; adult men, 5,102.

*Statistically significant at .10 level, **at .05 level, ***at .01 level (two-tailed test).

any other such study conducted to date as exact measures of program impact. To do so would wrongly endow these findings with "spurious precision." Nevertheless, as indicated in this and the following chapter, the level of precision of the findings in this report is adequate to provide a fairly clear indication of the successes and failures of JTPA programs at the 16 study sites.

Column 5 in Exhibit 4.4 expresses the dollar estimates of program impacts in column 3 as a percentage of the control group means in column 2. Statistical significance levels are not presented for the percentage impact estimates in order to simplify the presentation; they are the same as those for the estimates of impacts in dollars, however. For example, the $109 estimated impact of JTPA on adult women during the in-program period was 5.6 percent of the mean earnings of control group members during this period; both estimates were statistically significant at the 0.10 level.

Now consider the findings for adult assignees. First note that estimated program impacts per assignee for adult women were positive and statistically significant during the in-program period, during each of the two postprogram years, and for the 30-month follow-up period overall. These estimates ranged from program-induced earnings gains of 6 percent to gains of 11 percent. In total, JTPA increased the average earnings of adult women who were offered the opportunity to enter the program from $12,241 (the mean earnings of control group members) to $13,417 (the mean earnings of treatment group members), or by $1,176 (10 percent) per treatment group member (assignee). The standard error of this impact estimate is $336, which implies a 90 percent confidence interval of ±554 around the impact estimate of $1,176. Hence, it appears clear that JTPA increased the overall earnings of adult women in the 16 study sites during the 30-month follow-up period.

The findings in Exhibit 4.4 for men were similar to those for women, but were less striking. Adult men in the treatment group earned between 4 percent and 7 percent more than their counterparts in the control group during the three portions of the follow-up period. Only during the second postprogram year was this difference statistically significant, however. Nevertheless, the estimated impact for adult men during the overall 30-month follow-up period was a statistically significant increase of $978 per assignee, or 5 percent. The 90 percent confidence interval for the estimated impact on the total 30-month earnings of adult men was $978 ± $873.

The overall findings of statistically significant positive impacts on the earnings of both adult women and adult men reflect positive estimated impacts at 11 of the 16 sites for adult women and at 12 of the 16 sites for men (see Exhibit 4.5). Because of the relatively small samples available at the site level, the standard errors of site-specific impact estimates are quite large. Not surprisingly, then, the impact estimates were only statistically significant at two sites for women and at one site for men. Nevertheless, the predominance of positive impact estimates at the site level means that the positive overall impact findings for women and men are not the result of very large impact estimates in a few sites, but reflect instead a fairly consistent pattern of positive impact estimates at most sites in the study.

The estimated impacts at each site (point estimates) varied substantially, ranging from a positive $2,628 to a negative −$2,033 for women, and from a positive $5,310 to a negative −$2,637 for men (Exhibit 4.5). But this variation in impact estimates by site was not statistically significant for women or for men. In other words, although

Exhibit 4.5 IMPACTS ON EARNINGS PER ADULT ASSIGNEE, BY SITE

Rank of site, by size of estimated impact on target group	Adult women		Adult men	
	Impact estimate	(Standard error)	Impact estimate	(Standard error)
1	$2,628	($1,850)	$5,310**	($2,154)
2	2,308*	(1,244)	4,338	(5,454)
3	2,095	(1,393)	3,908	(3,120)
4	1,786**	(703)	2,533	(8,716)
5	1,190	(1,312)	2,335	(1,891)
6	1,181	(927)	2,197	(2,499)
7	1,109	(1,807)	1,655	(1,895)
8	1,069	(2,024)	1,540	(3,772)
9	844	(1,030)	1,212	(1,729)
10	787	(1,207)	721	(2,246)
11	309	(1,128)	710	(2,559)
12	−438	(1,962)	630	(1,039)
13	−1,008	(2,764)	−484	(1,950)
14	−1,369	(4,468)	−1,083	(1,814)
15	−1,410	(2,858)	−2,412	(4,290)
16	−2,033	(3,146)	−2,637	(2,337)
F-test, difference among sites	N.S.		N.S.	

Sources: Estimates based on First and Second Follow-up Survey responses and earnings data from state unemployment insurance (UI) agencies.
Notes: Sites were ranked separately for adult women and adult men, in order of size of estimated impact. Therefore, listings for adult women and adult men in each row do not necessarily refer to the same site. "N.S."—F-test for difference in impacts among study sites is not statistically significant.
*Statistically significant at .10 level, **at .05 level, *** at .01 level (two-tailed test).

the impact *estimates* varied markedly across sites, the data do not indicate that *true impacts* actually differ across the sites. Instead, the variation in impact estimates by site falls well within the range that could be produced by random sampling error, even if there were no differences in true average impacts by site. This again reflects the relatively small samples, and hence, large sampling error, for impact estimates at the site level.

Nevertheless, an exploratory analysis was conducted to attempt to identify local factors that might have influenced program impacts by site. Three types of factors were considered: (1) characteristics of the JTPA programs; (2) prevailing labor market conditions; and (3) the types of persons accepted into the programs. No clear patterns emerged from the analysis, and almost none of the factors analyzed had a statistically significant influence on earnings impacts. Our ability to detect such effects was severely limited, however, by the small samples at each site and the limited number of sites involved.[13]

The impact estimates in Exhibits 4.4 and 4.5 measure the *average* effect of JTPA on *all* treatment group members, regardless of whether or not they participated in the program. These estimates of impacts *per assignee* provide the most direct, reliable experimental evidence of JTPA impacts. As discussed earlier, however, not all JTPA assignees (treatment group members) actually enrolled in JTPA. Therefore, we also present estimates of average program impacts *per JTPA enrollee*. These estimates account for the fact that 34 percent of the women in the treatment group and 38 percent of the men in the treatment group did not enroll in JTPA.[14]

The adjustment for the treatment group's enrollment rate requires one to assume there was no JTPA impact on those members of the treatment group who did not formally enroll in the program. If some nonenrollees did experience positive effects from the program, the estimates of impacts per enrollee would overstate the impact on enrollees, because the adjustment would attribute these nonenrollee impacts to the enrollees.[15]

As described in chapter 3, we conducted a special study of JTPA services received by a subsample of nonenrolled treatment group members.[16] The findings of this study suggest that roughly half of all nonenrollees in the 18-month study sample received some form of JTPA service after their random assignment, in most cases job search assistance or referral to an employer for a possible on-the-job training position. Since these services were limited in scope and intensity, their impacts on nonenrollees were probably negligible. Nevertheless, we cannot be sure of this conclusion, and there is evidence to suggest that the validity of this conclusion may vary among sample members recommended for different service strategies.

We therefore consider our inferred impacts per JTPA *enrollee* to be estimates of the upper bound on the size of the average program impact on enrollees, since they may spread the total impact over too few treatment group members—that is, only those who formally enrolled. In contrast, we consider our estimates of impacts per JTPA *assignee* to be estimates of the lower bound on the true impacts on enrollees, since they spread the total impact over too many treatment group members; that is, they include some assignees who had no exposure to the program beyond the act of application.

Exhibit 4.6 presents estimates of impacts on the earnings of adult women and adult men who enrolled in JTPA, obtained using the estimation procedure described in Appendix B. Column 1 of the exhibit presents the mean earnings of treatment group members who enrolled in JTPA for each of the three segments of the follow-up period and for the follow-up period overall. As can be seen, adult women who enrolled in JTPA earned a total of $14,224, on average, during the 30-month follow-up period, and adult men who enrolled earned an average of $21,521.

The second column of Exhibit 4.6 presents estimates of the *impact* of JTPA on the earnings of enrollees, in dollars. These estimates of

Exhibit 4.6 IMPACTS ON EARNINGS PER ADULT ENROLLEE, BY FOLLOW-UP PERIOD

		Impact per enrollee		
	Mean earnings of enrollees	In dollars	(Standard error)	As percent
Adult women				
Months 1–6	$2,138	$170*	($94)	8.6%
Months 7–18	5,794	820***	(233)	16.5
Months 19–30	6,292	847***	(273)	15.6
Total	14,224	1,837***	(525)	14.8
Adult men				
Months 1–6	$3,718	$204	($160)	5.8%
Months 7–18	8,807	538	(386)	6.5
Months 19–30	8,996	856**	(437)	10.5
Total	21,521	1,599*	(865)	8.0

Sources: Estimates based on First and Second Follow-up Survey responses and earnings data from state unemployment insurance (UI) agencies.
Sample sizes: adult women, 6,102; adult men, 5,102.
*Statistically significant at .10 level, **at .05 level, ***at .01 level (two-tailed test).

impacts per enrollee are, by construction, a multiple of the estimates of impacts per assignee in Exhibit 4.4. For women, each estimated impact per enrollee in Exhibit 4.6 is 1.56 times its counterpart (per assignee) in Exhibit 4.4. As explained in Appendix B, this ratio was determined by the JTPA enrollment rate of the target group.[17] The estimated total impact on the earnings of adult women who enrolled in JTPA was therefore $1,837, or 1.56 times the corresponding estimate of the impact per assignee.

The approximate standard error (column 3 of Exhibit 4.6) of the estimated 30-month impact was $525, or 1.56 times the corresponding standard error of the estimated impact per assignee.[18] Hence, an approximate 90 percent confidence interval estimate for the total 30-month earnings impact per adult female JTPA enrollee is $1,837 ± $866. The point estimate of this impact, $1,837, is a 15 percent increase over what enrollees would have earned without the program (column 4 of Exhibit 4.6).

Men who enrolled in JTPA earned a total of $21,521 during their 30-month follow-up period (Exhibit 4.6). This was $1,599, or 8 percent, more than they would have earned if they had not enrolled in the program.[19] The 90 percent confidence interval around this estimate is $1,599 ± $1,427.

Decomposing Earnings Impacts Into Impacts on Hours Worked and Impacts on Hourly Earnings

Having established that JTPA increased the total earnings of both adult women and adult men during the 30-month follow-up period, we next attempted to measure the extent to which this earnings gain was produced by an increase in the amount of time that adults worked (an employment effect) versus an increase in the amount that adults were paid for the time they worked (a wage effect). Although there are certain limitations to any such decomposition analysis, the importance of the policy questions that it addresses warranted presenting the findings that were obtained from this exploratory analysis.

The approach used to study the relative contributions of increased hours worked and increased hourly earnings is described in Appendix B, but was briefly as follows. Using data from the follow-up surveys for the subsample of persons for whom these data were available, we obtained regression-adjusted estimates of the percentage impact of JTPA per assignee on the *average total number of hours worked* during the 30-month follow-up period and on *average hourly earnings*. The sum of these two percentage impacts on the components of earnings approximately equals the percentage impact on total earnings.[20] Hence, the magnitudes of these impacts on the components of earnings provide a measure of their relative contributions to the program-induced earnings gain. The estimated impacts are shown in Exhibit 4.7.

For adult women, JTPA produced an 8.6 percent increase in the total number of hours worked by treatment group members and increased their average hourly earnings by 2.2 percent (Exhibit 4.7). Hence, it appears that the program-induced earnings gain experienced by women was due mainly to an increase in the amount of time they worked. Indeed, their percentage increase in hours worked comprised four-fifths of the sum of the percentage increases in the two earnings components; hourly earnings comprised only one-fifth. Therefore, we conclude that increased hours worked produced about four-fifths of the program-induced earnings gain experienced by adult women; increased hourly earnings produced about one-fifth of these earnings.

JTPA increased total hours worked by adult men in the treatment group by 3.9 percent and increased their average hourly earnings by 2.7 percent (Exhibit 4.7). Hence, increased hours worked produced three-fifths of the program-induced earnings gain experienced by men, and increased hourly earnings produced about two-fifths of these earnings.

In interpreting these findings, several important points should be noted. First, the sample used to produce them included only those members of the 30-month earnings sample for whom follow-up survey data were available.[21] This was necessary because the UI earnings data used for the rest of the 30-month earnings sample do not provide information on hours worked. Fortunately, the earnings impact esti-

Exhibit 4.7 PERCENTAGE IMPACTS ON 30-MONTH EARNINGS, HOURS WORKED, AND HOURLY EARNINGS: ADULT ASSIGNEES

| | Estimated percentage impact on: | | | | |
	Earnings	(Standard error)	Hours worked	(Standard error)	Hourly earnings
Adult women	11.0***	(3.8)	8.6***	(2.9)	2.2
Adult men	6.7*	(3.8)	3.9	(2.6)	2.7

Sources: Estimates based on First and Second Follow-up Survey responses and earnings data from state unemployment insurance (UI) agencies. See text for sample sizes.
Note: Significance levels and standard errors were not calculated for final column of exhibit because estimates in that column were derived indirectly.
*Statistically significant at .10 level, **at .05 level, ***at .01 level (two-tailed test).

mates obtained for the full 30-month earnings sample (9.6 percent for women and 5.3 percent for men) were roughly comparable to those obtained for the earnings component analysis (11.0 percent for women and 6.7 percent for men—see Exhibit 4.7). Hence, we use the findings of the earnings component analysis to approximate the likely corresponding findings for the full 30-month earnings sample.

Second, the percentage impacts on the components of earnings do not exactly sum to the percentage impact on earnings overall. The exact relationship is nonlinear, and there is no clear way to define conceptually an exact measure of the relative contributions of impacts on hours worked and impacts on hourly earnings to the impact on total earnings. Nevertheless, for small earnings impacts within the range of those observed, the additive approximation is quite good.[22] Hence, this limitation is not a problem for the present analysis.

Third, and most important, it should be recognized that the estimated impacts on earnings per hour worked (wages) may reflect program effects on the composition of the subgroup of adult women or adult men who were employed, in addition to—or instead of—program impacts on the hourly earnings of specific individuals. If, for example, the additional employment generated by the program were concentrated among adults with high hourly earnings, the average hourly earnings calculated for all adult workers would increase even if the program had no effect on the hourly earnings of any individual worker. Conversely, gains in employment concentrated among low-wage workers could mask the effect of program-induced increases in the wage rates of individuals on the group average. Thus, the gain in average hourly earnings presented above is not necessarily a good indicator of the effects of JTPA on the wage rates of individual workers.

Incremental Impacts on Attainment of High School Diploma or GED Certificate

Exhibit 4.8 presents estimates of the impact of JTPA on the attainment of a high school diploma or a general educational development (GED) certificate by adult women and adult men who were school dropouts when they applied to the program.[23] This measure of program impact on educational attainment is reported because considerable past research suggests that a high school credential has an important influence on one's labor market prospects. The measure is reported only for sample members who were high school dropouts because only members of this subgroup could experience a change in their status according to this measure.

Exhibit 4.8 IMPACTS ON ATTAINMENT OF HIGH SCHOOL DIPLOMA OR GED:
ADULT HIGH SCHOOL DROPOUTS

	Percentage with GED or high school diploma 30 months after random assignment		Impact in percentage points per			
	Treatment group	Control group	Assignee	(Standard error)	Enrollee	(Standard error)
Adult women	32.0	20.4	11.6**	(5.6)	18.8**	(9.1)
Adult men	24.2	16.3	7.9	(5.1)	14.4	(9.3)

Source: Estimates based on Second Follow-up Survey responses.
Sample sizes: adult women, 301; adult men, 314.
*Statistically significant at .10 level, **at .05 level, *** at .01 level (two-tailed test).

The findings for adult women are clear: 32 percent of the treatment group members who were school dropouts initially attained a high school credential by the end of the 30-month follow-up period, whereas only 20 percent of the control group members did so (Exhibit 4.8). Hence, giving school dropouts in the adult female treatment group access to JTPA increased their likelihood of attaining a high school credential by 12 percentage points. This estimated impact per assignee dropout is statistically significant and translates into an estimate of 19 percentage points *per enrollee* dropout. These estimates of impacts on educational attainment had a wide margin of error. For example, the 90 percent confidence interval was 19 ± 15 percentage points per enrollee.[24]

Corresponding findings for adult men are less clear-cut than those for adult women, but they also suggest that JTPA had an appreciable impact on the attainment of a high school credential by school dropouts. Specifically, 24 percent of the adult male school dropouts in the treatment group attained a high school credential by the end of the 30-month follow-up period, whereas only 16 percent of the corresponding members of the control group did so (Exhibit 4.8). The difference, 8 percentage points, is a measure of the JTPA impact on this outcome per assignee. Although it is sizable, this treatment/control group difference was not statistically significant at conventional levels. Nevertheless, it was almost significant, so it *suggests* a true JTPA impact.[25] The 90-percent confidence interval estimate of the impact per enrollee was 14 ± 15 percentage points.

Overall then, it appears that JTPA produced a substantial and statistically significant impact on the attainment of a high school credential by adult female school dropouts, and the program *may have* produced a similar but less pronounced impact for adult male school dropouts. But in terms of the program's impact on the attainment of a high school credential by adult women and adult men overall, there was little effect, because only a fraction of the adults in JTPA at the 16 study sites were school dropouts. Because only 24 percent of the adult women in the study sample were school dropouts, the estimated impact of 12 percentage points per assignee for adult female dropouts in Exhibit 4.8 implies a 3 percentage point impact per assignee for adult women overall.[26] Likewise, the estimated impact of 8 percentage points per assignee for adult male dropouts in Exhibit 4.8 implies a 2 percentage point impact for adult men overall.

Impacts on AFDC and Food Stamp Benefits

Estimates of JTPA impacts on AFDC benefits received by adult sample members are presented in Exhibit 4.9. Corresponding estimates of impacts on food stamps benefits are shown in Exhibit 4.10. Both impacts are measured in terms of the total dollar amount of benefits received during the 30-month follow-up period (including zero for sample members who did not receive benefits). Because of gaps in data coverage due to state data system purge cycles and errors in the data provided by state staff, usable data on AFDC benefits were available for only six sites; usable data on food stamps benefits were available for five sites.[27]

Exhibit 4.9 IMPACTS ON RECEIPT OF AFDC BENEFITS: ADULT ASSIGNEES AND ENROLLEES IN AFDC SITES

| | Mean 30-month AFDC benefits | | Impact per | | | |
	Treatment group	Control group	Assignee	(Standard error)	Enrollee	(Standard error)
Adult women	$1,972	$2,049	$-77	($117)	$-130	($197)
Adult men	258	158	100**	(45)	164**	(74)

Sources: Estimates based on state welfare agency records and First and Second Follow-up Survey responses.
Notes: Sites represented in the sample are Butte, Mont.; Decatur, Ill.; Fort Wayne, Ind.; Larimer County, Colo.; Oakland, Calif.; and Providence, R.I.
Sample sizes: adult women, 2,433; adult men, 2,260.
*Statistically significant at .10 level, **at .05 level, ***at .01 level (two-tailed test).

Exhibit 4.10 IMPACTS ON RECEIPT OF FOOD STAMPS: ADULT ASSIGNEES AND ENROLLEES IN FOOD STAMPS SITES

	Mean 30-month food stamps benefits		Impact per			
	Treatment group	Control group	Assignee	(Standard error)	Enrollee	(Standard error)
Adult women	$1,496	$1,558	$ − 62	($85)	$ − 105	($144)
Adult men	698	598	100	(67)	170	(114)

Sources: Estimates based on state welfare agency records and First and Second Follow-up Survey responses.
Notes: Sites represented in the sample are Butte, Mont.; Fort Wayne, Ind.; Larimer County, Colo.; Northwest Minnesota; and Providence, R.I.
Sample sizes: adult women, 1,895; adult men, 1,750.
*Statistically significant at .10 level, **at .05 level, *** at .01 level (two-tailed test).

Exhibit 4.11 IMPACTS ON EARNINGS PER ADULT ASSIGNEE: AFDC SITES, FOOD STAMPS SITES, AND FULL 30-MONTH EARNINGS SAMPLE

	Impact on total 30-month earnings		
	AFDC sites	Food stamps sites	30-month earnings sample
Adult women	$2,027***	$2,062***	$1,176***
(Standard error)	(686)	(668)	(336)
Adult men	947	522	978*
(Standard error)	(1,057)	(966)	(529)

Sources: Estimates based on First and Second Follow-up Survey responses and earnings data from state unemployment insurance (UI) agencies.
Sample sizes: AFDC sites: adult women, 2,329; adult men, 2,136. Food stamps sites: adult women, 1,881; adult men, 1,734. Full 30-month earnings sample: adult women, 6,102; adult men, 5,102.
*Statistically significant at .10 level, **at .05 level, *** at .01 level (two-tailed test).

To help interpret the AFDC and food stamp impact estimates, which are based on subsamples of sites, Exhibit 4.11 presents estimates of JTPA impacts on total 30-month earnings separately for adults in three groups: the subsample in sites for which AFDC data are available, those in sites with food stamps data, and the full 30-month earnings sample. For adult women, it appears that average impacts on earnings in the sites with AFDC and food stamps data are considerably larger than the earnings impact in the 30-month earnings sample. Hence, the estimated impacts on AFDC and food stamps benefits received by adult women in the sites with AFDC and food stamps data *may over-state* the impacts on AFDC and food stamps received by women in the 30-month earnings sample. Earnings impact estimates for adult men in the 30-month earnings sample were about the same as those for men in sites with AFDC data and were larger than those in sites with food stamps data. Hence, the impacts on AFDC benefits estimated for men in the AFDC sites should reliably represent the impacts on AFDC benefits in the 30-month earnings sample, while the estimated impacts on food stamp benefits estimated for men in the food stamps sites may *understate* the impacts on men in the 30-month earnings sample.

As shown in Exhibit 4.9, adult women in the six AFDC sites who were assigned to the treatment group received an average of $1,972 in AFDC benefits during the 30-month follow-up period (including zero benefits for women who received no benefits during the period).[28] On average, adult women in the control group received a 30-month total of $2,049 in AFDC benefits. Hence, the estimated impact per adult female assignee was a −$77 reduction in average benefits over a 30-month period. This small estimated reduction was not statistically significant.

As expected, the average benefits received by adult men in the treatment group, $258 (see Exhibit 4.9), were a small fraction of those received by adult women, because men are less likely to receive benefits than are women.[29] Surprisingly, adult men in the control group received only $158 in AFDC benefits on average, which implies a JTPA-induced *increase* in benefits of $100 per assignee. This estimated impact was statistically significant and translates into an increase of $164 per enrollee. The 90 percent confidence interval estimate of the impact per enrollee was $164 ± $122.

The findings for food stamp benefits in Exhibit 4.10 indicate no statistically significant impacts for adult women or adult men. In addition, estimates of JTPA impacts on AFDC benefits and food stamps benefits for female youths, male youth non-arrestees, and male youth arrestees presented later in this chapter (Exhibits 4.19 and 4.20) indicate no statistically significant impacts for any of the youth target groups. Taking all of the AFDC and food stamps impact estimates for all of the target groups together, the one significant impact estimate (AFDC benefits for adult men) could well have occurred by chance, given the number of separate impact estimates that were computed. Hence, it is not clear whether the surprising positive impact estimate on AFDC benefits for men reflects a real impact or simply a chance result due to random sampling error.

This section presents the main study findings for out-of-school youths. The findings are presented separately for each of the three youth subgroups: *female youths*; *male youth non-arrestees* (male youths who did not report being arrested between their 16th birthday and their application to JTPA); and *male youth arrestees* (male youths who did report being arrested between their 16th birthday and their application to JTPA). As discussed previously, we report impact findings separately for male youth arrestees and male youth non-arrestees because of the major differences in findings for the two subgroups and because of the particular uncertainty that exists with respect to estimates of JTPA impacts for male youth arrestees (discussed later here). This section follows the same order as the previous section on adult impacts.

JTPA Enrollment Patterns Over Time: Youth Treatment Groups

Exhibit 4.12 illustrates the pattern of JTPA enrollment rates experienced by youth treatment group members during the first 18 months after random assignment. As was the case for adults, these enrollment rates were highest in the first month after random assignment and declined rapidly thereafter. For example, 57 percent of the female youths in the treatment group were enrolled in JTPA during the 1st month after random assignment, 26 percent were enrolled in follow-up month 7, and only 5 percent were enrolled in month 18. The corresponding rates for male youth non-arrestees were 59 percent in month 1, 18 percent in month 7, and 3 percent in month 18. The rates for male youth arrestees were 56 percent, 19 percent, and 3 percent, respectively.[30] This pattern of enrollment rates over time is consistent with the convention that we use to subdivide the 30-month follow-up period. As mentioned previously, follow-up months 1–6 are mainly the in-program period, months 17–18 are approximately the first postprogram year, and months 19–30 are roughly the second postprogram year.

Increase in Employment and Training Services due to JTPA: Measuring the Service Increment

The employment and training services received by youths in the treatment and control groups are described in Exhibit 4.13. Based on

Exhibit 4.12 PERCENTAGE ENROLLED DURING EACH OF THE FIRST 18 MONTHS AFTER RANDOM ASSIGNMENT: YOUTH TREATMENT GROUP MEMBERS

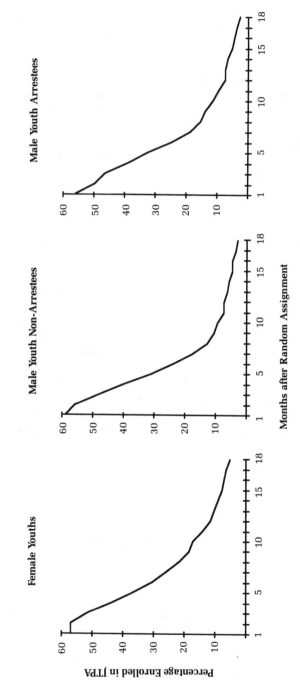

Sources: Unadjusted frequencies based on enrollment and tracking data from the 16 service delivery areas (SDAs).
Sample sizes: female youths, treatment group = 1,807; male youth non-arrestees, treatment group = 1,121; male youth arrestees, treatment group = 291.

Exhibit 4.13 EMPLOYMENT AND TRAINING SERVICES RECEIVED BY
YOUTH TREATMENT AND CONTROL GROUP MEMBERS

	Treatment group	Control group	Difference per			
			Assignee	(Standard error)	Enrollee	(Standard error)
Percentage receiving a service						
Female youths	66.1	44.3	21.8***	(2.2%)	33.9***	(3.4%)
Male youth non-arrestees	62.7	34.6	28.1***	(2.8%)	41.2***	(4.1%)
Male youth arrestees	54.9	27.4	27.5***	(5.1%)	42.4***	(7.9%)
Mean hours of services received						
Female youths	438	256	182***	(24)	283***	(37)
Male youth non-arrestees	406	231	175***	(34)	257***	(50)
Male youth arrestees	320	193	127**	(62)	195**	(95)
Mean cost of services received						
Female youths	$2,717	$1,824	$893***	($205)	$1,390***	($319)
Male youth non-arrestees	2,896	1,496	1,401***	(281)	2,055***	(412)
Male youth arrestees	2,315	1,173	1,142**	(487)	1,759**	(750)

Sources: Estimates based on First Follow-up Survey responses, published school expenditure data, SDA enrollment and expenditure records, and a telephone survey of
vocational/technical schools.
Sample sizes: female youths, 2,283; male youth non-arrestees, 1,338; male youth arrestees, 383.
*Statistically significant at .10 level, **at .05 level, ***at .01 level (two-tailed test).

treatment-control differences in service receipt, the exhibit also presents estimates of the incremental services received because of JTPA,
by treatment group members overall (assignees), and by JTPA enrollees in the treatment group. As discussed earlier, it is this *service
increment* that produced whatever impacts are observed for sample
members. And it is the cost of this service increment that must be
compared with the magnitude of the impacts produced by JTPA to
provide the basis for a benefit-cost analysis of the program.

To provide several perspectives on the JTPA service increment, it
was measured in three ways: the percentage of sample members who
received a service, the average number of hours of services received
by sample members (including zero hours for those who received no
services), and the average cost of services received by sample members
(including zero for those who received no services). As was the case
for adults, JTPA did indeed increase the amount of employment and
training services received by out-of-school youths beyond what they
would have received from other sources in the community. Among
female youths, 44 percent of the control group members received
employment and training services, whereas 66 percent of the treat-

ment group members did so (see Exhibit 4.13). Among male youth non-arrestees, 35 percent of the control group members received a service, compared to 63 percent of the treatment group members. Among male youth arrestees, 27 percent of the control group members received a service, compared to 55 percent of the treatment group members. These treatment and control group differences were statistically significant. In terms of incremental differences *per enrollee*, enrollment in JTPA increased the likelihood of receiving an employment and training service by 34 percentage points for female youths, by 41 percentage points for male youth non-arrestees, and by 42 percentage points for male youth arrestees.

These impacts on the likelihood of receiving an employment and training service produced a corresponding increase in the average number of hours of service received by sample members. Female youths who enrolled in JTPA received 283 additional hours of service, on average, beyond what they would have received had they not enrolled in the program. The corresponding figures for male youth non-arrestees and male youth arrestees were 257 and 195 additional hours of service, respectively. These increments are roughly comparable to an additional five to seven weeks of full-time training. As was the case for adults, youths in the treatment group who received services did so for roughly the same number of hours, on average, as did youths in the control group.[31] That is, most of the increase in employment and training services for youths reflects more sample members receiving services, not more intensive services for those who received them.

The additional hours of service received because of enrollment in JTPA translated into additional expenditures on services of $1,390, $2,055, and $1,759 per enrollee for female youths, male youth non-arrestees, and male youth arrestees, respectively. These incremental service expenditures are modest, but they equal or exceed the incremental services produced by JTPA for adults. Hence, if the services were effective, one would expect to observe positive JTPA impacts on the earnings of out-of-school youths.

Quarterly Earnings Trends:
Youth Treatment Groups and Control Groups

Exhibit 4.14 presents the earnings of treatment group members and control group members over the follow-up period, for female youths and male youth non-arrestees. Corresponding information is not presented for male youth arrestees, because their earnings patterns differ markedly depending on whether they are based on earnings data from

Exhibit 4.14 QUARTERLY EARNINGS: FEMALE YOUTHS AND MALE YOUTH
NON-ARRESTEES

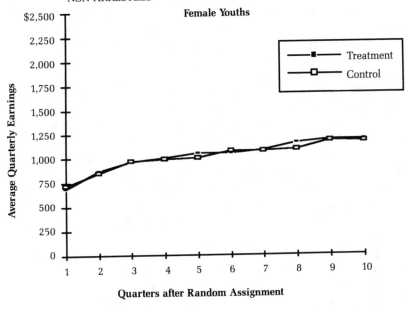

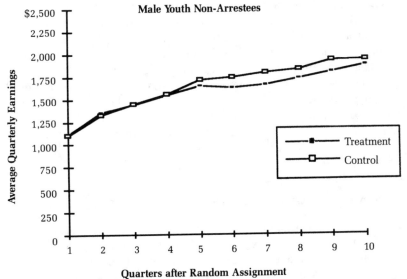

Sources: Estimates based on First and Second Follow-up Survey responses and earnings
data from state unemployment insurance (UI) agencies.
Sample sizes: Female youths: treatment group = 1,807, control group = 850. Male
youth non-arrestees: treatment group = 1,121, control group = 583.

follow-up surveys or earnings data from state unemployment insurance (UI) wage records (see discussion below).

As can be seen in Exhibit 4.14, the mean earnings of control group members increased appreciably during the 30-month follow-up period. Female youths in the control group earned $717, on average, during their 1st calendar quarter after random assignment, whereas they earned $1,166 during their 10th follow-up quarter (months 28–30). Male youth non-arrestees earned $1,101 during their 1st quarter after random assignment and $1,933 during their 10th follow-up quarter. Hence, as was the case for adults, out-of-school youths who applied to JTPA were able to increase their earnings substantially even without access to the program. This illustrates why it is important to have a randomly assigned control group, to enable us to measure the impact of the program as the difference between treatment group earnings and what treatment group members would have earned if they had been excluded from the program (as indicated by the control group's earnings).

Unlike the experience of adults in this study, youths in the treatment group did not increase their earnings during the follow-up period by more than the control group members. As can be seen in Exhibit 4.14, female youths in the treatment group earned almost exactly the same, on average, as their control group counterparts during all 10 follow-up quarters. Male youth non-arrestees in the treatment group earned almost exactly the same amount as their control group counterparts during the first 5 follow-up quarters and earned less than controls during the last 5 follow-up quarters.

Hence, there was virtually no treatment-control difference in overall earnings during the follow-up period for female youths. For male youth non-arrestees, treatment group members earned somewhat less than control group members overall during this period. These earnings trends are the basis for the impact estimates for youths presented in the next section.

Incremental Impacts on Earnings: JTPA Assignees and Enrollees

Estimates of the incremental impacts on earnings per assignee for youths are presented in Exhibit 4.15. These estimates reflect the incremental difference in employment and training services received by treatment group members and control group members presented in Exhibit 4.13, and they summarize the difference between the mean quarterly earnings patterns of treatment group members and control group members illustrated by Exhibit 4.14.

Exhibit 4.15 IMPACTS ON EARNINGS PER YOUTH ASSIGNEE,
BY FOLLOW-UP PERIOD

	Mean earnings		Impact per assignee		
	Treatment group (1)	Control group (2)	In dollars (3)	(Standard error) (4)	As percent of (2) (5)
Female youths					
Months 1–6	$1,565	$ 1,569	$ −4	($76)	−0.2
Months 7–18	4,064	4,030	34	(179)	0.8
Months 19–30	4,612	4,507	104	(223)	2.3
Total	10,241	10,106	135	(409)	1.3
Male youth non-arrestees					
Months 1–6	$ 2,471	$ 2,430	$ 41	(138)	1.7
Months 7–18	6,268	6,465	− 197	(313)	− 3.0
Months 19–30	7,046	7,481	− 434	(380)	− 5.8
Total	15,786	16,375	− 589	(710)	− 3.6
Male youth arrestees (Using survey data)					
Months 1–30	$14,633	$18,842	$ − 4,209**	(1,646)	− 22.3
Male youth arrestees (Using scaled UI data)					
Months 1–30	$14,148	$14,152	$ −4	(1,657)	0.0

Sources: Estimates based on First and Second Follow-up Survey responses and earnings
data from state unemployment insurance (UI) agencies.
Sample sizes: female youths, 2,657; male youth non-arrestees, 1,704; male youth arrestees, 416.
*Statistically significant at .10 level, **at .05 level, *** at .01 level (two-tailed test).

As shown in Exhibit 4.15, there was virtually no program impact
on the earnings of female youths during any portion of the follow-up
period. Female youths in the treatment group earned − $4 (0 percent)
less than their control group counterparts during the in-program period, $34 (1 percent) more during the 1st postprogram year, and $104
(2 percent) more during the 2nd postprogram year. Overall, female
youths in the treatment group earned $135 (1 percent) more than
controls during the follow-up period. None of these small differences
was statistically significant. Indeed, none was even half the size of its
standard error. The 90 percent confidence interval for the estimate of
the total 30-month impact on the earnings of female youths was $135
± $675 per assignee.

For male youth non-arrestees there was also no statistically significant impact on earnings during any portion of the follow-up period,

although the pattern of point estimates for male youth non-arrestees differed from that for female youths. Male youth non-arrestees in the treatment group earned $41 (2 percent) more than their control group counterparts during the in-program period, −$197 (−3 percent) less during the 1st postprogram year, and −$434 (−6 percent) less during the 2nd postprogram year (see Exhibit 4.15). Overall, male youth non-arrestees in the treatment group earned −$589 (−4 percent) less than did control group members during the 30-month follow-up period. This difference was smaller than its estimated standard error, however, and its 90 percent confidence interval was $589 ± $1,172.

Two sets of estimates are presented for male youth arrestees in Exhibit 4.15: one based on earnings measures obtained from unemployment insurance (UI) wage records and one based on follow-up survey data. The two estimates are presented for the subsample of male youth arrestees for whom earnings measures were available from both data sources. Hence, any differences between the two sets of estimates of earnings impacts must be attributable to differences between the two data sources for the same individuals. To simplify the exhibit, only estimates of JTPA impacts on total 30-month earnings are reported.

According to earnings measures obtained from the follow-up surveys, male youth arrestees in the treatment group earned −$4,209 (−22 percent) less than male youth arrestees in the control group (Exhibit 4.15). This major difference was statistically significant and thus cannot be explained by random sampling error. Hence, according to survey data, it would appear that access to JTPA reduced the subsequent earnings of male youth arrestees by −$4,209 per assignee. In contrast, UI wage records indicate that the mean earnings of treatment group members during the 30-month follow-up period differed from those of control group members by only −$4 (0 percent). Hence, according to this data source, JTPA had virtually no impact on the subsequent earnings of male youth arrestees.

The striking difference in the impact estimates obtained for male youth arrestees from the two data sources reflects the fact that the relationship between mean earnings from the surveys and mean earnings from UI wage records was quite different for the treatment group and the control group. For control group members, the ratio of mean survey earnings to mean UI earnings was much higher than it was for treatment group members. This was not the case for adult women, adult men, female youths, and male youth non-arrestees; hence, there was no major discrepancy between the impact estimates from these two data-sources for those target groups (see Appendix B). The major discrepancy for male youth arrestees, however, raises the question: "Which source is correct?"

A variety of comparisons between the two data sources were made to help explain their differences, but no clear explanation was found.[32] Therefore, it is not clear whether JTPA had no effect on the future earnings of male youth arrestees at the study sites or whether it actually reduced the future earnings of this target group. What is clear is that JTPA did not achieve its goal of increasing the earnings of this target group; neither data source shows positive impacts on earnings.

Estimates of JTPA impacts on total 30-month earnings per assignee by site for female youths and male youth non-arrestees are presented in Exhibit 4.16. Because of the small samples of male youth arrestees at each site, their impact estimates are not presented by site. In this

Exhibit 4.16 IMPACTS ON EARNINGS PER YOUTH ASSIGNEE, BY SITE

Rank of site, by size of estimated impact on the target group	Female youths		Male youth non-arrestees	
	Impact estimate	(Standard error)	Impact estimate	(Standard error)
1	$3,372*	($1,971)	$9,473**	($4,387)
2	2,320	(1,518)	5,464	(5,435)
3	1,404	(1,131)	1,918	(2,214)
4	1,222	(3,106)	1,414	(2,160)
5	649	(1,258)	1,192	(5,041)
6	556	(1,939)	1,090	(3,977)
7	244	(3,067)	973	(4,363)
8	117	(1,023)	119	(1,756)
9	−432	(1,066)	−204	(5,453)
10	−1,064	(3,556)	−1,298	(3,427)
11	−1,298	(1,282)	−2,206	(1,573)
12	−1,471	(1,555)	−2,876	(3,789)
13	−2,179	(2,293)	−3,029	(2,265)
14	−2,355	(4,082)	−4,147	(2,687)
15	−3,821*	(2,271)	−5,836	(4,031)
F-test, difference among sites	N.S.		N.S.	

Sources: Estimates based on First and Second Follow-up Survey responses and earnings data from state unemployment insurance (UI) agencies.
Notes: Sites were ranked separately for female youths and male youth non-arrestees, in order of size of estimated impact. Therefore, listings for female youths and male youth non-arrestees in each row do not necessarily refer to the same site. Does not include Oakland; no youth assigned in that site. N.S. means the F-test for difference in impacts among study sites is not statistically significant.
*Statistically significant at .10 level, **at .05 level, ***at .01 level (two-tailed test).

exhibit, sites are ordered by size of impact on *each* target group; this means that the impacts shown on the same line for females and males do not necessarily represent the same site for the two target groups. As can be seen, the site-specific impact estimates for female youth assignees ranged from a positive $3,372 to a negative −$3,821, with a broad range of both negative and positive values between these two extremes. Hence, the overall near-zero impact for female youths was not dominated by the results of a few idiosyncratic sites. Instead, it reflects the central tendency of a broad range of site-specific results. Only the most positive and the most negative site-specific impact estimates were statistically significant for female youths. Indeed, most of the estimates were smaller than their standard errors. And as a group, the site-specific impact estimates were not statistically different from each other.[33] Hence, even though the point estimates of the impacts varied substantially by site, there was no evidence that the actual impact of the program varied across the sites.

A similar pattern of site-specific impact estimates was observed for male youth non-arrestees. These estimates range from $9,473 to −$5,836, with roughly an even balance of sites having positive and negative impact estimates (see Exhibit 4.16). Hence, the overall insignificant impact estimates for this target group reflects the central tendency of a broad range of site-specific findings. Only the most positive impact estimate was statistically significant, and as a group, the 15 site-specific estimates were not significantly different from each other. It is important to note that in a group of 30 impact estimates, one would expect about 3 to be statistically significant at the .10 level by chance alone. Therefore, it is likely that the three significant site-specific impact estimates for youths represent sampling error, rather than real program impacts.

Exhibit 4.17 presents estimates of mean impacts per enrollee for female youths and male youth non-arrestees for each of three sub-periods and for the follow-up period overall. Corresponding impact estimates are not presented for male youth arrestees because of the discrepancy between the impact estimates based on the follow-up surveys and those based on UI wage records for this group. The estimated impacts per enrollee account for the fact that 33 percent of the female youths in the treatment group and 30 percent of the male youth non-arrestees in the treatment group did not enroll in JTPA. These estimates also account for the fact that 2.4 percent of the female youths and 1.5 percent of the male youth non-arrestees in the control group enrolled in JTPA.

Exhibit 4.18 IMPACTS ON ATTAINMENT OF HIGH SCHOOL DIPLOMA OR GED: YOUTH HIGH SCHOOL DROPOUTS

	Percentage with GED or high school diploma 30 months after random assignment		Impact in percentage points per			
	Treatment group	Control group	Assignee	(Standard error)	Enrollee	(Standard error)
Female youths	39.4	31.7	7.7*	(4.2)	10.6*	(5.8)
Male youth non-arrestees	36.8	36.3	0.5	(5.3)	0.7	(7.7)
Male youth arrestees	29.9	28.9	1.0	(9.9)	1.7	(17.2)

Source: Estimates based on Second Follow-up Survey responses.
Sample sizes: female youths, 605; male youth non-arrestees, 413; male youth arrestees, 118.
*Statistically significant at .10 level, **at .05 level, ***at .01 level (two-tailed test).

this outcome. The estimated impact per enrollee dropout was 11 percentage points, and its 90 percent confidence interval was 11 ± 10 percentage points. This impact estimate was somewhat smaller than the corresponding estimate for adult school dropouts (see Exhibit 4.8).

When interpreting these findings, it is important to note that only about half of the female youths in the study sample were high school dropouts when they applied to JTPA. Hence, the 11 percent estimated impact on female youths who were school dropouts implies only about a 5 percentage point increase in the percentage of all female youths in the treatment group who attained a high school credential during the follow-up period. Even if the attainment of a high school credential leads to higher earnings, an increase in educational attainment of this magnitude is unlikely to have a detectable effect on the average earnings of female youths overall. Therefore, this result, combined with those given earlier for earnings, should not be interpreted as implying that attainment of a high school credential does not lead to higher earnings.

The findings for male youths were less encouraging. There was no sign of a statistically significant JTPA impact on the attainment of a high school credential by school dropouts who were either male youth arrestees or male youth non-arrestees.

Incremental Impacts on AFDC Benefits and Food Stamp Benefits

Estimates of JTPA impacts on the average total AFDC benefits received by youths during the 30-month follow-up period (including zeros for those who received no benefits) are presented in Exhibit 4.19. The corresponding estimates of JTPA impacts on food stamp benefits are shown in Exhibit 4.20. As was the case for adults, usable data on AFDC benefits and food stamp benefits were only available for some study sites. Each type of data was available for five sites.[37]

None of the estimates of JTPA impacts on AFDC benefits in Exhibit 4.19 or on food stamp benefits in Exhibit 4.20 are statistically significant. Hence, there is no evidence of a program impact on the average amount of either AFDC or food stamp benefits received by female youths, male youth non-arrestees, or male youth arrestees in the sites for which these data are available.

To help interpret the impact estimates for AFDC and food stamp benefits received by youths, Exhibit 4.21 presents estimates of program impacts on earnings for youths in the full 30-month earnings sample, youths in the sites with AFDC data, and youths in the sites with food stamps data. Although the point estimates vary substan-

Exhibit 4.19 IMPACTS ON AFDC BENEFITS: YOUTH ASSIGNEES AND ENROLLEES IN AFDC SITES

	Mean 30-month AFDC benefits		Impact per			
	Treatment group	Control group	Assignee	(Standard error)	Enrollee	(Standard error)
Female youths	$1,699	$1,734	$ −125	($208)	$ −193	($320)
Male youth non-arrestees	158	150	8	(82)	12	(126)
Male youth arrestees	251	69	182	(132)	274	(198)

Sources: Estimates based on state welfare agency records and First and Second Follow-up Survey responses.
Notes: Sites represented in sample are Butte, Mont.; Decatur, Ill.; Fort Wayne, Ind.; Larimer County, Colo.; and Providence, R.I.
Sample sizes: female youths, 731; male youth non-arrestees, 580; male youth arrestees, 202.
*Statistically significant at .10 level, **at .05 level, ***at .01 level (two-tailed test).

Exhibit 4.20 IMPACTS ON RECEIPT OF FOOD STAMP BENEFITS: YOUTH ASSIGNEES AND ENROLLEES, IN FOOD STAMPS SITES

	Mean 30-month food stamps benefits		Impact per			
	Treatment group	Control group	Assignee	(Standard error)	Enrollee	(Standard error)
Female youths	$1,370	$1,490	$ −120	($136)	$ −186	($211)
Male youth non-arrestees	446	378	68	(86)	107	(135)
Male youth arrestees	543	333	210	(149)	317	(225)

Sources: Estimates based on state welfare agency records and First and Second Follow-up Survey responses.
Notes: Sites represented in sample are Butte, Mont.; Fort Wayne, Ind.; Larimer County, Colo.; Northwest Minnesota; and Providence, R.I.
Sample sizes: female youths, 731; male youth non-arrestees, 569; male youth arrestees, 196.
*Statistically significant at .10 level, ** at .05 level, *** at .01 level (two-tailed test).

Exhibit 4.21 IMPACTS ON EARNINGS PER YOUTH ASSIGNEE: AFDC SITES, FOOD
STAMPS SITES, AND FULL 30-MONTH EARNINGS SAMPLE

	Impact on total 30-month earnings		
	AFDC sites	Food stamps sites	30-month earnings sample
Female youths	$426	$491	$135
(Standard error)	(859)	(865)	(409)
Male youth non-arrestees	−1,456	−1,821	−589
(Standard error)	(1,277)	(1,265)	(710)

Sources: Estimates based on First and Second Follow-up Survey responses and earnings
data from state unemployment insurance (UI) agencies.
Sample sizes: AFDC sites—female youths, 717; male youth non-arrestees, 570. Food
stamps sites—female youths, 717; male youth non-arrestees, 559. Full 30-month earnings sample—female youths, 2,657; male youth non-arrestees, 1,704.

tially, none of the estimates of JTPA impacts on earnings for these
three different samples are statistically significant. Hence, there is no
firm evidence that the impacts on earnings for those in the sites where
AFDC or food stamps data are available differ from those for the full
30-month earnings sample. Therefore, there is no strong reason to
believe that these results would be substantially different if data were
available for the full study sample.

Incremental Impacts on Arrest Rates

Estimates of the impacts of JTPA on the arrest rates of youths in the
study sample are shown in Exhibit 4.22.[38] The top panel in the exhibit
is based on arrests reported on the First Follow-up Survey, and the
bottom panel is based on arrests reported on both the First and Second Follow-up Surveys. Because the follow-up surveys were administered to different sample members at somewhat different times after
random assignment, the follow-up periods for measuring arrest rates
varied accordingly. The average first follow-up period for the sample
in Exhibit 4.22 was 21 months, and the average period covered by the
First and Second Follow-up Surveys was 36 months.[39]

In terms of their variation across groups and over time, the arrest
rates measured from self-reports on the follow-up surveys exhibit
clear and plausible patterns. As was the case in previous studies (for
example, Cave and Doolittle, 1991) the arrest rates for female youths
(both treatment and control group members) were considerably lower
than those for male youths (see Exhibit 4.22). This held both for the
first follow-up period and for the full follow-up period. In addition,

Exhibit 4.22 IMPACTS ON ARREST RATES OF YOUTHS

	Percentage arrested during follow-up period		Impact per			
	Treatment group	Control group	Assignee	(Standard error)	Enrollee	(Standard error)
			During first follow-up period[a]			
Female youths	4.4%	3.6%	0.8%	(0.8%)	1.3%	(1.3%)
Male youth non-arrestees	14.1	9.6	4.5**	(1.8)	6.5**	(2.6)
Male youth arrestees	43.3	42.6	0.7	(5.3)	1.1	(8.3)
			During full follow-up period[b]			
Female youths	7.0	5.3	1.7	(1.2)	2.7	(1.8)
Male youth non-arrestees	25.8	18.7	7.1**	(2.8)	10.4**	(4.1)
Male youth arrestees	59.2	55.7	3.5	(6.7)	5.5	(10.5)

Sources: Estimates based on First and Second Follow-up Survey responses.
Sample sizes: First follow-up period—female youths, 2,294; male youth non-arrestees, 1,337; male youth arrestees, 390. Full follow-up period—female youths, 1,153; male youth non-arrestees, 708; male youth arrestees, 198.
a. The first follow-up period began at random assignment and ended 21 months later, on average (with a minimum of 12 and a maximum of 37 months).
b. The full follow-up period began at random assignment and ended 36 months later, on average (with a minimum of 23 and a maximum of 48 months).
*Statistically significant at .10 level, **at .05 level, ***at .01 level (two-tailed test).

as would be expected, the arrest rates during the follow-up period were considerably higher for male youths with prior arrests (the arrestee target group) than for male youths without prior arrests (the non-arrestee target group).

A third pattern apparent in Exhibit 4.22 is the considerable extent to which arrest rates continued to increase over time during the follow-up period. Cumulative arrest rates were noticeably higher at the end of the full follow-up period than they were at first follow-up. The JTPA impact estimates for two of the three target groups, female youths and male youth arrestees, are straightforward to interpret. Essentially, there was no observable effect on the arrest rates of these two groups during the follow-up period. The impact estimates were quite small (especially for female youths), and they were not statistically significant.

But the impact estimates for male youth non-arrestees are puzzling. During the first follow-up period, it appears that enrollment in JTPA *increased* the arrest rate of this group by a statistically significant 6 percentage points per enrollee. This estimated impact increased to a statistically significant 10 percentage points by the end of the full follow-up period (Exhibit 4.22). There is no clear explanation of why this increase in arrest rates occurred. More detailed analysis indicates, however, that the finding was not produced by methodological artifacts. For example, these results were not produced by extreme impacts concentrated in a few sites.[40]

Notes

1. Recall that the sample of male youth arrestees was only a small fraction of the size of that for the other target groups, and hence its potential for certain analyses was limited accordingly.

2. Although 66 percent of the adult female treatment group were enrolled in JTPA Title II at some point during the follow-up period, only 52 percent were enrolled in the first follow-up month, because some treatment group members enrolled later.

3. It is not possible to derive separate experimental impact estimates for the inprogram and postprogram periods defined by the actual JTPA enrollment and termination dates for treatment group members because there is no way to define corresponding periods for control group members.

4. It is important to note that the counterfactual represented by the control group is exclusion from JTPA, holding the availability of non-JTPA services fixed, not complete elimination of JTPA. Complete elimination of JTPA would likely result in changes in the availability of non-JTPA services that could not be measured in this study. In any

case, the impact of access to JTPA relative to exclusion from JTPA may be more relevant for policy, since it may more accurately represent the effect of marginal changes in the size of the program.

5. In the benefit-cost analysis presented in chapter 6, we take account of the fact that we measure only incremental impacts by comparing program benefits (impacts) with the incremental costs of the program.

6. See Appendixes A and B for more details on the measurement of service receipt and cost.

7. Appendix B describes how impacts per enrollee were computed and outlines the underlying logic of this computation.

8. See Appendix B for a detailed explanation of the derivation of the incremental cost of employment and training services.

9. Throughout this chapter, earnings and impact estimates are expressed in nominal dollars. The follow-up period varied across individuals, beginning as early as November 1987 and ending as late as December 1990.

10. The earnings estimates shown in Exhibit 4.3 and subsequent exhibits include wages paid to JTPA participants in on-the-job training positions. During the 18-month follow-up period, the program reimbursed employers a total of about $650 per adult female *OJT participant*. Among all adult women in the sample, OJT reimbursements totaled about $80 *per treatment group member* over the 18-month follow-up period.

11. To increase the statistical precision of these estimates, we used ordinary least squares regressions. This reduced the standard errors of the impact estimates but did not appreciably affect the point estimates, because the average values of the independent variables (mainly the baseline characteristics of the treatment and control groups) were virtually the same for the two groups. See Appendix B for a full description of these procedures.

12. A 90 percent confidence interval is directly related to a two-tailed significance test at the 0.10 level. Specifically, if the 90 percent confidence interval *includes* the value zero, then the impact estimate *is not* statistically significantly different from zero at the 0.10 level (two-tail). If the 90 percent confidence interval *does not contain* the value zero, then the impact estimate *is* significant at the 0.10 level (two-tail).

13. Bloom et al., (1993) presented this analysis, which was based on estimates of impacts on earnings per assignee over 18 months.

14. Estimates of program impacts per enrollee also account for the fact that 1.1 percent of the men in the control group and 1.7 percent of the women actually enrolled in JTPA, despite the experiment's 18-month embargo on doing so. As explained in Appendix B, the adjustment factor used to derive impacts per enrollee from impacts per assignee is $1/(r\text{-}c)$, where r is the enrollment rate (the proportion of treatment group members who enrolled in JTPA) and c is the crossover rate (the proportion of control group members who were enrolled in JTPA). Since these two rates are fixed for any given group or subgroup, the ratio of impacts per enrollee to impacts per assignee is also fixed for any given group or subgroup. Thus, for example, for the adult female target group the impact per enrollee is 1.56 times the impact per assignee for all outcomes in all time periods, and for adult men this ratio was 1.63.

15. This assumes that the program impact on nonenrolled treatment group members was of the same sign as the impact on the enrollees. In the unlikely event that the effects on the two groups were of the opposite sign, the estimated impacts per enrollee would understate the magnitude of the average impact on enrollees.

16. See Bloom et al. (1993, Appendix F) for a detailed description of this study and its findings.

17. The approach used to compute estimates of impacts per enrollee was developed by Bloom (1984). It adjusts the experimental comparison of treatment group earnings and control group earnings to account for "no-shows" (treatment group members who do not enroll in JTPA) and "crossovers" (control group members who did enroll in JTPA). The same approach was developed independently for use in medical clinical trials (see Haynes and Dantes, 1987, for a discussion). More recently, in a study of the effect of Vietnam veteran status on future earnings, Angrist (1990) used an instrumental variables approach that is equivalent to the enrollee adjustment procedure in the present report. Angrist indicated that his approach is a special case of an estimator originally developed by Wald (1940).

18. The estimate of the standard error of the impact estimate is *conditional* on the specific JTPA enrollment rate for which the estimate of impact per enrollee was computed. To compute the *unconditional* standard error would require a knowledge of the covariance between the impact estimate per assignee and the JTPA enrollment rates of treatment and control group members, which is not known. The unconditional standard error may be either larger than or smaller than the conditional standard error, depending upon whether the covariance is positive or negative (Cave, 1988).

19. Note that the estimated impact per adult male enrollee is 1.63 times the estimated impact per adult male assignee, and the corresponding approximate standard error for enrollees is 1.63 times that for assignees.

20. The exact relationship among these impacts is as follows:

$$1 + r_E = (1 + r_H)(1 + r_W)$$

where:

r_E = the *proportional* impact on total earnings,

r_H = the *proportional* impact on total hours worked,

r_W = the *proportional* impact on average hourly earnings.

21. The 30-month earnings sample used to estimate the impacts on earnings reported in earlier sections of this chapter contained 6,102 women and 5,102 men. Data from First Follow-up Surveys used to estimate hours worked during months 1–18 after random assignment were available for 5,312 women and 4,107 men. Data from Second Follow-up Surveys used to estimate hours worked during months 19–30 after random assignment were available for 1,262 women and 1,127 men. Smaller samples were available for the latter part of the follow-up period because the second follow-up survey was only conducted for a random subsample of the experimental sample. Appendix B describes how this information was used to produce the results presented in this section.

22. For women in the earnings component sample, the estimated earnings impact was 11.0 percent, whereas the sum of the component impacts was 10.8 percent; for men, the corresponding findings were 6.8 percent and 6.6 percent, respectively.

23. The measure of educational attainment was obtained from answers to a question on the Second Follow-up Survey that asked sample members if they had a high school diploma or a GED certificate at the time of the interview and, if so, the date they received it. This information was used to determine whether the respondent had the credential 30 months after random assignment. School dropouts were defined as sample members who indicated on their Background Information Form when they applied to JTPA that they had neither a high school diploma nor a GED certificate.

The basic results reported in this chapter are similar to those in the 18-month impact report (Bloom et al., 1993) for all target groups except male youths. Findings from the two reports are not directly comparable, however, because they are based on two different samples and two different measures of educational attainment. The analysis in the 18-month report was based on all respondents to the First Follow-up Survey, for which interviews were attempted with the entire experimental sample; the 30-month analysis is based on respondents to the Second Follow-up Survey, which included only a random subset of the experimental sample. Moreover, the 18-month analysis used a more restrictive measure of educational attainment, based on whether the sample member reported having received a high school diploma or GED *through participation in an education or training program.*

24. Note that the standard errors of the estimates of impacts per enrollee are simply the standard errors for the estimates of the impact per assignee, scaled by the same factor used to convert the point estimates of impacts per assignee into estimates of impacts per enrollee. As discussed earlier, this standard error is *conditional* on the JTPA enrollment rates of the sample involved.

25. The difference would have been significant at the .12 level (i.e., its p value was .12).

26. The implied impact per assignee for the full adult female target group is equal to the estimated impact per school dropout (11.6 percentage points) times the proportion of target group members that were dropouts at random assignment (.24).

27. Usable AFDC data were obtained for: Butte, Decatur, Fort Wayne, Larimer County, Oakland, and Providence. Usable food stamps data were obtained for Butte, Fort Wayne, Larimer County, Northwest Minnesota, and Providence.

28. The average AFDC benefit received per recipient in the adult female treatment group was $6,086.

29. The average AFDC benefits per adult male recipient in the treatment group were $3,850. Note, however, that only 6.7 percent of the adult men in the treatment group received AFDC benefits during the follow-up period, whereas 32.4 of the adult women in the treatment group did so.

30. The percentage of treatment group members enrolled in JTPA at any time during the follow-up period was 67 percent for female youths, 69 percent for male youth non-arrestees, and 64 percent for male youth arrestees. This percentage is greater than the percentage of each group enrolled during the first month after random assignment because some treatment group members enrolled later.

31. The mean number of hours of services received by sample members who received a service (per recipient) can be obtained by dividing the mean number of hours of services received overall by a treatment group or a control group by the corresponding *proportion* of its members who received a service.

32. Survey data reported more earnings, on average, than did unemployment insurance (UI) wage records, although the ratio of average earnings from the survey to average earnings from UI wage records was virtually the same for treatment and control group members in all target groups except male youth arrestees (see Bloom et al., 1993, Appendix E). For male youth arrestees, the ratio of survey earnings to UI earnings was much higher for control group members than it was for treatment group members. No clear explanation of this difference could be found. The difference could not be attributed to exaggerated survey reports of earnings by control group members, because the mainly low skill jobs and low wage rates they reported were quite plausible. Neither could the difference be attributed to "outliers" (individuals with unusually high earnings) in the survey data, because dropping the outliers from the data did not eliminate the difference. Finally, the difference could not be attributed to systematic under-reporting of jobs by UI wage records, because the employment rates measured by the survey and those measured using UI wage data were not sufficiently different to explain the discrepancy in earnings reported by the two data sources.

33. This finding is based on an *F*-test of the null hypothesis that all of the site-specific impacts were the same.

34. If non-enrollees in the treatment group experienced a negative program impact on earnings, the estimates of impacts per enrollee presented in this report would under-

state the true average JTPA impacts on enrollees. A previous analysis reported in Bloom et al. (1993, Appendix F) indicates that about half of the non-enrollees in the treatment group subsequently received some—usually minimal—JTPA services. Because these services were quite limited, it is unlikely that they had much of an effect, either positive or negative. Hence, it is most likely that the estimates of program impacts per enrollee presented in this report provide a reasonable approximation of the true average program impacts on enrollees.

35. The statements in this paragraph and in note 34 hold when the estimated impact is positive. If the estimated impact is negative, impact per assignee and impact per enrollee represent lower and upper bounds, respectively, of the *absolute value* of the true impact when the impact on non-enrollees is zero or negative. If the estimated impact is negative and the impact on non-enrollees is positive, the estimated impact per enrollee understates the absolute value of the true impact.

36. Recall that youths were not included in the experimental sample at the Oakland site.

37. Usable AFDC data for youths were obtained from: Butte; Decatur; Fort Wayne; Larimer County; and Providence. Because youths were not included in the study sample at the Oakland site, the fact that usable AFDC data were available from this site (and used for adults) was not relevant for youths. Usable food stamps data for youths were obtained for Butte; Fort Wayne; Larimer County; Northwest Minnesota; and Providence.

38. Data on arrests were collected for youths but not for adults because past evaluations of employment and training programs for youths focused considerable attention on this outcome, whereas it has not been considered an important outcome for adults.

39. A sample member was recorded as having been arrested during the first follow-up period (top panel in Exhibit 4.22) if he or she reported such an arrest on the First Follow-up Survey. A sample member was recorded as having been arrested anytime during the full follow-up period (bottom panel in Exhibit 4.22) if he or she reported such an arrest on either the First or Second Follow-up Survey.

40. Nor can these results be attributed to outliers in the data, which are not possible for a zero/one outcome, such as being arrested or not, or to a poor match of the treatment and control groups on the baseline value of the outcome, since by definition none of the treatment or control non-arrestees reported having been arrested before random assignment.

Chapter Five

PROGRAM IMPACTS ON THE
EARNINGS OF SUBGROUPS

The impact estimates presented in the previous chapter were averages for all sample members in each target group. They therefore reflect the effects of JTPA on a wide variety of different types of individuals who received a number of different employment and training services. This chapter examines the impacts of the program on the earnings of a number of subgroups within each of the major target groups.

The first section focuses on subgroups of the adult target groups. We begin by describing the employment and training services received by treatment and control group members in each service strategy subgroup and the personal characteristics of the adult women and men in each. We then present estimates of the impact of the program on the earnings of adult enrollees in each of the service strategy subgroups and other key subgroups of interest to policymakers and program planners. The section concludes by analyzing the effects of JTPA on the earnings of adult women who were receiving AFDC at the time of application to JTPA.

The second section of the chapter presents corresponding findings for female youths and male youth non-arrestees, by service strategy and other key subgroups. We do not present impact estimates for subgroups of male youth arrestees because their sample sizes are too small to do so.

FINDINGS FOR ADULTS, BY SERVICE STRATEGY AND OTHER KEY SUBGROUPS

As explained in chapter 2, the service strategy subgroups were defined on the basis of services *recommended* by program intake staff, not the services actually *received* by sample members, because there is no way to identify the control group members who would have received a particular service had they been allowed to enter JTPA. Because service recommendations were made before random assignment, control group members *can* be matched to treatment group members on the basis of recommended services. As a result, we can obtain purely experimental impact estimates for subgroups defined on the basis of recommended services.

Applicants for whom classroom training in occupational skills was recommended were placed in the *classroom training subgroup*. Those for whom on-the-job training (OJT) was recommended were placed in the *OJT/JSA subgroup* (so named because many of the treatment group members in this subgroup were enrolled in job search assistance (JSA) while searching for either an on-the-job training position or an unsubsidized job). Because JTPA staff sometimes recommend combinations and sequences of services, any of several other services may also have been recommended for applicants placed in these subgroups, including job search assistance, basic education, work experience, or miscellaneous other services. Those applicants for whom program staff recommended one or more of these services— but neither classroom training in occupational skills nor on-the-job training—were placed in the *other services subgroup*.[1]

As explained in chapter 3 (Exhibit 3.14), classroom training was much more likely to be recommended for women, and OJT was more likely to be recommended for men. Intake staff recommended classroom training in occupational skills for 38 percent of the adult women in the 30-month earnings sample, but only 20 percent of the adult men; the staff recommended OJT for 50 percent of the men and only 37 percent of the women. The other services subgroup, for whom neither of these major services was recommended, comprises about a quarter of both the adult target groups.

Treatment-Control Service Increment, by Service Strategy Subgroup: Adult Women and Men

As discussed earlier, the JTPA impacts measured by the present study are incremental impacts produced by the *incremental* employment and training services received by treatment group members, beyond the services they would have received if they had been excluded from JTPA. We measure the services the treatment group would have received if they had been excluded from JTPA by the services received by controls, who *were* excluded from JTPA. Exhibits 5.1 and 5.2 show the percentage of adult treatment and control group members in each service strategy subgroup who received each of six types of employ-

Exhibit 5.1 RECEIPT OF SPECIFIC EMPLOYMENT AND TRAINING SERVICES: ADULT WOMEN TREATMENT AND CONTROL GROUPS, BY SERVICE STRATEGY

	Percentage receiving service			Mean hours of service		
	Treatment group	Control group	Difference in % pts.	Treatment group	Control group	Difference in hours
Classroom training subgroup						
Classroom training in occupational skills	50.1	29.9	20.2% pts.	387	258	129***
Basic education	10.6	6.6	4.0***	39	21	18***
OJT	4.4	0.9	3.5***	39	3	36***
Work experience	6.0	0.0	6.0***	41	0	41***
JSA	3.9	2.7	1.2	8	4	5*
Other	11.7	6.3	5.4***	50	33	17
Any service	71.9%	42.6%	29.3%***	564	318	246***
OJT/JSA subgroup						
Classroom training in occupational skills	12.6	13.9	−1.2	58	66	−7
Basic education	4.1	4.1	0.0	10	4	6**
OJT	31.5	1.0	30.5***	116	3	113***
Work experience	2.6	0.0	2.6***	14	0	14***
JSA	7.4	1.9	5.5***	5	0	5***
Other	6.5	5.3	1.2	17	16	1
Any service	53.2%	24.6%	28.6%***	220	89	131***
Other services subgroup						
Classroom training in occupational skills	21.2	16.5	4.7**	111	96	15
Basic education	12.3	8.3	4.0**	36	27	8
OJT	6.3	0.0	6.3***	45	0	45***
Work experience	2.6	0.0	2.6***	20	0	20***
JSA	9.7	1.8	7.9***	11	2	9***
Other	10.5	7.5	3.0*	30	20	10
Any service	49.9%	31.6%	18.3%***	251	145	106***

Sources: Estimates based on First Follow-up Survey responses and enrollment and tracking data from 16 SDAs.
Sample sizes: classroom training subgroup, 2,007; OJT/JSA subgroup, 1,999; other services subgroup, 1,247.
*Statistically significant at .10 level, **at .05 level, ***at .01 level (two-tailed test).

Exhibit 5.2 RECEIPT OF SPECIFIC EMPLOYMENT AND TRAINING SERVICES: ADULT MEN TREATMENT AND CONTROL GROUPS, BY SERVICE STRATEGY

	Percentage receiving service			Mean hours of service		
	Treatment group	Control group	Difference in % pts.	Treatment group	Control group	Difference in hours
Classroom training subgroup						
Classroom training in occupational skills	43.7	26.9	16.8***	352	225	127***
Basic education	7.8	4.0	3.8**	33	20	13
OJT	9.4	0.4	9.0***	74	2	71***
Work experience	1.8	0.0	1.8***	11	0	11***
JSA	2.7	0.0	2.7***	5	0	5***
Other	13.3	6.7	6.6***	44	33	12
Any service	68.3%	36.8%	31.6%***	520	280	239***
OJT/JSA Subgroup						
Classroom training in occupational skills	10.2	9.1	1.2	51	55	−4
Basic education	2.5	4.6	−2.1**	6	7	−2
OJT	29.6	1.3	28.3***	135	6	129***
Work experience	2.4	0.0	2.4***	10	0	10***
JSA	7.1	1.8	5.3***	5	1	5
Other	6.3	4.6	1.7	17	19	−2
Any service	48.8%	19.4%	29.4%***	224	87	137***
Other services subgroup						
Classroom training in occupational skills	13.3	9.0	4.3**	55	41	15
Basic education	5.0	4.5	0.5	19	17	2
OJT	6.3	1.0	5.3***	42	10	32***
Work experience	0.6	0.0	0.6**	6	0	6
JSA	6.6	1.8	4.8***	5	5	0
Other	9.5	6.3	3.3**	26	37	−11
Any service	36.1%	21.6%	14.6%***	153	110	43*

Sources: Estimates based on First Follow-up Survey responses and enrollment and tracking data from 16 SDAs.
Sample sizes: classroom training subgroup, 818; OJT/JSA subgroup, 2,095; other services subgroup, 1,113.

ment and training service and the average number of hours of each type of service received (including zeros for those who did not receive a particular service).

The figures in Exhibits 5.1 and 5.2 include both JTPA and non-JTPA services.[2] Receipt of classroom training in occupational skills, basic education, job search assistance, and "other" services was measured from follow-up survey data. Survey data may understate the receipt of these services, especially minor services such as job search assistance, which may easily be forgotten. Nevertheless, the follow-up surveys are the only feasible source of comparable information for both JTPA and non-JTPA services. In chapter 6, we conduct a sensitivity test to determine the potential effects of survey underreporting on the benefit-cost results.

Receipt of on-the-job training and work experience was measured with data from SDA records, because in most communities these services are provided only by JTPA and because survey respondents were unlikely to be able to distinguish on-the-job training and work experience from regular jobs.

As shown in Exhibits 5.1 and 5.2, not all sample members received the services that were recommended for them. Nevertheless, the three service strategy subgroups did receive distinctly different mixes of services. Moreover, for both women and men, the principal difference in services received by the treatment and control groups in the classroom training and OJT/JSA subgroups was that substantially higher percentages of the treatment groups in those two subgroups received classroom training and OJT, respectively, than among the controls. Thus, the impacts observed for adults in the classroom training subgroups are primarily the result of incremental classroom training, and the impacts we observe for adults in the OJT/JSA subgroups are primarily the result of incremental on-the-job training.

The service increment in the other services subgroup was spread more broadly across several different services, with no single service showing a treatment-control differential of more than 8 percentage points in the percentage receiving the service. In part, however, this may reflect underreporting on the follow-up survey of the less intensive services such as job search assistance.

The differences in hours of service shown in the right-hand panels of Exhibits 5.1 and 5.2 reflect very similar patterns. For both adult women and adult men, over half the total service increment in the classroom training subgroup was attributable to additional hours of classroom training in occupational skills, and in the OJT/JSA subgroup about half was due to additional hours of on-the-job training. In the other services subgroup, the service differential reflected small increments of hours of a number of different services. (Again, these figures may reflect underreporting of minor services such as job search assistance.)

Exhibit 5.3 shows three summary measures of the service increment in each adult service strategy subgroup. The first panel shows the percentages of treatment and control group members receiving any service, along with the treatment-control difference per assignee and per enrollee. As seen in chapter 4 at the target group level, not all treatment group members received employment and training services, and many controls did receive services. Nevertheless, as shown in the exhibit, assignment to the treatment group increased the likelihood of receiving services by statistically significant margins in each service strategy subgroup.

In terms of total hours of service, the service increment was greatest for the classroom training subgroup. Adult women and men in that subgroup received about 320 additional hours of service per enrollee, as compared with about 230 additional hours per enrollee in the OJT/JSA subgroup (Exhibit 5.3). Women enrolled in the other services subgroup received 181 additional hours of service, whereas men enrolled in that subgroup received only 70 additional hours. The treatment-control service differential in the other services subgroup may be understated, however, because of underreporting of less-intensive services such as job search assistance in the follow-up surveys.

It is important to bear in mind that the mean hours of service shown in these exhibits are averaged across all treatment and control group members, whether they received services or not. Mean hours of service for service recipients can be derived by dividing mean hours for all treatment or control group members by the proportion of that group who received services. Such calculations reveal that, in each subgroup, treatment group members *who received some service* received about the same number of hours of service as controls *who received services*. This means that the service increment primarily took the form of more individuals receiving services, not more intensive services to those who received them.

The bottom panel of Exhibit 5.3 shows the service differential in terms of cost of services received. Although the classroom training strategy involved a substantially larger service increment in terms of hours per enrollee than the OJT/JSA strategy, the incremental cost of the OJT/JSA strategy was actually higher for adult men—$1,461 per enrollee—versus $964 per enrollee for classroom training. For adult women, classroom training was more expensive, at $1,657 per enrollee, as compared with $1,201 for OJT/JSA. The incremental cost of the other services strategy was much lower in both target groups— $825 per enrollee for adult women and $297 for adult men. In summary, then, for both adult women and adult men:

- Although not all treatment group members received the services that were recommended for them, the service recommendations of JTPA intake workers created three groups that received distinctly different mixes of employment and training services;
- The service increment in the classroom training subgroup reflects primarily a higher likelihood of receiving classroom training in occupational skills;
- The service increment in the OJT/JSA subgroup reflects primarily a higher likelihood of receiving on-the-job training;
- The service increment in the other services subgroup was spread more broadly across several different services;
- The service increment was greatest for the classroom training strat- egy (about 320 hours per enrollee), followed by the OJT/JSA strategy (about 230 hours), and least for the other services strategy (70–181 hours). The incremental cost of the classroom training strategy exceeded that of the OJT/JSA strategy for adult women, while the reverse was true for adult men; the other services strategy was substantially cheaper for both target groups; and,
- The service increment primarily took the form of more individuals receiving services, not more intensive services for those who re- ceived them.

The experimental design thus succeeded in creating three subgroups that received systematically different services, with a sta- tistically significant treatment-control service differential in each. In absolute terms, however, the service increments created by access to JTPA were relatively modest in size, especially in the other services subgroups. The largest service increment represents only about eight weeks of full-time training per enrollee. An increment of this size is likely to have commensurately modest impacts on earnings and other outcomes.

Differences in Baseline Characteristics across Service Strategy Subgroups: Adult JTPA Assignees

It is important to bear in mind that the differences in estimated im- pacts of JTPA across the service strategy subgroups reflect not only differences in the mix of services received among these subgroups

Exhibit 5.3 INCREMENT IN EMPLOYMENT AND TRAINING SERVICES RECEIVED BY ADULTS FROM ANY SOURCE, BY SERVICE STRATEGY SUBGROUP

Service strategy subgroup	Treatment group	Control group	Difference per assignee	(Standard error)	Enrollee	(Standard error)
Percentage receiving any service						
Adult women						
Classroom training	71.9	42.6	29.3***	(2.3)	38.3***	(3.0)
OJT/JSA	53.2	24.6	28.6***	(2.2)	49.9***	(3.8)
Other services	49.9	31.6	18.3***	(2.9)	31.1***	(4.9)
Adult men						
Classroom training	68.3	36.8	31.6***	(3.6)	41.9***	(4.8)
OJT/JSA	48.8	19.4	29.4***	(2.0)	51.1***	(3.5)
Other services	36.1	21.6	14.6***	(2.7)	23.9***	(4.5)
Mean hours of services received						
Adult women						
Classroom training	564	318	246***	(33)	321***	(43)
OJT/JSA	220	89	131***	(16)	229***	(28)
Other services	251	145	106***	(25)	181***	(43)
Adult men						
Classroom training	520	280	239***	(53)	318***	(70)
OJT/JSA	224	87	137***	(16)	237***	(28)
Other services	153	110	43*	(23)	70*	(37)

Mean cost of services received

Adult women					
Classroom training	$3,295	$2,028	$1,267***	($248)	$1,657***	($324)
OJT/JSA	1,430	742	688***	(164)	1,201***	(286)
Other services	1,450	965	485**	(195)	825**	(332)
Adult men					
Classroom training	2,883	2,158	726*	(410)	964*	(544)
OJT/JSA	1,424	583	841***	(129)	1,461***	(224)
Other services	827	646	181	(160)	297	(263)

Sources: Estimates based on First Follow-up Survey responses, published school expenditure data, SDA enrollment and expenditure records, and a telephone survey of vocational/technical schools.

Sample sizes: Adult women—classroom training subgroup, 2,007; OJT/JSA subgroup, 1,999; other services subgroup, 1,247. Adult men—classroom training subgroup, 818; OJT/JSA subgroup, 2,095; other services subgroup, 1,113.

*Statistically significant at .10 level, **at .05 level, ***at .01 level (two-tailed test).

148   *Does Training for the Disadvantaged Work?*

but also differences in the characteristics of the enrollees in the subgroups. Exhibit 5.4 shows selected baseline characteristics of adult assignees in each of the service strategy subgroups.[3]

The service strategy subgroups differ noticeably in their ethnic composition. Those assigned to the OJT/JSA subgroup were more likely to be white than those in the other two subgroups (Exhibit 5.4). This was true in the sites where blacks and Hispanics were concentrated, as well as in predominantly white sites. This disparity in assignment rates apparently reflects a judgment on the part of intake workers that black and Hispanic enrollees were not as job-ready as white enrollees. Among adult women, the OJT/JSA subgroup contained a smaller proportion of Hispanics than did the other two subgroups.

Although most of the differences among the three subgroups in the other characteristics shown in Exhibit 5.4 were not large, among adult women it does appear that program staff tended to recommend the OJT/JSA or other services strategy for the most job-ready applicants. Adult women in the classroom training subgroup were more likely than those in the other two subgroups to be facing the barriers to employment represented by welfare receipt or limited recent work experience, although fewer of them were high school dropouts. Women in the classroom training subgroup were also less likely to have worked before and were likely to have had lower earnings in the year preceding their application than those in the other two subgroups. Women in the other services subgroup were slightly less well educated than those in the other two subgroups. In other respects, the other services subgroup of adult women tended to be intermediate between the classroom training and OJT/JSA subgroups.

Among adult men, there was no clear pattern of differences in barriers to employment or work and training history across the three service strategy subgroups (Exhibit 5.4). Men in the classroom training subgroup were somewhat less likely to face barriers to employment than those in the other two subgroups, but men in the OJT/JSA subgroup were slightly more likely to have had prior work experience.

Because of these differences among the assignees in the three service strategy subgroups, one must be careful in comparing program impacts across the three groups. The impacts presented in the next subsections reflect the effects of the program on the kinds of people recommended for each subgroup. If the same service strategy were recommended for a different set of people, there is no guarantee that the same impacts would be obtained. Thus, although the analysis can identify a strategy (or strategies) that was working, or not working, for

Exhibit 5.4 ETHNICITY, BARRIERS TO EMPLOYMENT, AND WORK AND
TRAINING HISTORIES: ADULT ASSIGNEES BY SERVICE STRATEGY

| | Service strategy | | |
Characteristic	Classroom training	OJT/JSA	Other services
Adult women			
Ethnicity			
White, non-Hispanic	54.4%	67.2%	55.5%
Black, non-Hispanic	29.2	24.2	27.0
Hispanic	14.2	7.2	14.5
Other	2.2	1.4	3.1
Barriers to employment			
Receiving cash welfare[a]	41.6	26.7	33.7
No high school diploma or GED	23.1	28.6	30.9
Worked less than 13 weeks in past 12 months	56.3	46.9	50.7
Number of barriers			
None of the above	26.6	35.0	32.3
One of the above	36.0	37.0	33.2
Two of the above	28.6	22.4	24.7
Three of the above	8.8	5.6	9.8
Work and training histories			
Ever employed	82.8%	92.1%	87.1%
Mean earnings in past 12 months	$2,075	$2,860	$2,569
Previously received occupational training	45.8%	44.8%	44.2%
Adult men			
Ethnicity			
White, non-Hispanic	49.9%	71.6%	51.5%
Black, non-Hispanic	36.2	16.4	33.4
Hispanic	9.4	9.6	10.9
Other	4.5	2.3	4.2
Barriers to employment			
Receiving cash welfare[a]	11.7	3.2	6.7
No high school diploma or GED	21.3	32.3	34.9
Worked less than 13 weeks in past 12 months	39.3	38.2	44.8
Number of barriers			
None of the above	44.6	39.8	35.9
One of the above	39.3	40.8	43.8
Two of the above	14.4	16.6	17.4
Three of the above	1.6	2.7	2.9
Work and training histories			
Ever employed	89.0%	94.3%	87.4%
Mean earnings in past 12 months	$3,946	$4,091	$3,907
Previously received occupation training	47.6%	45.9%	48.4%

Source: Estimates based on Background Information Form data.
Sample sizes: Adult women—classroom training subgroup, 2,343; OJT/JSA subgroup,
2,284; other services subgroup, 1,475. Adult men—classroom training subgroup, 1,034;
OJT/JSA subgroup, 2,571; other services subgroup, 1,497. Sample sizes for certain rows
are slightly smaller because of missing data.
a. AFDC, General Assistance, or other welfare except food stamps.

the group of people for whom that strategy was recommended, we cannot tell whether the labor market outcomes of one subgroup could be improved by substituting a different set of services.[4]

Impacts on Earnings: Adult Women and Men, by Service Strategy Subgroup

As shown in Exhibits 5.5 and 5.6, the quarterly earnings profiles of the treatment and control groups over the follow-up period were markedly different across the three service strategy subgroups, both in the level of control group earnings and in the contrast between treatment group earnings and control group earnings. Earnings levels for the control groups in the three service strategy subgroups support the hypothesis that program staff tended to assign the more employable applicants to the OJT/JSA service strategy. For both women and men, earnings in the absence of JTPA, as measured by the control group level, were much higher for the OJT/JSA group than for the classroom training group in the first year or more after random assignment. Control group earnings in the other services subgroup were intermediate between these two subgroups. In all three subgroups, earnings in the absence of JTPA services (the control level) showed a pronounced upward trend over the first year of the follow-up period. Treatment group earnings were above the earnings of controls throughout most of the follow-up period in all three subgroups, for both adult women and adult men, suggesting positive impacts on earnings.

Estimates of those impacts per enrollee are shown in Exhibit 5.7. The pattern of impacts shown in the exhibit is consistent with what one would expect for each of the three service strategies. The *classroom training strategy* involves an initial investment of time in classroom training that can be expected to delay participants' employment and temporarily reduce their earnings. Once trained, however, participants should command higher earnings than they would have without training. Moreover, to the extent that classroom training improves trainees' human capital, these gains should persist over time.

As shown in Exhibit 5.7, this is exactly the pattern of impacts estimated for both adult women and adult men in the classroom training subgroup. For both target groups, the estimated impact during the in-program period is negative, with positive impacts in each of the post-program periods.[5] In neither case, however, are the estimated impacts statistically significant; thus, we cannot be confident that the classroom training strategy increased the earnings of either adult women,

Exhibit 5.5 AVERAGE QUARTERLY EARNINGS OF ADULT WOMEN: TREATMENT GROUP AND CONTROL GROUP, BY SERVICE STRATEGY SUBGROUP

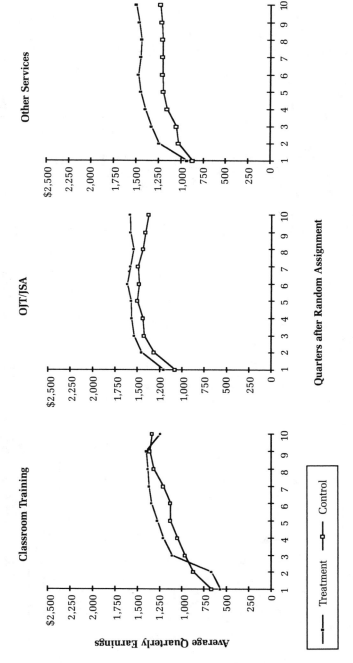

Sources: Estimates based on First and Second Follow-up Survey responses and earnings data from state unemployment insurance (UI) agencies.

Sample sizes: classroom training subgroup, 2,343; OJT/JSA subgroup, 2,284; other services subgroup, 1,475.

Exhibit 5.6 AVERAGE QUARTERLY EARNINGS OF ADULT MEN: TREATMENT GROUP AND CONTROL GROUP, BY SERVICE STRATEGY SUBGROUP

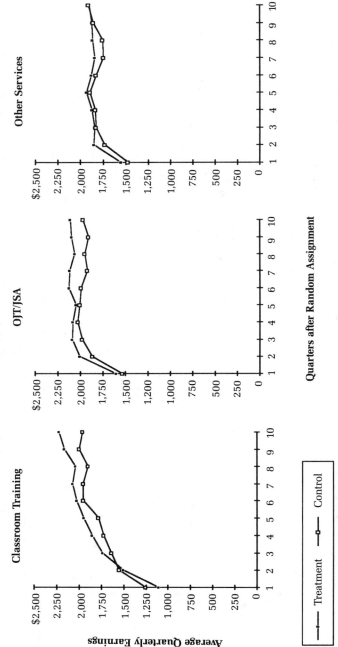

Sources: Estimates based on First and Second Follow-up Survey responses and earnings data from state unemployment insurance (UI) agencies.

Sample sizes: classroom training subgroup, 1,034; OJT/JSA subgroups, 2,571; other services subgroup, 1,497.

Exhibit 5.7 IMPACTS ON EARNINGS OF ADULT ENROLLEES, BY SERVICE
STRATEGY AND FOLLOW-UP PERIOD

	Mean earnings of enrollees	Impact per enrollee		
		In dollars	(Standard error)	As percent
Adult women				
Classroom training				
Months 1–6	$1,372	$ – 169	(112)	– 11.0
Months 7–18	4,810	434	(297)	9.9
Months 19–30	5,826	365	(366)	6.7
Total	12,008	630	(670)	5.5
OJT/JSA				
Months 1–6	3,164	484***	(188)	18.1
Months 7–18	7,128	787*	(451)	12.4
Months 19–30	7,027	1,021*	(525)	17.0
Total	17,319	2,292**	(1,023)	15.3
Other services				
Months 1–6	2,187	478**	(224)	28.0
Months 7–18	5,838	1,763***	(552)	43.3
Months 19–30	6,166	1,708***	(635)	38.3
Total	14,191	3,949***	(1,246)	38.6
Adult men				
Classroom training				
Months 1–6	2,558	– 255	(273)	– 9.1
Months 7–18	7,896	632	(696)	8.7
Months 19–30	8,896	910	(842)	11.4
Total	19,349	1,287	(1,582)	7.1
OJT/JSA				
Months 1–6	4,368	374	(250)	9.4
Months 7–18	9,665	611	(592)	6.7
Months 19–30	9,588	1,125*	(659)	13.3
Total	23,621	2,109	(1,335)	9.8
Other services				
Months 1–6	3,711	339	(310)	10.1
Months 7–18	8,219	233	(737)	2.9
Months 19–30	8,093	368	(822)	4.8
Total	20,023	941	(1,628)	4.9

Sources: Estimates based on First and Second Follow-up Survey responses and earnings
data from state unemployment insurance (UI) agencies.
Sample sizes: Adult women—classroom training subgroup, 2,343; OJT/JSA subgroup,
2,284; other services subgroup, 1,475. Adult men—classroom training subgroup, 1,034;
OJT/JSA subgroup, 2,571; other services subgroup, 1,497.
*Statistically significant at .10 level, **at .05 level, ***at .01 level (two-tailed test).

taken by themselves, or adult men, taken by themselves. If the two target groups are combined, however, the estimated impacts on the earnings of all adults are statistically significant in both postdemonstration years.[6]

The *OJT/JSA strategy*, which attempts to place participants immediately in either subsidized or unsubsidized jobs, should involve no delay in participants' employment. If anything, JTPA assignees in this subgroup should show earnings gains early in the follow-up period, because of quicker job placements than they would have experienced in the absence of the program. And if participants in on-the-job training positions improve their human capital or develop labor market attachments or job search skills that prevent or shorten subsequent spells of unemployment, the early earnings gains should persist over time. In fact, for both adult women and adult men the estimated impacts on earnings are positive throughout the 30-month follow-up period. For women, earnings gains ranging from $484 per enrollee in the first 6 months of the follow-up period to $1,021 in the last 12 months, for a total gain of $2,292 per enrollee, are statistically significant both overall and in all three subperiods. For adult men, only the $1,125 earnings gain in the second postprogram year is significant. The total estimated gains over the 30-month period represent a 15 percent increase in the earnings of adult women and a 10 percent increase in the earnings of adult men.

The *other services strategy* can be expected to have relatively rapid effects, because it comprises a variety of short-term, less-intensive services, many of which are directed toward immediate employment. The expected duration of these effects is less clear, however, than it is for the other two subgroups, because many of these services are not intended to develop human capital. As shown in Exhibit 5.7, the other services strategy had immediate, large, statistically significant impacts on the earnings of adult women that persisted throughout the follow-up period. Adult women in this subgroup gained a total of $3,949 per enrollee over the 30-month period, a 39 percent increase in earnings. In contrast, the other services strategy had no significant effect on the earnings of adult men. The estimated impacts for this group were not significant in any subperiod nor for the follow-up period as a whole. This is perhaps not surprising, given the very modest service increment observed for this subgroup—only 70 additional hours of service, at an incremental cost of less than $300 per enrollee.[7]

To summarize the effects of the various service strategies on the earnings of adult women and men:

- As expected, both women and men in the *classroom training* subgroup experienced earnings losses during the in-program period, with earnings gains in the post-program period. None of these estimated impacts are statistically significant when adult women and adult men are analyzed separately, but when the two target groups are combined, statistically significant impacts on earnings are found in both postprogram years;
- Also as expected, women in the *OJT/JSA strategy* had immediate, statistically significant earnings gains that persisted throughout the follow-up period; men in this subgroup had estimated effects that were quite similar in magnitude, but were only statistically significant in the second postprogram year; and,
- The *other services strategy* had large, statistically significant positive effects on the earnings of adult women throughout the follow-up period, but no significant impacts on the earnings of adult men.

In interpreting these results, it is important to remember that what matters from a policy perspective is not just the absolute size of the impacts but whether these effects outweigh the costs of the incremental services provided. Chapter 6 presents a benefit-cost analysis that compares the impacts of each of the service strategies with its costs, to determine which were cost-effective. It should also be borne in mind that these results reflect not only the differences among the three service strategies in the services provided but also differences among the subgroups of participants for whom these strategies were recommended. There is no guarantee that a service strategy that is shown to be cost-effective for one group will be cost-effective for another.

Impacts on Earnings: Adult Women and Men in Selected Key Subgroups

We have so far presented impact estimates for all adult women and men, and for those in each service strategy subgroup. To better understand the distribution of program effects, we now examine the impacts of JTPA on a number of other subgroups of women and men of interest to both policymakers and program administrators: those defined in terms of their ethnicity, barriers to employment, work history, welfare history, household composition, family income, and age. This analysis allows us to distinguish the groups for which JTPA was particularly effective, which in turn should help policymakers target future research into the factors that lead to program success. And by identifying any groups for which the program was not working well, the analysis should help policymakers and program administrators target their efforts for improvement.

It is important to note at the outset that any comparison of program impacts across these key subgroups must take into account the fact that effects may vary for any of a large number of reasons, reflecting the many dimensions in which subgroups may differ from one another beyond the single, selected characteristic defining them. On average, white women, for example, differ from black women in a variety of ways beyond ethnicity, such as in where they live, their education, and their work experience.

Furthermore, some subgroups that exhibit especially large earnings impacts may have been concentrated in sites with particularly effective programs. Other successful subgroups may have received a particularly effective mix of program services. But the ability of any one of these groups to benefit more from the program may also have been due to factors not directly related to the JTPA program, such as conditions in the local labor market or other personal characteristics of the subgroup members themselves.[8]

The exhibits in this subsection provide two different types of information. First, they provide the usual information about the size and statistical significance of the estimated impact for each subgroup. This tells us whether the program is having the desired effect for the subgroup in question. Second, the exhibits show whether the *difference* in impacts across subgroups defined by a particular characteristic is statistically significant (see the F-test at the end of each panel). This tells us whether we can be confident that the program is working *better* for one subgroup than for another.

The results for adult women by ethnic group in the first panel of Exhibit 5.8 can be used to illustrate how to interpret these estimates and their tests of significance. These results show that the program had statistically significant effects on the earnings of white and black women, but not on the earnings of Hispanic women. We can be confident, therefore, that JTPA improved the earnings of white and black women, but we have no conclusive evidence of a positive effect on the earnings of Hispanic women. At the same time, the estimated impacts for these three ethnic groups were not significantly different from one another, as indicated by the F-test for the ethnicity panel. This means that we cannot be confident that Hispanic women benefited *less* from the program than white or black women, either. In effect, the evidence is simply not strong enough to determine the effects of the program on the earnings of Hispanic women relative to

Exhibit 5.8 IMPACTS ON TOTAL 30-MONTH EARNINGS: ADULT WOMEN ASSIGNEES AND ENROLLEES, BY KEY SUBGROUP

Subgroup defined by:	Sample size	Control mean	Impact per			
			Assignee	(Standard error)	Enrollee	(Standard error)
Ethnicity						
White, non-Hispanic	3,636	13,200	$1,283***	(433)	$1,973***	(666)
Black, non-Hispanic	1,613	10,838	1,121*	(657)	1,927*	(1,129)
Hispanic	728	10,702	328	(959)	467	(1,365)
F-test, difference among subgroups			N.S.		N.S.	
Barriers to employment (in italics)						
Receiving cash welfare[a]	2,106	8,769	1,510***	(572)	2,359***	(894)
No cash welfare	3,505	14,551	1,056**	(452)	1,634**	(699)
F-test, difference among subgroups			N.S.		N.S.	
No high school diploma or GED	1,600	9,379	878	(646)	1,499	(1,103)
High school diploma or GED	4,132	13,484	1,152***	(410)	1,753***	(624)
F-test, difference among subgroups			N.S.		N.S.	
Worked less than 13 weeks in past 12 months	2,774	8,774	1,334***	(499)	2,100***	(786)
Worked 13 weeks or more in past 12 months	2,604	16,466	682	(515)	1,029	(777)
F-test, difference among subgroups			N.S.		N.S.	
Number of barriers						
None of the above	1,423	17,893	917	(705)	1,365	(1,049)
One of the above	1,611	13,011	1,133*	(668)	1,712*	(1,009)
Two of the above	1,266	8,952	981	(739)	1,562	(1,177)
All three of the above	418	5,745	535	(1,268)	910	(2,157)
F-test, difference among subgroups			N.S.		N.S.	

(Continued)

Exhibit 5.8 IMPACTS ON TOTAL 30-MONTH EARNINGS: ADULT WOMEN ASSIGNEES AND ENROLLEES, BY KEY SUBGROUP
(continued)

Subgroup defined by:	Sample size	Control mean	Impact per			
			Assignee	(Standard error)	Enrollee	(Standard error)
Work history						
Never employed	802	6,887	788	(910)	1,270	(1,467)
Earned < $4 hourly in last job	1,836	10,979	943	(614)	1,437	(936)
Earned $4 or more hourly in last job	2,798	14,528	1,626***	(495)	2,540***	(773)
F-test, difference among subgroups			N.S.		N.S.	
AFDC history						
Never AFDC case head	3,036	14,513	563	(478)	883	(750)
AFDC case head less than 2 years	1,388	12,358	1,018	(703)	1,582	(1,092)
AFDC case head 2 years or more	1,544	8,056	2,255***	(664)	3,519***	(1,036)
F-test, difference among subgroups			N.S.		N.S.	
JTPA required for welfare, food stamps, or WIN program[b]						
Yes	710	7,763	1,195	(989)	2,190	(1,812)
No	5,117	13,033	1,022***	(370)	1,560***	(565)
F-test, difference among subgroups			N.S.		N.S.	

	Sample size					
Household composition						
No spouse or own children present	1,143	12,949	558	(783)	$920	(1,291)
Own children under age 4, no spouse present	1,076	10,824	1,685**	(808)	2,519**	(1,208)
Own children, 4 or older, no spouse present	1,790	13,781	391	(623)	598	(953)
Spouse present, with or without own children	1,229	11,962	1,698**	(768)	2,617**	
F-test, difference among subgroups			N.S.		N.S.	
Family income in past 12 months						
$6,000 or less	3,633	10,770	760*	(436)	1,199*	(688)
More than $6,000	2,003	15,446	1,620***	(591)	2,448***	(893)
F-test, difference among subgroups			N.S.		N.S.	
Age at random assignment						
22–29 years	2,656	11,754	1,121**	(513)	1,746**	(799)
30–54 years	3,177	12,766	1,283***	(464)	2,020***	(731)
> 54 years	269	9,603	557	(1,603)	833	(2,397)
F-test, difference among subgroups			N.S.		N.S.	
Full sample	6,102	12,241	1,176***	(336)	1,837***	(525)

Sources: Estimates based on First and Second Follow-up Survey responses and earnings data from state unemployment insurance (UI) agencies.

Notes: Sample sizes for mutually exclusive subgroups within a panel do not necessarily sum to sample size for target group as a whole, because persons in omitted subgroups or with missing data on the variable used to define the subgroup are excluded. "N.S."—F-test is not statistically significant.

a. AFDC, General Assistance, or other welfare except food stamps.

b. WIN is the federal Work Incentive program.

*Statistically significant at the .10 level, **at the .05 level, ***at the .01 level (two-tailed test).

women in other ethnic groups—in part because of the small sample of Hispanic women available for the analysis.

In fact, although the estimated impacts vary widely across subgroups and there are a number of statistically significant estimated subgroup impacts in Exhibits 5.8 and 5.9, in only one case do the impacts for subgroups defined by any particular characteristic differ significantly from one another—adult men with spouses present had substantially and significantly larger program-induced earnings gains than adult men without spouses present. This may reflect greater motivation on the part of men with family responsibilities. It may also reflect the fact that in a set of 20 statistical tests such as those performed in these two exhibits, one or two tests could be expected to be significant at the .10 level by chance alone. In general, the results of these tests indicate that if the impact of JTPA differs among subgroups defined on the basis of the characteristics considered here, our sample is not large enough to allow us to detect those differences.

The results do, however, provide solid evidence of program-induced earnings gains for a number of subgroups of adult women and several subgroups of adult men. There is no particular pattern to these significant positive impacts, however. On the basis of these results, and the general lack of statistically significant differences among subgroups, we conclude that the benefits of JTPA are broadly distributed across a wide variety of different types of adult women and men.

Impacts on Earnings: Adult Women, by Receipt of AFDC at Application to JTPA

A subgroup of particular interest for policy is women receiving welfare. The previous section showed that JTPA had positive effects on the earnings of adult women receiving cash welfare when they applied to JTPA (including general assistance and other cash welfare, as well as AFDC). This section examines in more detail the effects of the program on adult women receiving AFDC at application.

For comparison, we present the corresponding results for adult women who were *not* receiving AFDC at application. These results are of interest not only as a benchmark for assessing the results for AFDC recipients but also because they represent the first experimental estimates of the effects of an employment and training program for nonwelfare women. Prior experimental studies have focused on welfare recipients.

As might be expected, the women who were receiving AFDC when they applied to JTPA were noticeably more disadvantaged than the

Exhibit 5.9 IMPACTS ON TOTAL 30-MONTH EARNINGS: ADULT MEN ASSIGNEES AND ENROLLEES, BY KEY SUBGROUP

					Impact per		
Subgroup defined by:	Sample size	Control mean	Assignee	(Standard error)	Enrollee	(Standard error)
Ethnicity						
White, non-Hispanic	3,144	19,796	$707	(670)	$1,171	(1,110)
Black, non-Hispanic	1,296	15,483	931	(1,047)	1,529	(1,720)
Hispanic	497	19,007	1,784	(1,706)	2,680	(2,563)
F-test, difference among subgroups			N.S.		N.S.	
Barriers to employment (in italics)						
Receiving cash welfare[a]	568	13,608	305	(1,576)	549	(2,837)
No cash welfare	3,977	18,986	1,529**	(599)	2,456**	(962)
F-test, difference among subgroups			N.S.		N.S.	
No high school diploma or GED	1,464	14,520	1,353	(995)	2,359	(1,735)
High school diploma or GED	3,313	20,018	931	(659)	1,478	(1,046)
F-test, difference among subgroups			N.S.		N.S.	
Worked less than 13 weeks in past 12 months	1,857	13,874	735	(891)	1,211	(1,468)
Worked 13 weeks or more in past 12 months	2,791	21,859	1,140	(722)	1,815	(1,150)
F-test, difference among subgroups			N.S.		N.S.	
Number of barriers[b]						
None of the above	1,605	23,717	1,438	(945)	2,225	(1,462)
One of the above	1,588	13,011	1,479	(969)	2,370	(1,553)
Two of the above	639	8,952	1,463	(1,528)	2,549	(2,662)
F-test, difference among subgroups			N.S.		N.S.	

(continued)

Exhibit 5.9 IMPACTS ON TOTAL 30-MONTH EARNINGS: ADULT MEN ASSIGNEES AND ENROLLEES, BY KEY SUBGROUP (continued)

Work history						
Never employed	427	14,368	-2,104	(1,850)	-3,463	(3,045)
Earned < $4 hourly in last job	835	14,268	245	(969)	391	(2,095)
Earned ≥ $4 hourly in last job	3,058	19,353	1,647**	(1,528)	2,699**	(1,103)
F-test, difference among subgroups			N.S.		N.S.	
Household composition						
No spouse present	3,139	16,413	248	(672)	418	(1,133)
Spouse present	1,716	22,749	2,759***	(925)	4,282***	(1,436)
F-test, difference among subgroups			**		**	
Family income in past 12 months						
$6,000 or less	2,898	15,099	733	(707)	1,233	(1,189)
More than $6,000	1,884	24,159	1,556*	(882)	2,405*	(1,363)
F-test, difference among subgroups			N.S.		N.S.	
Age at random assignment[c]						
22–29 years	2,270	19,092	1,221	(798)	1,961	(1,282)
30–54 years	2,660	18,001	1,152	(731)	1,916	(1,216)
F-test, difference among subgroups			N.S.		N.S.	
Full sample	5,102	18,496	978*	(529)	1,599*	(865)

Sources: Estimates based on First and Second Follow-up Survey responses and earnings data from state unemployment insurance (UI) agencies.

Notes: Sample sizes for mutually exclusive subgroups within a panel do not necessarily sum to sample size for target group as a whole, because persons in omitted subgroups or with missing data on the variable used to define the subgroup are excluded. "N.S."—F-test is not statistically significant.

a. AFDC, General Assistance, or other welfare except food stamps.
b. Sample of men facing all three barriers too small for analysis.
c. Sample of men age 55 or older too small for analysis.
*Statistically significant at .10 level, **at .05 level, ***at .01 level (two-tailed test).

nonwelfare women who applied to JTPA. Most notably, 58 percent of the welfare women were minorities, as compared with only 29 percent of those not receiving welfare. Thirty-one percent of those receiving AFDC lacked a high school diploma or GED, as did 26 percent of those not on AFDC; and the average age of AFDC recipients was 30, as compared with an average of 35 for nonrecipients.

Estimated impacts on the earnings of AFDC recipients and non-recipients in each of the service strategy subgroups are shown in Exhibit 5.10. As shown earlier, JTPA had a significant positive impact on the earnings of both welfare recipients and nonrecipients overall.[9] The estimated impacts for the service strategy subgroups reveal, however, that the overall impacts for the two groups arise from different sources. For AFDC recipients, OJT/JSA was the only service strategy that led to significant earnings gains—nearly $5,000 per enrollee over the 30-month follow-up period. For nonrecipients, the other services subgroup experienced large, significant earnings increases—nearly $4,000 per enrollee—and those in OJT/JSA did not. Although the estimated impact of the other services strategy on the earnings of AFDC recipients was relatively large ($2,900), it was not statistically significant. In neither case was the impact of classroom training on earnings statistically significant.

Whereas the estimated impacts and their significance differ substantially between AFDC recipients and nonrecipients in both the OJT/JSA and the other services subgroups, only the difference in impacts between the two OJT/JSA subgroups is significant (at the .10 level; tests not shown in Exhibit 5.10). Moreover, for neither AFDC recipients nor for nonrecipients are the differences among service strategy subgroups statistically significant (tests not shown in exhibit). Thus, although we can be confident that the OJT/JSA strategy had a positive effect on the earnings of AFDC recipients and that that effect was greater than the effect of the same strategy for nonwelfare women, we cannot be sure that OJT/JSA was more effective for AFDC recipients than were the other two service strategies. Similarly, although we have solid evidence that the other services strategy increased the earnings of nonwelfare women, we cannot be confident that it was more effective than the other two service strategies for nonrecipients, or that it was more effective for nonwelfare women than for AFDC recipients.

The large effects of OJT/JSA on the earnings of AFDC recipients are consistent with the two prior experimental studies of programs that provided subsidized employment for AFDC recipients. The Supported Work Demonstration and the AFDC Homemaker–Home Health Aide

Exhibit 5.10 IMPACTS ON TOTAL 30-MONTH EARNINGS: ADULT WOMEN ASSIGNEES AND ENROLLEES, BY RECEIPT OF AFDC AND SERVICE STRATEGY SUBGROUP

Service strategy subgroup	Sample size	Mean earnings of control group	Impact per			
			Assignee	(Standard error)	Enrollee	(Standard error)
AFDC Recipients						
Classroom training	912	$8,273	$790	($779)	$1,077	(1,062)
OJT/JSA	507	9,786	2,930***	(1,048)	4,833***	(1,729)
Other services	443	7,833	1,632	(1,123)	2,900	(1,995)
All recipients	1,862	8,582	1,570***	(545)	2,387***	(829)
Nonrecipients						
Classroom training	1,395	12,656	521	(737)	683	(966)
OJT/JSA	1,749	15,517	820	(655)	1,499	(1,197)
Other services	1,014	12,918	2,231**	(882)	3,744**	(1,480)
All nonrecipients	4,158	13,952	1,053**	(428)	1,668**	(678)

Sources: Estimates based on First and Second Follow-up Survey responses and earnings data from state unemployment insurance (UI) agencies.

Notes: "AFDC recipients" indicated on Background Information Form that they were receiving AFDC at time of application to JTPA. "Nonrecipients" indicated the contrary.

*Statistically significant at .10 level, **at .05 level, ***at .01 level (two-tailed test).

Demonstrations, which offered up to 12 months of subsidized employment for AFDC recipients, both found large impacts on post-demonstration earnings.[10] In Supported Work, gains in quarterly earnings averaged $310 in the last quarter of the 27-month follow-up period. In the seven state-run Home Health Aide Demonstations, quarterly earnings gains ranged from $39 to $573 at the end of the 32-month follow-up period. The estimated OJT/JSA impacts of nearly $500 per quarter over the 30-month follow-up period compare quite favorably with these results. Subsequent analyses of the Supported Work and Home Health Aide Demonstration samples based on longer-term follow-up data confirm that significant earnings gains persisted throughout a five-year postprogram period for the Home Health Aide Demonstrations and for eight years in the Supported Work sample, although in both cases the gains declined over time.[11]

These earlier demonstrations were much more intensive interventions than JTPA. But their basic approach was similar to the JTPA OJT/JSA strategy, in that they focused on getting AFDC recipients into real jobs, in order to teach them the work skills and habits needed to be employable. They were also, like JTPA, voluntary programs. Taken together, these results seem to suggest that, at least for volunteers, actual work experience may be a more effective device for raising the earnings of AFDC recipients than other services, such as classroom training in occupational skills or basic education. This conclusion is, however, subject to the qualification that the personal characteristics of the women for whom the OJT/JSA strategy was recommended differed from those of the women in other service strategies; therefore, it may have been the characteristics of the women themselves, rather than the services they received, that led to more positive results for that subgroup.

FINDINGS FOR YOUTHS, BY SERVICE STRATEGY AND OTHER KEY SUBGROUPS

This section presents results for youth subgroups corresponding to those analyzed above for adults.

Treatment-Control Service Increment, by Service Strategy Subgroup: Female Youths and Male Youth Non-Arrestees

The specific employment and training services received by female youths and male youth non-arrestees in each of the three service strategy subgroups are shown in Exhibits 5.11 and 5.12. As with the corresponding figures for adults, these exhibits include both JTPA and non-JTPA services. Receipt of classroom training in occupational skills, basic education, job search assistance, and "other" services was measured with follow-up survey data. Because of respondent recall error, these data may understate somewhat the receipt of these services—especially minor services such as job search assistance—but are the only feasible source of comparable information for treatment and control group members. Receipt of on-the-job training and work experience was measured with data from SDA records, because these services are generally provided only by JTPA.

As with adults, the recommendations of JTPA intake staff created service strategy subgroups that received distinctly different mixes of employment and training services. Moreover, for both female youths and male youth non-arrestees (Exhibits 5.11 and 5.12), the largest difference in services received by the treatment and control groups in the classroom training and OJT/JSA subgroups was that substantially higher percentages of the treatment groups in those two subgroups received classroom training and OJT, respectively, than among the controls. Thus, the impacts we observe for youths in the classroom training subgroups are primarily the result of incremental classroom training, and the impacts we observe for youths in the OJT/JSA subgroups are primarily the result of incremental on-the-job training. The service increment in the other services subgroup was spread more broadly across several different services, with only one service showing a treatment-control differential of more than 8 percentage points in the percentage receiving the service. In part, however, this may reflect underreporting of the less-intensive services such as job search assistance on the follow-up survey.

The differences in hours of service shown in the right-hand panels of Exhibits 5.11 and 5.12 reflect very similar patterns. For female youths, over half the total service increment in the classroom training subgroup was attributable to additional hours of classroom training in occupational skills, and virtually the entire service increment in the OJT/JSA subgroup was due to additional hours of on-the-job training. For male youth non-arrestees, about two-thirds of the service increment in these two service strategies was due to additional hours of the defining service. In the other services subgroup, the service differential reflected small increments of hours of a number of different services. (Again, these figures may reflect underreporting of minor services such as job search assistance.)

Exhibit 5.11 RECEIPT OF SPECIFIC EMPLOYMENT AND TRAINING SERVICES: FEMALE YOUTH TREATMENT AND CONTROL GROUPS, BY SERVICE STRATEGY

	Percentage receiving service			Mean hours of service		
	Treatment group	Control group	Difference in percentage points	Treatment group	Control group	Difference in hours
Classroom training subgroup						
Classroom training in occupational skills	48.4	33.2	15.2***	400	228	173***
Basic education	17.4	15.4	2.0	79	47	32**
OJT	3.6	0.0	3.6***	30	0	30
Work experience	6.2	0.9	5.3***	36	4	32
JSA	3.9	0.9	3.0***	9	2	8
Other	12.6	3.0	9.6***	48	5	43
Any service	75.3	48.9	26.4***	603	285	319
OJT/JSA Subgroup						
Classroom training in occupational skills	18.5	19.0	-0.5	129	123	6
Basic education	5.6	7.4	-1.7	20	24	-4
OJT	34.3	0.0	34.3***	124	0	124***
Work experience	2.7	0.0	2.7***	10	0	10***
JSA	4.3	0.6	3.7***	4	0	4*
Other	5.4	7.4	-2.0	16	13	2
Any service	56.0	33.1	22.9***	297	167	130***
Other services subgroup						
Classroom training in occupational skills	26.0	28.1	-2.1	146	184	-38
Basic education	23.3	18.4	4.9	75	78	-3
OJT	5.0	0.0	5.0*	35	0	35***
Work experience	2.9	0.9	2.0***	16	3	13**
JSA	8.9	2.2	6.7***	10	6	4
Other	8.9	2.6	6.3**	42	8	33**
Any service	61.4	45.6	15.7***	324	280	45

Sources: Estimates based on First Follow-up Survey responses and enrollment and tracking data from 15 SDAs.
Sample sizes: classroom training subgroup, 1,004; OJT/JSA subgroup, 536; other services subgroup, 743.
*Statistically significant at .10 level, **at .05 level, *** at .01 level (two-tailed test).

Exhibit 5.12 RECEIPT OF SPECIFIC EMPLOYMENT AND TRAINING SERVICES: MALE YOUTH NON-ARRESTEE TREATMENT AND CONTROL GROUPS, BY SERVICE STRATEGY

	Percentage receiving service			Mean hours of service		
	Treatment group	Control group	Difference in percentage points	Treatment group	Control group	Difference in hours
Classroom training subgroup						
Classroom training in occupational skills	45.9	23.5	22.5***	383	213	170**
Basic education	14.3	12.9	1.4	83	37	46*
OJT	5.0	0.0	5.0***	32	0	32***
Work experience	3.9	0.8	3.1**	23	2	21***
JSA	1.2	0.8	0.4	4	1	3
Other	0.9	0.7	0.2	53	44	9
Any service	68.3	43.9	24.4***	578	297	281***
OJT/JSA subgroup						
Classroom training in occupational skills	19.3	10.6	8.7***	144	50	94***
Basic education	5.2	7.3	-2.1	9	56	-47*
OJT	37.6	0.7	36.9***	148	4	144***
Work experience	1.0	0.0	1.0*	3	0	3
JSA	6.2	0.0	6.2***	10	0	10**
Other	5.9	4.0	1.9	27	20	7
Any service	58.5	21.9	36.6***	341	130	210***
Other services subgroup						
Classroom training in occupational skills	26.0	24.4	1.7	154	165	-11
Basic education	28.4	15.4	13.1***	118	93	26
OJT	5.7	0.0	5.7***	22	0	22***
Work experience	1.8	1.3	0.5	8	10	-2
JSA	3.3	0.6	2.7**	6	0	6**
Other	9.0	1.3	7.7***	25	5	19**
Any service	62.3	39.1	23.2***	333	273	60

Sources: Estimates based on First Follow-up Survey responses and enrollment and tracking data from 15 SDAs.
Sample sizes: classroom training subgroup, 391; OJT/JSA subgroup, 457; other services subgroup, 490.
*Statistically significant at .10 level **at .05 level ***at .01 level (two-tailed test)

Exhibit 5.13 shows three summary measures of the service increment in each youth service strategy subgroup. The first panel of the exhibit shows the percentages of treatment and control group members receiving any service, along with the treatment-control difference per assignee and per enrollee. As can be seen in the exhibit, assignment to the treatment group increased the likelihood of receiving services by statistically significant margins in each service strategy subgroup.

In terms of total hours of service, the service increment was greatest for the classroom training subgroup. Female and male youths enrolled in that subgroup received 429 and 378 additional hours of service, respectively, as compared with 224 additional hours for females and 329 for males in the OJT/JSA subgroup and only 81 and 90 additional hours, respectively, in the other services subgroup (Exhibit 5.13). The service increments in the other services subgroup were not statistically significant, indicating that JTPA may not have provided any more services to youths in this subgroup than they could have obtained outside of JTPA. Thus, it would not be surprising if the program had little effect on these subgroups. However, the service increments for youths in the classroom training and OJT/JSA subgroups are larger than those observed for adults; thus, any absence of program impacts in these subgroups cannot be explained by a lack of treatment-control service differential.

The mean hours of service shown in these exhibits are averaged across all treatment and control group members, whether they received services or not. In each subgroup, treatment group members *who received some service* received about the same number of hours of service as controls *who received services* (numbers not shown in the exhibits). This means that the service increment primarily took the form of more individuals receiving services, not more intensive services to those who received them. The bottom panel of Exhibit 5.13 shows the service differential in terms of the cost of the additional services received. Although the classroom training strategy involved a substantially larger service increment in terms of hours per enrollee than the OJT/JSA strategy, the latter cost more—$2,091 per enrollee for female youths and $3,754 for male youths, as compared with about $1,860 per enrollee for both females and males in the classroom training subgroup. The relatively small service increment in the other services strategy cost only $47 per enrollee for female youths and $739 for male youth non-arrestees. Thus, there was essentially no treatment-control difference in service costs for female youths in the other services subgroup.

Exhibit 5.13 INCREMENT IN EMPLOYMENT AND TRAINING SERVICES RECEIVED BY YOUTHS FROM ANY SOURCE, BY SERVICE STRATEGY SUBGROUP

	Treatment group	Control group	Difference per			
			Assignee	(Standard error)	Enrollee	(Standard error)
			Percentage receiving any service			
Female youths						
Classroom training	75.3	48.9	26.4***	(3.2)	35.5***	(4.3)
OJT/JSA	56.0	33.1	22.9***	(4.5)	39.4***	(7.7)
Other services	61.4	45.6	15.7***	(3.9)	28.2***	(7.0)
Male youth non-arrestees						
Classroom training	68.3	43.9	24.4***	(5.2)	32.9***	(7.0)
OJT/JSA	58.5	21.9	36.6***	(4.4)	57.2***	(6.9)
Other services	62.3	39.1	23.2***	(4.7)	34.4***	(7.0)
			Mean hours of services received			
Female youth						
Classroom training	603	285	319***	(39)	429***	[52]
OJT/JSA	297	167	130***	(40)	224***	[69]
Other services	324	280	45	(42)	81	[78]
Male youth non-arrestees						
Classroom training	578	297	281***	(73)	378***	[98]
OJT/JSA	341	130	210***	(49)	329***	[77]
Other services	333	273	60	(55)	90	[83]

Mean cost of services received

Female youths					
Classroom training	$3,241	$1,855	$1,386***	($295)	$1,867***	($397)
OJT/JSA	2,474	1,259	1,215***	(370)	2,091***	(637)
Other services	2,209	2,183	26	(407)	47	(736)
Male youth non-arrestees					
Classroom training	3,469	2,089	$1,380**	(645)	1,860**	(869)
OJT/JSA	3,097	693	2,404***	(418)	3,754***	(653)
Other services	2,268	1,771	498	(395)	739	(586)

Sources: Estimates based on First Follow-up Survey responses, published school expenditure data, SDA enrollment and expenditure records, and telephone survey of vocational/technical schools.

Sample sizes: Adult women—classroom training subgroup, 1,004; OJT/JSA subgroup, 536; other services subgroup, 743. Adult men—classroom training subgroup, 391; OJT/JSA subgroup, 457; other services subgroup, 490.

*Statistically significant at .10 level, **at .05 level, ***at .01 level (two-tailed test).

The patterns of services received by female youths and male youth non-arrestees can be summarized as follows:

- Although not all treatment group members received the services that were recommended for them, the service recommendations of JTPA intake workers created three groups that received distinctly different mixes of employment and training services;
- The service increment in the classroom training subgroup reflects primarily a higher likelihood of receiving classroom training in occupational skills;
- The service increment in the OJT/JSA subgroup reflects primarily a higher likelihood of receiving on-the-job training;
- The service increment in the other services subgroup was spread more broadly across several different services;
- The service increment was greatest for the classroom training strategy, followed by the OJT/JSA strategy, and least for the other services strategy. The service increments for the other services subgroups were small and statistically insignificant; those in the classroom training and OJT/JSA subgroups were larger than the corresponding increments for adults;
- The incremental cost of the classroom training strategy was about $1,860 per enrollee for both female and male youths, as compared with $2,091 for female youths and $2,908 for males in the OJT/JSA subgroup; the other services strategy was substantially cheaper for males, at $739 per enrollee, and there was virtually no incremental cost for female youths in the other services subgroup; and,
- The service increment primarily took the form of more individuals receiving services, not more intensive services for those who received them.

Differences in Baseline Characteristics across Service Strategy Subgroups: Female Youths and Male Youth Non-Arrestees

As noted earlier, it is important to recognize that the effects of the program estimated for different subgroups of enrollees reflect not only differences in the program services received by those subgroups but also differences among the subgroups in the characteristics of their members. Exhibit 5.14 shows selected baseline characteristics of female youths and male youth non-arrestees in each of the service strategy subgroups. For both female and male youths, the ethnic composition of the three subgroups varied widely. As with adults, youths in the OJT/JSA subgroup were much more likely to be white than those

Exhibit 5.14 ETHNICITY, BARRIERS TO EMPLOYMENT, AND WORK AND
TRAINING HISTORIES: YOUTH ASSIGNEES, BY SERVICE STRATEGY

	Service strategy		
Characteristic	Classroom training	OJT/JSA	Other services
Female youths			
Ethnicity			
White, non-Hispanic	51.8%	65.2%	43.8%
Black, non-Hispanic	23.9	22.4	45.9
Hispanic	22.6	10.7	9.0
Other	1.8	1.6	1.3
Barriers to employment			
Receiving cash welfare[a]	33.4	21.5	29.8
No high school diploma or GED certificate	47.8	35.8	56.6
Worked less than 13 weeks in past 12 months	59.1	44.1	68.7
Number of barriers			
None of the above	20.9	34.6	14.5
One of the above	32.6	36.6	31.9
Two of the above	32.0	21.9	36.6
Three of the above	14.4	6.9	17.0
Work and training histories			
Ever employed	76.1	88.8	75.0
Mean earnings in past 12 months	$1,266	$1,940	$1,092
Previously received occupational training	20.9%	32.0%	25.6%
Male youth non-arrestees			
Ethnicity			
White, non-Hispanic	46.9%	74.2%	44.5%
Black, non-Hispanic	25.5	12.6	44.2
Hispanic	25.8	11.3	9.5
Other	1.8	1.9	3.7
Barriers to employment			
Receiving cash welfare[a]	10.2	8.5	11.2
No high school diploma or GED certificate	60.1	38.9	70.4
Worked less than 13 weeks in past 12 months	50.0	32.9	54.4
Number of barriers			
None of the above	21.8	39.7	13.9
One of the above	39.1	43.6	41.3
Two of the above	34.6	14.2	37.0
Three of the above	4.5	2.4	7.8
Work and training histories			
Ever employed	79.4	92.9	79.6
Mean earnings in past 12 months	$1,672	$3,024	$1,817
Previously received occupational training	25.7%	33.0%	33.1%

Source: Estimates based on Background Information Form data.
Sample sizes: Female youths—classroom training subgroup, 1,150; OJT/JSA subgroup,
614; other services subgroup, 893. Male youth non-arrestees—classroom training
subgroup, 489; OJT/JSA subgroup, 554; other services subgroup, 661. Sample sizes for
certain rows are slightly smaller because of missing data.
a. AFDC, General Assistance, or other welfare except food stamps.

for whom the other two service strategies were recommended. Unlike adults, however, among youths the highest proportion of blacks was found in the other services subgroup. Hispanics comprised a larger proportion of the classroom training subgroups than of the other two subgroups. Again, these patterns do not necessarily represent ethnic discrimination in service recommendations. They may instead simply reflect differences in overall service mix among the sites where the different ethnic groups were concentrated.

The remaining characteristics shown in Exhibit 5.14 display a clear pattern of assignment of the most job-ready youths to the OJT/JSA service strategy. Both female and male youths in this subgroup were less likely to face each of the three barriers to employment shown in the exhibit, were more likely to have worked for pay, and had higher earnings in the previous 12 months than those in the other two service strategy subgroups. Female youths in the OJT/JSA subgroup were also somewhat more likely to have had prior occupational training than those in the other two subgroups. The differences in these character-istics between the classroom training and other services subgroups were much smaller.

These differences among the assignees in the three service strategy subgroups mean that the impacts estimated for each subgroup are applicable only to the individuals in that subgroup. If that service strategy were adopted for the individuals in another subgroup, there is no guarantee that the same impacts would be obtained. Thus, al-though the analysis can identify a strategy (or strategies) that was working, or not working, for the group of people for whom that strat-egy was recommended, we cannot tell whether the labor market out-comes of one subgroup could be improved by substituting a different set of services.[12]

Impacts on Earnings: Female Youths and Male Youth Non-Arrestees, by Service Strategy Subgroup

The quarterly earnings trends of youths in the treatment and control groups in each service strategy subgroup are shown in Exhibits 5.15 and 5.16. The control earnings levels strongly support the conclusion that the most job-ready youths were assigned to the OJT/JSA subgroup. For both female and male youths, controls in this subgroup earned more throughout the follow-up period than those in the other two subgroups. Earnings for controls in all six subgroups also show the same strong upward trend observed for adults, indicating that

Exhibit 5.15 AVERAGE QUARTERLY EARNINGS OF FEMALE YOUTHS: TREATMENT GROUP AND CONTROL GROUP, BY SERVICE STRATEGY SUBGROUP

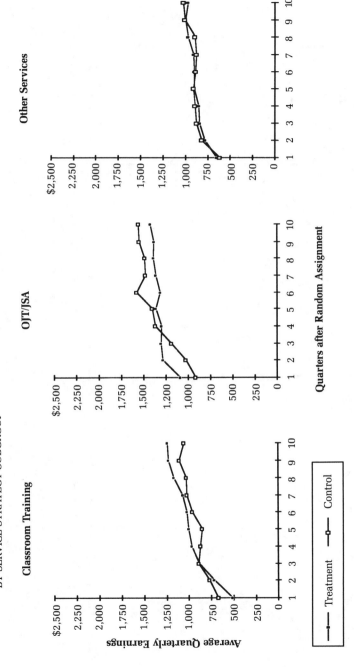

Sources: Estimates based on First and Second Follow-up Survey responses and earnings data from state unemployment insurance (UI) agencies.

Sample size: classroom training subgroup, 1,150; OJT/JSA subgroup, 614; other services subgroups, 893.

Exhibit 5.16 AVERAGE QUARTERLY EARNINGS OF MALE YOUTH NON-ARRESTEES: TREATMENT GROUP AND CONTROL GROUP, BY SERVICE STRATEGY SUBGROUP

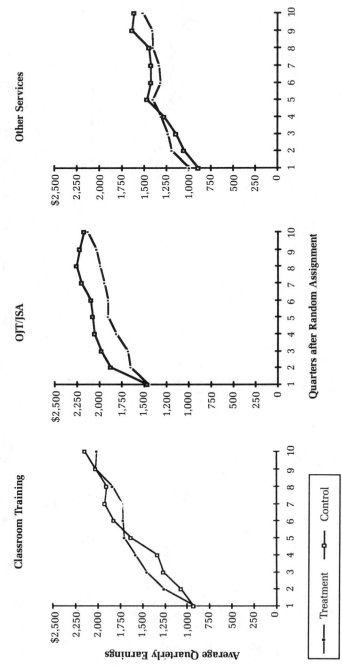

Sources: Estimates based on First and Second Follow-up Survey responses and earnings data from state unemployment insurance (UI) agencies.
Sample sizes: classroom training subgroup, 489; OJT/JSA subgroup, 554; other services subgroup, 661.

many of the youths who applied to JTPA would have found employment even in the absence of JTPA services.

The separation between the earnings paths of the treatment and control groups is much less marked than was the case for adults, however, and in some cases the control level lies *above* the treatment group level, suggesting a program-induced *loss* of earnings. The impacts implied by these treatment-control differences, and tests of their statistical significance, are shown in Exhibit 5.17. As shown in the exhibit, there were no statistically significant impacts on total 30-month earnings in any of the six youth service strategy subgroups. The only significant impacts occurred during the first six months of the follow-up period—a significant earnings *loss* for female youths in the classroom training subgroup and a significant earnings *gain* for those in the OJT/JSA service strategy. It is likely, however, that among the 24 estimates shown in the exhibit, this many would be statistically significant by chance alone.

On the basis of these results, then, there is no evidence that any of the JTPA service strategies improved the earnings of either female youths or male youth non-arrestees. This finding is not surprising for youths in the other services subgroup, who received no significant increase in services. For both females and males in the other two service strategies, however, the service increment was as large as that for adults; thus, the lack of program effects cannot be explained by a lack of additional services.

Impacts on Hours of Employment or Training: Female Youths and Male Youth Non-Arrestees, by Service Strategy Subgroup

In the case of youths, JTPA has traditionally viewed "success" more broadly than in the case of adults. Whereas JTPA performance standards for adults have focused on placement in jobs, standards for youths have been defined in terms of "positive terminations." Positive terminations include not only entering employment but also returning to school full-time; completing elementary, secondary, or post-secondary school; attainment of recognized employment competencies established by the Private Industry Council; enrolling in other training programs or apprenticeships; or enlisting in the military. Although data are not available to estimate the impact of JTPA on all of these activities and accomplishments in our sample, we are able to estimate impacts on total hours spent in employment and training over the follow-up period.

Exhibit 5.17 IMPACT ON EARNINGS OF YOUTH ENROLLEES,
BY SERVICE STRATEGY AND FOLLOW-UP PERIOD

	Mean earnings of enrollees	Impact per enrollee		
		In dollars	(Standard error)	As percent
Female youths				
Classroom training				
Months 1–6	$1,181	$ − 284*	($145)	− 19.4
Months 7–18	4,051	458	(347)	12.7
Months 19–30	5,047	665	(459)	15.2
Total	10,279	839	(791)	8.9
OJT/JSA				
Months 1–6	2,717	762**	(339)	39.0
Months 7–18	5,768	− 441	(825)	− 7.1
Months 19–30	5,771	− 899	(963)	− 13.5
Total	14,256	− 578	(1,883)	− 3.9
Other services				
Months 1–6	1,386	− 15	(220)	− 1.1
Months 7–18	3,352	− 115	(726)	− 3.3
Months 19–30	3,548	97	(607)	2.8
Total	8,286	− 33	(1,125)	− 0.4
Male youth non-arrestees				
Classroom training				
Months 1–6	2,000	248	(372)	14.2
Months 7–18	6,444	547	(818)	9.3
Months 19–30	7,918	− 543	(1,041)	− 6.4
Total	16,362	251	(1,916)	1.6
OJT/JSA				
Months 1–6	3,843	− 366	(432)	− 8.7
Months 7–18	8,347	− 1,448	(993)	− 14.8
Months 19–30	8,911	− 1,198	(1,158)	− 11.9
Total	21,101	− 3,012	(2,222)	− 12.5
Other services				
Months 1–6	2,229	340	(289)	18.0
Months 7–18	5,211	− 91	(661)	− 1.7
Months 19–30	5,380	− 688	(808)	− 11.3
Total	12,819	− 438	(1,474)	− 3.3

Sources: Estimates based on First and Second Follow-up Survey responses and earnings data from state unemployment insurance (UI) agencies.
Notes: Results were inferred from findings for all treatment and control group members, with the following sample sizes. Female youths—classroom training subgroup, 1,150; OJT/JSA subgroup, 614; other services subgroup, 893. Male youth non-arrestees—classroom training subgroup, 489; OJT/JSA subgroup, 554; other services subgroup, 661.
*Statistically significant at .10 level, **at .05 level, ***at .01 level (two-tailed test).

Exhibit 5.18 IMPACTS ON HOURS OF EMPLOYMENT OR TRAINING: YOUTH
ASSIGNEES AND ENROLLEES, BY SERVICE STRATEGY SUBGROUP

	Sample size	Control mean	Impact per assignee	(Standard error)	Impact per enrollee
Female youths					
Classroom training	585	2,309	260*	(150)	335*
OJT/JSA	299	3,016	−165	(243)	−278
Other services	378	2,110	120	(193)	223
All female youths	1,262	2,390	154	(106)	234
Male youth non-arrestees					
Classroom training	212	3,703	14	(254)	18
OJT/JSA	242	3,689	53	(243)	84
Other services	241	3,313	−167	(240)	−259
All male youths	695	3,566	−47	(141)	−70

Sources: Estimates based on First and Second Follow-up Survey responses and earnings
data from state unemployment insurance (UI) agencies.
*Statistically significant at .10 level, **at .05 level, ***at .01 level (two-tailed test).

Exhibit 5.18 shows the estimated impacts for each of the youth
service strategy subgroups.[13] As shown in the exhibit, the only
subgroup for which JTPA significantly increased total hours of employment and training was the classroom training subgroup of female
youths. The increase in total hours of employment and training for
that subgroup (335 hours per enrollee) was approximately equal to
the incremental hours of training attributable to participation in JTPA
(429 hours per enrollee) (see Exhibit 5.13). Thus, for this subgroup,
JTPA succeeded in increasing the amount of time enrollees spent in
training without markedly reducing the amount of time they were
employed.

For the other youth subgroups, the program did not significantly
increase total hours of employment and training. In these subgroups
(with the possible exception of female youths in the other services
subgroup), the added hours of training came primarily at the expense
of time spent working. This implies that hours of employment lost
during the in-program period, if any, were not made up through enhanced employment during the post-program period.

Impacts on Earnings: Female Youths and Male Youth Non-Arrestees in Selected Key Subgroups

To determine whether particular types of youths may have benefited
more from JTPA than the overall youth target groups or those assigned

to each of the service strategy subgroups, we estimated impacts for key subgroups of youths defined in terms of their baseline characteristics, similar to those analyzed for adults. In particular, we estimated program effects on 30-month earnings for youth subgroups defined in terms of ethnicity, barriers to employment, work history, family income, and age at random assignment. The results are displayed in Exhibits 5.19 and 5.20.

Among the 39 subgroups for whom impacts were estimated, only one estimate was statistically significant—an outcome that could well have occurred by chance, given the number of estimates derived. Nor were the estimated impacts within any given set of subgroups (e.g., the different ethnic groups or those facing different numbers of barriers to employment) significantly different from one another.

On the basis of these results, we conclude that the lack of program effectiveness for youths was pervasive across a broad range of different types of youths. In fact, we cannot identify *any* group of youths who benefited, in terms of earnings gains, from participation in JTPA.

Exhibit 5.19 IMPACTS ON TOTAL 30-MONTH EARNINGS: FEMALE YOUTH
ASSIGNEES AND ENROLLEES, BY KEY SUBGROUP

Subgroup defined by:	Sample size	Control mean	Impact per Assignee	Impact per Enrollee
Ethnicity				
White, non-Hispanic	1,369	$11,088	$285	$432
Black, non-Hispanic	829	9,536	−735	−1,381
Hispanic	417	7,730	1,268	1,598
F-test, difference among subgroups			N.S.	
Barriers to employment (in italics)				
Receiving cash welfare[a]	789	7,043	211	337
No cash welfare	1,653	11,532	116	177
F-test, difference among subgroups			N.S.	
No high school diploma or GED	1,232	6,673	517	751
High school diploma or GED	1,315	13,510	−433	−707
F-test, difference among subgroups			N.S.	
Worked less than 13 weeks in past 12 months	1,397	7,940	−410	−636
Worked 13 weeks or more in past 12 months	1,004	12,916	503	770
F-test, difference among subgroups			N.S.	
Number of barriers				
None of the above	477	15,513	859	1,271
One of the above	689	11,645	−318	−501
Two of the above	661	7,703	−709	−1,112
All three of the above	312	3,306	1,425	2,052
F-test, difference among subgroups			N.S.	
Work history				
Never employed	563	5,687	34	54
Earned < $4 hourly in last job	1,161	10,081	449	680
Earned ≥ $4 hourly in last job	768	12,933	−43	−68
F-test, difference among subgroups			N.S.	
Family income in past 12 months				
$6,000 or less	1,802	9,440	59	92
More than $6,000	607	11,926	389	599
F-test, difference among subgroups			N.S.	
Age at random assignment				
16–19	1,610	9,019	112	177
20–21	1,047	11,654	180	272
F-test, difference among subgroups			N.S.	
Full sample	2,657	10,106	135	210

Sources: Estimates based on First and Second Follow-up Survey responses and earnings data from state unemployment insurance (UI) agencies.
Notes: Sample sizes for mutually exclusive subgroups within a panel do not necessarily sum to sample size for target group as a whole, because persons in omitted subgroups or with missing data on the variable used to define the subgroup are excluded. "N.S."— F-test is not statistically significant.
a. AFDC, General Assistance, or other welfare except food stamps.
*Statistically significant at .10 level, **at .05 level, ***at .01 level (two-tailed test).

Exhibit 5.20 IMPACTS ON TOTAL 30-MONTH EARNINGS: MALE YOUTH
NON-ARRESTEE ASSIGNEES AND ENROLLEES, BY KEY SUBGROUP

Subgroup defined by:	Sample size	Control mean	Impact per Assignee	Impact per Enrollee
Ethnicity				
White, non-Hispanic	$922	$19,355	$ − 540	$ − 767
Black, non-Hispanic	484	11,047	1,068	1,817
Hispanic	256	16,913	− 3,280*	− 4,350*
F-test, difference among subgroups			N.S.	
Barriers to employment (in italics)				
Receiving cash welfare[a]	160	14,625	− 3,087	− 4,510
No cash welfare	1,363	16,993	− 348	− 516
F-test, difference among subgroups			N.S.	
No high school diploma or GED	927	14,394	− 1,064	− 1,506
High school diploma or GED	696	19,605	− 484	− 747
F-test, difference among subgroups			N.S.	
Worked less than 13 weeks in past 12 months	727	13,158	− 1,294	− 1,872
Worked 13 weeks or more in past 12 months	834	19,558	− 252	− 375
F-test, difference among subgroups			N.S.	
Number of barriers				
None of the above	337	20,953	580	863
One of the above	567	18,255	− 1,828	− 2,872
Both of the above	382	11,343	627	844
F-test, difference among subgroups			N.S.	
Work history				
Never employed	264	11,052	587	845
Earned < $4 hourly in last job	527	16,543	− 1,198	− 1,825
Earned ≥ $4 hourly in last job	735	19,056	− 1,727	− 2,504
F-test, difference among subgroups			N.S.	
Family income in past 12 months				
$6,000 or less	1,009	16,143	− 1,251	− 1,801
More than $6,000	522	17,473	395	581
F-test, difference among subgroups			N.S.	
Age at random assignment				
16−19	1,035	15,047	− 133	− 189
20−21	669	18,671	− 1,277	− 1,991
F-test, difference among subgroups			N.S.	
Full sample	1,704	16,375	− 589	− 868

Sources: Estimates based on First and Second Follow-up Survey responses and earnings
data from state unemployment insurance (UI) agencies.
Notes: Sample sizes for mutually exclusive subgroups within a panel do not necessarily
sum to sample size for target group as a whole, because persons in omitted subgroups
or with missing data on the variable used to define the subgroup are excluded. "N.S."—
F-test is not statistically significant.
a. AFDC, General Assistance, or other welfare except food stamps.
*Statistically significant at .10 level, **at .05 level, ***at .01 level (two-tailed test).

Notes

1. For a few applicants in the other services subgroup, both classroom training in occupational skills and on-the-job training were recommended as part of "customized training."

2. See Appendixes A and B for a detailed explanation of the derivation of the service receipt measures in Exhibits 5.1 and 5.2.

3. For a more detailed description of the baseline characteristics of these subgroups, see Bloom (1991). Note, however, that the data in Bloom (1991) cover all JTPA applicants randomly assigned to treatment or control status, whereas Exhibit 5.4 includes only adults in the 30-month earnings sample.

4. The best summary measure of differences among subgroups in terms of labor market outcomes is probably the earnings of the control group, which are unaffected by the differential treatments received by the three subgroups. As shown in later sections, the earnings of controls differed substantially across the three service strategy subgroups, for both adult women and adult men. Although one cannot be certain that differences that affect the *level* of earnings would also affect program impacts, these differences suggest caution in extrapolating impacts from one subgroup to another.

5. The change in impact from the in-program period to the first postprogram year was statistically significant for both adult women and adult men. The only other period-to-period change in impact estimates that was statistically significant for the adult service strategy subgroups was the change from the in-program period to the first postprogram year for adult women in the other services subgroup.

6. For all adults combined, the estimated impact on earnings in months 7–18 was $580 per enrollee (11.2 percent), which was significant at the .05 level. In months 19–30, the estimated impact was $611 (9.9 percent), which was significant at the .10 level.

7. As noted earlier, these figures may understate the service differential in this subgroup because of underreporting of minor services such as job search assistance in the follow-up surveys.

8. In our earlier analysis of impacts over the first 18 months after random assignment, we presented impact estimates for each subgroup that were adjusted for differences across subgroups in their distributions across sites and in their distributions across both sites and service strategies. Except for very small subgroups and subgroups defined on the basis of ethnicity, these adjustments generally did not have large effects on the size or significance of the estimated impacts. For ethnic subgroups, adjustment for differences in distributions across sites had a large effect on the estimated impacts for Hispanics, who tended to be concentrated in only a few sites. Because of the apparent insensitivity of the estimates to these adjustments, they have not been made in this analysis.

9. The impact estimates shown in Exhibit 5.10 for all AFDC recipients and all nonrecipients differ slightly from those shown in Exhibit 5.8 for all women receiving cash welfare and all women not receiving cash welfare, because the recipient sample in Exhibit 5.8 includes some women (244 out of 2,106) who received cash welfare other than AFDC.

10. In the Supported Work Demonstration, participants worked under the close supervision of demonstration staff, who enforced standards of attendance and performance that gradually increased in stringency until they resembled those in regular unsubsidized jobs. In the AFDC Homemaker–Home Health Aide Demonstrations, participants received four to six weeks of vocational training as homemaker–home health aides before being employed on a subsidized basis by a regular public or private home care agency.

11. See Couch (1992a) and Bell et al. (1995).

12. As noted earlier, the best summary measure of differences among subgroups in terms of labor market outcomes is probably the earnings of the control group, which are unaffected by the differential treatments received by the three subgroups. As discussed in later sections, the earnings of controls differed substantially across the three service strategy subgroups, for both female youths and male youth non-arrestees. Although one cannot be certain that differences that affect the *level* of earnings would also affect program impacts, these differences suggest caution in extrapolating impacts from one subgroup to another.

13. See Appendix B for a detailed explanation of how total hours of employment and training were measured.

Chapter Six

BENEFITS AND COSTS OF TITLE II YEAR-ROUND PROGRAMS

The previous chapters of this volume have presented estimates of the impacts of JTPA on the earnings, welfare benefits, and other outcomes of members of the study sample. Although beneficial impacts on these outcomes for at least some groups of participant are evidence that the program is achieving its objectives for those groups, for the program to be worthwhile to society its beneficial effects must outweigh its costs. Therefore, this chapter compares the estimated benefits of JTPA with its costs.

We begin by discussing the conceptual framework for the benefit-cost analysis, including the specific benefits and costs that might be expected to result from the program. We then present estimated benefits and costs for each target group. The following two sections present the corresponding estimates for each service strategy subgroup of adults and youths. We then examine the sensitivity of the results to the measurement techniques employed in the analysis and compare the results to those of earlier benefit-cost analyses of employment and training programs. The chapter concludes with a discussion of the implications of the findings.

CONCEPTUAL FRAMEWORK FOR BENEFIT-COST ANALYSIS

We measure both the benefits and costs of JTPA as the *changes* from what would have occurred if sample members had not enrolled in the program. Thus, costs are defined as the *incremental* resources devoted to employment and training services as a result of the program, plus any adverse effects on treatment group members or others that would not have occurred if sample members had not been allowed to enroll in JTPA. This approach is consistent with the approach we have taken in earlier chapters in deriving the estimates of program impacts that will serve as the basis for our estimates of the benefits of JTPA. As a summary measure of the overall effects of the program, we estimate *net benefits*—the algebraic sum of all program benefits and costs. If the incremental benefits of the program exceed its incremental costs, net benefits are positive; if costs exceed benefits, net benefits are negative.

As in most public programs, the benefits and costs of JTPA are likely to accrue to different people. For example, taxpayers bear the costs of JTPA services, whereas program participants receive the benefit of increased earnings. Therefore, this chapter assesses net benefits from several different perspectives: that of the participants, of the rest of society, and of society as a whole. Comparing the benefits and costs to enrollees with those to the rest of society allows us to examine the redistributional consequences of the program. Programs are generally viewed as worthwhile if their net benefits to society are positive and their redistributional consequences are acceptable.

Exhibit 6.1 shows the potential benefits and costs of the program from each of the perspectives just described. Benefits and costs to society as a whole, shown in the last column of the exhibit, are the sum of the benefits and costs to the subgroups of society shown in the first two columns. In each column, a " + " indicates a benefit from that perspective, a " − " indicates a cost, and a "0" indicates that this item has no effect from that perspective. A " ± " indicates that we cannot predict a priori whether this item will be a benefit or cost from the perspective in question. The potential benefits and costs of the program are enumerated as comprehensively as possible in the exhibit, to indicate not only those that are measured in this study but also those that are not.

Exhibit 6.1 POTENTIAL BENEFITS AND COSTS OF JTPA

	Enrollees	Rest of society	Society
Earnings gain (minus OJT subsidy)	+	0	+
OJT wage subsidy	+	−	0
Fringe benefits	+	0	+
Increased taxes on earnings	−	+	0
Welfare benefit reduction	−	+	0
Incremental training cost	±	−	−
Increased work-related expenses	−	0	−
Reduced leisure time and home production	−	0	−
Reduced criminal activity	+	+	+
Psychological benefits of increased employment	+	+	+

The principal benefit expected to accrue to enrollees is *earnings gains* resulting from more employment or employment in better jobs. We separate *OJT wage subsidies* from other earnings gains because OJT wage subsidies represent a cost to the rest of society, whereas increases in regular wages do not.[1] Increases in regular wages, then, are a benefit to enrollees and an equal benefit to society as a whole (see Exhibit 6.1). OJT wage subsidies are a benefit to enrollees and an equal cost to the rest of society; from the perspective of society as a whole, then, these benefits and costs cancel out.

In addition to increasing money wages, JTPA may increase the *fringe benefits* received by enrollees (e.g., vacation, sick leave, and Social Security, unemployment insurance, and workers' compensation entitlements). Like regular earnings gains, increases in fringe benefits are a benefit to enrollees and to society as a whole (see Exhibit 6.1). Because we were unable to collect data on the value of fringe benefits associated with the jobs held by sample members, we are unable to reliably estimate this impact. Therefore, in the estimates presented in the next section, we take the conservative approach of excluding the value of fringe benefits. In a subsequent section, however, we examine the effect of including an estimate of the value of fringe benefits.

The *increased taxes* enrollees pay on their higher earnings are a cost to enrollees and an equal benefit to the rest of society. Enrollees' earnings gains may also result in *reduced benefits from income-tested programs* such as AFDC and food stamps. Such reductions are a cost to enrollees and an offsetting benefit to the rest of society, resulting in no monetary gain or a loss to society as a whole (Exhibit 6.1).[2]

The principal cost of the program is the *incremental cost of employment and training services*. As explained in chapter 4, our measures of service receipt include both JTPA and non-JTPA services, and our cost measures represent the full resource cost of employment and training services.[3] The cost of the incremental services received by JTPA enrollees is borne primarily by the rest of society. Participation in JTPA may, however, displace employment and training services that the treatment group members would have paid for themselves in the absence of the program, resulting in savings to the enrollees. It is also possible, however, that participation in JTPA encourages enrollees to increase their investment in training; therefore, in Exhibit 6.1 we show the effect on enrollees' training costs as indeterminant (a " ± " sign).

The remaining entries in Exhibit 6.1 are potential benefits and costs of the program to which we cannot assign a monetary value, either because of the conceptual difficulties of valuing these impacts in monetary terms or because the data to do so are not available. *In-*

creased work-related expenses, such as child care and transportation costs, are a cost to enrollees and, therefore, to society as a whole. Enrollees also bear the cost of reduced leisure time and home production because of their participation in the program and the increased time they spend working. Although we can measure the number of hours of leisure time lost by enrollees, we do not attempt to place a monetary value on this cost. Similarly, we estimate the effect of the program on criminal activity, but do not attempt to value this impact in monetary terms. Finally, both enrollees and taxpayers derive psychological benefits from the knowledge that enrollees are working more and/or are less dependent on public transfers; we have not measured these effects.

BENEFITS AND COSTS

We turn now to the measurement of those program benefits and costs to which we can assign a monetary value. We begin with a discussion of the benefits and costs to adult women and men overall; the following section presents the corresponding findings for youths. Most of the estimates of benefits and costs shown here are derived directly from the impact estimates presented in earlier chapters. All estimates are expressed as benefits or costs per enrollee. Use of a different base—such as benefits and costs per assignee or total benefits and costs—would change the absolute magnitude of the estimates but would not change their relative size or, most importantly, the sign of any of the estimates of net benefits.

In all cases, we use the point estimate of each benefit or cost, regardless of its statistical significance, as our best estimate of the effect of the program. The reader should keep in mind, however, that each of these estimates is subject to some error. For those benefit or cost estimates that are based on impact estimates, standard errors of estimate were provided in the previous chapters. We cannot, however, derive an estimate of the sampling error for estimates of net benefits, which combine the individual benefit and cost estimates, because we cannot calculate the covariances of those estimates. Nor can we measure the nonsampling error of any of these estimates.

Although it would be desirable to provide estimates of the uncertainty associated with these estimates, it should be noted that they would serve a different purpose than the standard errors of the impact estimates. The standard errors of the impact estimates were used in tests of statistical significance to identify the program components and participant subgroups for which we could confidently say that the program had nonzero effects. In that hypothesis-testing framework, impact estimates that were statistically insignificant were simply regarded as inconclusive tests—i.e., as neither evidence of a nonzero impact nor evidence that the program has no effect. In the benefit-cost analysis, our purpose is somewhat different. Here, we ask whether the government's investment in the program (or a particular component) was worthwhile. In the end, the government must answer this question with a definite yes or no; it cannot simply say that the test was inconclusive. Thus, although we would like to know the uncertainty associated with that answer, the best evidence on which to base such an answer is the point estimates of the benefits and costs.

Adult Women and Men Overall

The first row of each panel of Exhibit 6.2 shows the estimated earnings gains of adult enrollees, net of OJT wage subsidies, over the 30-month follow-up period.[4] We did not attempt to project earnings gains beyond the follow-up period, as is sometimes done in benefit-cost analyses, because doing so would require strong assumptions about the time path of program effects beyond the period we observed and, in any case, would not change the main conclusions of the analysis. For adults, the earnings gains during the follow-up period were sufficient

Exhibit 6.2 BENEFITS AND COSTS OF JTPA PER ENROLLEE:
ADULT WOMEN AND MEN

	Enrollees	Rest of society	Society
Adult women			
Earnings gain (minus OJT subsidy)	$1,683	$0	$1,683
OJT wage subsidy	154	−154	0
Increased taxes on earnings	−236	236	0
Incremental training cost	56	−1,227	−1,171
Welfare benefit reduction	−235	235	0
Net benefits	1,422	−910	512
Adult men			
Earnings gain (minus OJT subsidy)	1,355	0	1,355
OJT wage subsidy	244	−244	0
Increased taxes on earnings	−211	211	0
Incremental training cost	100	−931	−831
Welfare benefit reduction	334	−334	0
Net benefits	1,822	−1,298	524

to offset the social costs of the program. For youths, the earnings impacts observed during the follow-up period were negligible or even negative; no reasonable projection of these impacts would produce sufficient benefits to offset the social costs of the incremental services they received.

As shown in Exhibit 6.2, over the 30-month follow-up period, adult women who enrolled in JTPA enjoyed added earnings of $1,683 (not including OJT wage subsidies, which are shown separately in the exhibit). The corresponding gains for adult men over the follow-up period were $1,355.[5] These were the principal benefits of the program for both the enrollees and society as a whole. As noted earlier, we do not include the value of any increase in fringe benefits associated with these earnings gains. In a subsequent section, we examine the effect of including an estimate of the program's effect on fringe benefits.

In addition to receiving increased wages from employers, adult women received OJT wage subsidies averaging $154 per enrollee (including those receiving no OJT subsidy), and adult men received $244 per enrollee in OJT wage subsidies (see Exhibit 6.2). Unlike regular wages, these subsidies entailed an equal cost to taxpayers and therefore resulted in no net benefit to society as a whole. Out of their added earnings, adult women and adult men paid an estimated $236 and $211, respectively, in additional federal and state taxes.[6] These taxes are a cost to enrollees and an exactly offsetting benefit to the rest of society. Therefore, they represent neither a benefit nor a cost to society as a whole.

The principal social cost of the program was the cost of the additional employment and training services provided to enrollees. As shown in Exhibit 6.2, participation in JTPA displaces some services that the enrollees would have paid for themselves, resulting in a savings to the enrollees themselves of $56 per adult woman and $100 per adult man. The net incremental training cost to society as a whole was − $1,171 per enrollee for adult women and − $831 per enrollee for adult men.

The increased employment and earnings of enrollees resulted in only minor changes in AFDC and food stamp benefits (see the discussion in chapter 4). Adult women lost − $235 per enrollee in welfare benefits from these two programs over the follow-up period, while welfare benefits to adult men actually increased by $334 per enrollee. There were exactly offsetting benefits (in the case of women) or costs (in the case of men) to taxpayers, so that the net effect of these distributional changes was zero from the standpoint of society as a whole.

We did not project effects on welfare benefits beyond the follow-up period because the estimated impacts during the follow-up period were so small that there was no reliable basis for extrapolating them into the future. Nor did we attempt to estimate the effect of these small impacts on the administrative costs of AFDC or food stamps. Since there were no significant impacts on months of benefit receipt, we would expect the effect on administrative costs to be negligible.

The net result of these various benefits and costs is shown in the bottom row of each panel of Exhibit 6.2 as the net benefit to each subgroup of society and to society as a whole. The net benefit to each group is the algebraic sum of all the benefits and costs to that group. As shown in the exhibit, adult women enjoyed net benefits of $1,422 per enrollee (see last row of panel, first column), at a cost of $-$910 to the rest of society. Thus, for every dollar the program cost the rest of society, adult female enrollees gained $1.56. Since benefits to enrollees exceeded the costs to the rest of society, the net benefit to society as a whole was $512 per enrollee for this target group.

The results for adult men were similar. Enrollee net benefits of $1,822 more than offset costs of $-$1,298 per enrollee to the rest of society. The resulting social net benefit for adult men was $524 per enrollee. For each dollar spent on the program by the rest of society, then, adult men received a benefit of $1.40.

It should be borne in mind that these net benefit estimates do not include several benefits and costs that could not be measured in monetary terms: enrollees' increased fringe benefits and work-related expenses and their loss of leisure time and home production; reduced costs to society as a result of any reduction in criminal activity; and the psychological benefits to enrollees and taxpayers of increased enrollee employment and earnings. Unless the omitted costs outweigh the omitted benefits by a large margin, however, these estimates indicate that JTPA is cost-effective for both adult women and adult men overall. In a subsequent section, we examine program benefits and costs for the service strategy subgroups within each of these target groups. We also test the sensitivity of the net benefit estimates to the omission of fringe benefits.

Female Youths and Male Youth Non-Arrestees Overall

This section presents the estimated benefits and costs of JTPA for out-of-school youths. Because of the inconsistent impact results for male youths who had been arrested prior to random assignment, this analysis excludes arrestees from the male youth target group.

Exhibit 6.3 shows estimated benefits and costs for the two youth target groups, in the same format as the adult estimates in Exhibit 6.2. As expected, neither female youths nor male youth non-arrestees experienced sufficient earnings gains to offset incremental training costs of −$1,316 and −$1,955, respectively. From the standpoint of society as a whole, therefore, the program resulted in net costs of −$1,180 per female youth enrollee and −$2,923 per male youth enrollee.

Even when taken by themselves, enrollees did not derive positive net benefits from the program. For female youths, very small gains in aftertax earnings, reductions in out-of-pocket training costs, and OJT wage subsidies were more than offset by losses of welfare benefits. Male youth non-arrestees lost more in after-tax earnings than they gained in OJT wage subsidies, reduced out-of-pocket training costs, and slightly higher welfare benefits (Exhibit 6.3).

Adult Women and Men, by Service Strategy Subgroup

As shown in the previous chapter, the impact of JTPA varied across the three service strategy subgroups. Similarly, the costs of service varied with the type of service provided. Therefore, this section presents estimated benefits and costs for each service strategy subgroup within the adult target groups; the next section presents the corresponding results for youths.

Exhibit 6.3 BENEFITS AND COSTS OF JTPA PER ENROLLEE: FEMALE YOUTHS AND MALE YOUTH NON-ARRESTEES

	Enrollees	Rest of society	Society
Female youths			
Earnings gain (minus OJT subsidy)	$136	$0	$136
OJT wage subsidy	74	−74	0
Increased taxes on earnings	−28	28	0
Incremental training cost	76	−1,392	−1,316
Welfare benefit reduction	−379	379	0
Net benefits	−121	−1,059	−1,180
Male youth non-arrestees			
Earnings gain (minus OJT subsidy)	−968	0	−968
OJT wage subsidy	100	−100	0
Increased taxes on earnings	109	−109	0
Incremental training cost	110	−2,065	−1,955
Welfare benefit reduction	119	−119	0
Net benefits	−530	−2,393	−2,923

As shown in Exhibit 6.4, net benefits to society were positive in five of the six adult service strategy subgroups, ranging from $323 to $3,124 per enrollee. The sole exception was the classroom training subgroup of adult women, where earnings gains of $612 per enrollee over the follow-up period were insufficient to offset incremental training costs of −$1,639 per enrollee, resulting in a social cost of −$1,027. It is, of course, possible that this subgroup will experience sufficient earnings gains beyond the 30-month follow-up period to reverse this finding. However, it would require nearly three additional years of earnings gains at the level estimated for the last year of the follow-up period ($365 per enrollee) to convert this social cost into a net social benefit.[7]

In all six adult subgroups, including classroom training for adult women, enrollees experienced positive net benefits and the rest of society bore net costs. Net benefits to enrollees ranged from $287 to $3,538 per enrollee, while the costs to the rest of society varied from −$414 to −$1,694 (Exhibit 6.4). For adult women, the benefits to enrollees for each dollar the program cost the rest of society ranged from $.22 in the classroom training subgroup to $8.55 in the other services subgroup. Among adult men, benefits to enrollees per dollar spent by the rest of society varied from $1.19 in the classroom training subgroup to $2.52 in the other services subgroup.

These findings illustrate the importance of comparing the impacts of JTPA with the costs of the program, rather than simply focusing on program impacts. For example, the earnings gains to adult men in the other services subgroup were much smaller than those in the other two service strategy subgroups, but so were the costs of that service strategy. As a result, the net benefit to society in the other services subgroup of adult men ($644 per enrollee) compared quite favorably with those in the other two subgroups ($323 in classroom training and $648 in OJT/JSA).

Female Youths and Male Youth Non-Arrestees, by Service Strategy Subgroup

The corresponding estimates for female youths and male youth non-arrestees are presented in Exhibit 6.5. Net benefits to society as a whole were negative in all six youth service strategy subgroups, with net costs ranging from −$80 (for female youths in the other services subgroup) to −$6,766 (for male youth non-arrestees in the OJT/JSA subgroup). Only youths who enrolled in the classroom training strategy experienced positive net benefits ($1,100 for female youths and

Exhibit 6.4 BENEFITS AND COSTS OF JTPA PER ENROLLEE:
ADULT WOMEN AND MEN, BY SERVICE STRATEGY SUBGROUP

	Enrollees	Rest of society	Society
Adult women—classroom training			
Earnings gain (minus OJT subsidy)	$612	$0	$612
OJT wage subsidy	18	−18	0
Increased taxes on earnings	−81	81	0
Incremental training cost	147	−1,786	−1,639
Welfare benefit reduction	−409	409	0
Net benefits	287	−1,314	−1,027
Adult women—OJT/JSA			
Earnings gain (minus OJT subsidy)	1,918	0	1,918
OJT wage subsidy	374	−374	0
Increased taxes on earnings	−300	300	0
Incremental training cost	−9	−818	−827
Welfare benefit reduction	−288	288	0
Net benefits	1,695	−604	1,091
Adult women—other services			
Earnings gain (minus OJT subsidy)	3,849	0	3,849
OJT wage subsidy	100	−100	0
Increased taxes on earnings	−509	509	0
Incremental training cost	−28	−697	−725
Welfare benefit reduction	126	−126	0
Net benefits	3,538	−414	3,124
Adult men—classroom training			
Earnings gain (minus OJT subsidy)	1,238	0	1,238
OJT wage subsidy	49	−49	0
Increased taxes on earnings	−167	167	0
Incremental training cost	294	−1,209	−915
Welfare benefit reduction	603	−603	0
Net benefits	2,017	−1,694	323
Adult men—OJT/JSA			
Earnings gain (minus OJT subsidy)	1,678	0	1,678
OJT wage subsidy	431	−431	0
Increased taxes on earnings	−279	279	0
Incremental training cost	34	−1,064	−1,030
Welfare benefit reduction	368	−368	0
Net benefits	2,232	−1,584	648
Adult men—other services			
Earnings gain (minus OJT subsidy)	858	0	858
OJT wage subsidy	83	−83	0
Increased taxes on earnings	−123	123	0
Incremental training cost	64	−278	−214
Welfare benefit reduction	185	−185	0
Net benefits	1,067	−423	644

Exhibit 6.5 BENEFITS AND COSTS OF JTPA PER ENROLLEE:
FEMALE YOUTHS AND MALE YOUTH NON-ARRESTEES,
BY SERVICE STRATEGY SUBGROUP

	Enrollees	Rest of society	Society
Female youth—classroom training			
Earnings gain (minus OJT subsidy)	$820	$0	$820
OJT wage subsidy	19	−19	0
Increased taxes on earnings	−108	108	0
Incremental training cost	68	−1,916	−1,848
Welfare benefit reduction	301	−301	0
Net benefits	1,100	−2,128	−1,028
Female youth—OJT/JSA			
Earnings gain (minus OJT subsidy)	−789	0	−789
OJT wage subsidy	210	−210	0
Increased taxes on earnings	71	−71	0
Incremental training cost	100	−1,981	−1,881
Welfare benefit reduction	−595	595	0
Net benefits	−1,003	−1,667	−2,670
Female youth—other services			
Earnings gain (minus OJT subsidy)	−101	0	−101
OJT wage subsidy	68	−68	0
Increased taxes on earnings	3	−3	0
Incremental training cost	71	−50	21
Welfare benefit reduction	−724	724	0
Net benefits	−683	603	−80
Male youth non-arrestees—classroom training			
Earnings gain (minus OJT subsidy)	228	0	228
OJT wage subsidy	23	−23	0
Increased taxes on earnings	−33	33	0
Incremental training cost	354	−2,190	−1,836
Welfare benefit reduction	243	−243	0
Net benefits	815	−2,423	−1,608
Male youth non-arrestees—OJT/JSA			
Earnings gain (minus OJT subsidy)	−3,253	0	−3,253
OJT wage subsidy	241	−241	0
Increased taxes on earnings	383	−383	0
Incremental training cost	−80	−3,433	−3,513
Welfare benefit reduction	228	−228	0
Net benefits	−2,481	−4,285	−6,766
Male youth non-arrestees—other services			
Earnings gain (minus OJT subsidy)	−481	0	−481
OJT wage subsidy	43	−43	0
Increased taxes on earnings	55	−55	0
Incremental training cost	59	−754	−695
Welfare benefit reduction	−15	15	0
Net benefits	−339	−837	−1,176

$815 for male youths). In the OJT/JSA and other services subgroups, enrollees actually suffered net losses ranging from −$339 to −$2,481 per enrollee, primarily because of reduced earnings and/or welfare benefits.

The rest of society bore net costs ranging from −$837 to −$4,285 per enrollee in all of the youth service strategy subgroups, except the other services subgroup of female youths (Exhibit 6.5). In that subgroup, the net increment in training received by enrollees, as compared with what they would have received from non-JTPA sources had they been excluded from JTPA, was virtually zero ($21 per enrollee in direct training costs plus an average OJT wage subsidy of $68). As a result, JTPA had almost no impact on earnings in this subgroup. Nevertheless, enrollees in this subgroup received substantially less welfare benefits than they would have in the absence of the program; this estimated loss of −$724 per enrollee dominates the benefit-cost calculation for this subgroup, resulting in a net loss to enrollees and a net gain to the rest of society.

In interpreting these results, it must be borne in mind that these estimates are based on relatively small samples, and each component of net benefits is subject to substantial sampling error (see the standard errors of the impact estimates in chapter 5). Thus, caution must be exercised in interpreting even large differences in benefits or costs across subgroups.

SENSITIVITY OF THE RESULTS TO MEASUREMENT TECHNIQUES

This section examines the extent to which the results just presented are dependent on several measurement techniques employed in this analysis. First, we consider the potential bias that might result from the use of survey data on receipt of employment and training services in deriving the estimates of incremental training costs. Second, we examine the effect on the estimates of omitting the value of fringe benefits from the estimated earnings gains of enrollees. Finally, we calculate the effect on the net benefit estimates of rescaling survey earnings to UI earnings levels, rather than the reverse procedure, which was used in combining survey and UI data for the impact analyses presented in chapters 4 and 5.

Bias in Survey Reports of Service Receipt

Receipt of employment and training services was measured primarily through self-reports on the follow-up surveys because that was the only way to obtain information about receipt of both JTPA and non-JTPA services by both treatment and control group members. Only for on-the-job training and work experience—two services provided only by JTPA in most communities—did we use SDA records to measure service receipt. Use of SDA administrative records to measure the receipt of other services would have overstated the treatment-control difference in service receipt, because controls were more likely to receive non-JTPA services.

Survey data may, however, be subject to significant underreporting of service receipt because of respondent recall errors. This is particularly likely to be the case with minor services such as job search assistance, which survey respondents may simply forget. Comparison of Exhibit 3.17 in chapter 3 with Exhibits 5.1, 5.2, 5.11, and 5.12 in chapter 5 suggests that the follow-up survey data may in fact understate the amount of employment and training services received. These exhibits show the percentage of the treatment group in each target group who received JTPA services. In Exhibit 3.17, service receipt was measured with data from SDA records. In the exhibits in chapter 5, receipt of classroom training in occupational skills, basic education, job search assistance, and "other" services was measured with follow-up survey data.[8] In many cases, the percentages based on survey data are noticeably lower than those based on SDA records. This is particularly true for classroom training in occupational skills in the classroom training subgroups, and for job search assistance in all subgroups.

Unfortunately, we have the necessary data for this comparison only for treatment group members. Even if both treatment group members and controls understated their receipt of employment and training services by a similar proportion—as seems likely if the source of the discrepancy is respondent recall error—the effect would be to understate the treatment-control difference by the same proportion. Thus, there is reason to believe that our estimates of the incremental cost of training are biased downward.

To put an upper bound on the effect of this potential bias on the benefit-cost results, we calculated a measure of incremental training costs that is biased *upward* and recomputed the net benefit estimates shown in Exhibits 6.2–6.5. For all JTPA enrollees who reported no employment or training services in the follow-up survey, we imputed training costs on the basis of the services reported in SDA records.

This almost certainly overstates incremental training costs, because it adjusts for the underreporting of JTPA enrollees, virtually all of whom were treatment group members, without making any adjustment for underreporting of non-JTPA services by controls.

Exhibit 6.6 shows the results of this sensitivity test. The net social benefits based on survey reports of service receipt presented in earlier sections of this chapter are repeated in the first column of the exhibit; the adjusted measure is shown in the second column. Both measures show positive net benefits for the two adult target groups and negative net benefits for the two youth groups. At the service strategy subgroup level, the adjustment changed the sign of only 2 of the 12 estimates of net social benefits: those for adult men in the classroom training subgroup, which went from $323 to −$153, and for adult men in the other services subgroup, which fell from $644 to −$90. Since the adjustment yields an upper bound on incremental training costs, and

Exhibit 6.6 NET SOCIAL BENEFITS OF JTPA PER ENROLLEE, BY TARGET GROUP
AND SERVICE STRATEGY—ALTERNATIVE DATA SOURCES

	Net social benefits	
	Based on survey-reported services	Based on both survey-reported services and JTPA records
Adult women		
Classroom training	−$1,027	−$1,565
OJT/JSA	1,091	998
Other services	3,124	2,721
All adult women	512	151
Adult men		
Classroom training	323	−153
OJT/JSA	648	563
Other services	644	−90
All adult men	524	176
Female youths		
Classroom training	−1,028	−1,911
OJT/JSA	−2,670	−2,808
Other services	−80	−2,776
All female youths	−1,180	−2,422
Male youth non-arrestees		
Classroom training	−1,608	−2,612
OJT/JSA	−6,766	−6,983
Other services	−1,176	−4,088
All male youth non-arrestees	−2,923	−4,374

since our estimates of net benefits do not include any effects on fringe benefits or earnings gains beyond the 30-month follow-up period, it seems likely that true net social benefits are also positive in these cases, as reported in Exhibit 6.4.

Omission of Fringe Benefits

As explained earlier, the earnings gains reported here reflect the impact of JTPA on money wages paid to enrollees; they do not include any effect the program may have on the value of fringe benefits received by enrollees. Since we did not collect data on the value of fringe benefits associated with jobs held by the sample, we cannot estimate this impact directly. We can, however, place plausible values on the fringe benefit component of employee compensation, using national data.

Exhibit 6.7 shows the estimated cost of fringe benefits as a percentage of hourly wages for several different categories of private industry workers in March 1990, roughly the midpoint of the 30-month follow-up period. As shown in the exhibit, the cost of fringe benefits ranges from about 31 percent of money wages for service workers to 45 percent for blue-collar workers. It is important to recognize, however, that these *average* relationships between fringe benefits and money wages may not apply to the *incremental* program-induced earnings of enrollees, depending on the source of the increase in enrollees' earnings. If, for example, that increase was entirely in the form of higher earnings per hour, with no increase in employment rates or hours worked, fringe benefits would probably not increase proportionally. If, on the other hand, earnings gains came entirely in the form of more weeks of employment at the same hourly rate, fringe benefits could be expected to rise commensurately. (In fact, as noted in chapter 4, most of the impact of JTPA on the earnings of adults

Exhibit 6.7 AVERAGE HOURLY WAGES AND FRINGE BENEFITS, PRIVATE INDUSTRY WORKERS BY OCCUPATIONAL CATEGORY, MARCH 1990

Occupational category	Average hourly wage	Benefit cost per hour	Benefits as percent of wages
White-collar	$12.99	$4.60	35%
Blue-collar	10.04	4.53	45
Service	5.84	1.82	31
All private workers	10.84	4.13	38

Source: U.S. Department of Labor (1993).

appears to have been an effect on hours employed, not on hourly earnings.)

It is also quite possible that the kinds of jobs held by JTPA enrollees are either more or less likely than those held by the average private industry worker to have fringe benefits at all. Finally, if JTPA *affects* the likelihood that an enrollee will find a job with fringe benefits, the impact of the program on fringe benefits could be quite different from its impact on money wages. For all of these reasons, national data on the cost of fringe benefits should be used with caution in this context. Nevertheless, it is useful to consider the sensitivity of the benefit-cost results to inclusion of some reasonable increase in fringe benefits. Exhibit 6.8 shows the effect on net social benefits of assuming that the increase in fringe benefits is 31 percent of the increase in money wages. This is the average relationship between the cost of fringe benefits and money wages for service workers in private industry earning $5.84 per hour—about the wage rate JTPA enrollees earned.[9]

Exhibit 6.8 NET SOCIAL BENEFITS OF JTPA PER ENROLLEE, BY TARGET GROUP AND SERVICE STRATEGY—WITH AND WITHOUT ESTIMATED EFFECTS ON FRINGE BENEFITS

	Net social benefits	
	Without fringe benefits	With estimated fringe benefits
Adult women		
Classroom training	− $1,027	− $831
OJT/JSA	1,091	1,814
Other	3,124	4,353
All adult women	512	1,081
Adult men		
Classroom training	$323	$725
OJT/JSA	648	1,323
Other	644	942
All adult men	524	1,034
Female youths		
Classroom training	− $1,028	− $767
OJT/JSA	− 2,670	− 2,841
Other	− 80	− 87
All female youths	− 1,180	− 1,112
Male youth non-arrestees		
Classroom training	− $1,608	− $1,529
OJT/JSA	− 6,766	− 7,689
Other	− 1,176	− 1,309
All male youth nonarrestees	− 2,923	− 3,186

As shown in Exhibit 6.8, the addition of fringe benefits does not change any of the qualitative conclusions of the analysis. For adults, impacts on earnings were positive for all subgroups, so that the estimated impact on fringe benefits was also positive. Therefore, the addition of fringe benefits increases net social benefits somewhat in all cases; however, the increment is not sufficient to change the sign of the only negative net benefit in these two target groups (that for adult women in classroom training). For youths, the estimated impact on fringe benefits was generally negative because the estimated impacts on earnings were negative in most subgroups. In those subgroups, the addition of fringe benefits simply increased the absolute magnitude of negative net benefits. Even where impacts on earnings and fringe benefits were positive (for all female youths, female youths in the classroom training subgroup, and male youths in classroom training), net social benefits remain negative after the addition of fringe benefits.

Scaling of UI Earnings Data

The estimated impacts on earnings presented in chapters 4 and 5 are based on a combination of data from the follow-up surveys and UI earnings records. For those sample members for whom survey data were available for the entire 30-month follow-up period, they were used; for all other sample members, UI earnings data were used if they were available. Because UI earnings records systematically reported lower earnings than the follow-up surveys in the sample for whom both were available, UI earnings were scaled upward by the ratio of total survey earnings to total UI earnings in each target group.[10]

Because this ratio was virtually identical for treatment and control groups in all target groups except male youth arrestees, this rescaling had almost no effect on the estimated *percentage* impacts on earnings. It did, however, increase the *absolute* size of the estimated impacts, relative to the alternative of scaling survey earnings *down* to UI earnings levels. Since the absolute level of earnings gains enters into the computation of net benefits, the rescaling of UI earnings therefore affects the estimated net benefits of the program.

To test the importance of this effect, we recalculated net social benefits on the basis of the earnings gains that would have been estimated if survey earnings had been rescaled to UI earnings levels. The results are shown in Exhibit 6.9. The first column of the exhibit shows net social benefits as calculated earlier in this chapter, with UI earnings scaled to survey levels. The second column shows the result of

Exhibit 6.9 NET SOCIAL BENEFITS OF JTPA PER ENROLLEE, BY TARGET GROUP
AND SERVICE STRATEGY—ALTERNATIVE SCALING OF SURVEY
AND UI EARNINGS

	Net social benefits	
	UI earnings scaled to survey level	Survey earnings scaled to UI level
Adult women		
Classroom training	−$1,027	−$1,135
OJT/JSA	1,091	779
Other	3,124	2,443
All adult women	512	225
Adult men		
Classroom training	323	9
OJT/JSA	648	263
Other	644	436
All adult men	524	207
Female youths		
Classroom training	−1,028	−1,234
OJT/JSA	−2,670	−2,450
Other	−80	−45
All female youths	−1,180	−1,207
Male youth non-arrestees		
Classroom training	−1,608	−1,683
OJT/JSA	−6,766	−5,631
Other	−1,176	−1,005
All male youth nonarrestees	−2,923	−2,579

rescaling survey earnings to UI levels. As can be seen, this rescaling
did not change the sign of net social benefits for any target group or
service strategy subgroup, although it virtually eliminates the small
net social benefit of the classroom training strategy for adult men.

FINDINGS IN COMPARISON WITH OTHER BENEFIT-COST ANALYSES OF EMPLOYMENT AND TRAINING PROGRAMS

The findings presented here are generally consistent with those of
previous experimental studies of employment and training programs.
This section reviews those results. Because differences in study populations, programs, and methodology make these studies somewhat
noncomparable to the present study, however, we do not attempt to

compare the specific estimates obtained in each of those studies with those presented here.

Adult Women

Almost all previous experimental evaluations of employment and training programs for adult women have focused on welfare recipients; the National JTPA Study is the first large-scale experimental study of the effects of such programs on nonwelfare women. Moreover, unlike JTPA, participation in some of these programs was mandatory, and in some cases the services provided differed greatly from those offered by JTPA. Nevertheless, the results of these studies provide a useful context within which to view the present findings.

During the late 1970s and early 1980s, a number of state Work Incentive (WIN) programs and demonstrations were evaluated with experimental methods. These studies included seven low-intensity programs that offered primarily group and individual job search and unpaid work experience; two moderate-intensity programs that provided these services as well as occupational training and basic education for up to a quarter of the participants; and two demonstrations that emphasized on-the-job training.[11]

The low-intensity WIN programs were probably most comparable to JTPA's other services strategy, while the OJT demonstrations are most comparable to the OJT/JSA strategy. The moderate-intensity WIN programs were roughly comparable to the JTPA classroom training strategy in terms of intensity of service.

The low-intensity programs ranged in cost from $250 to $1,400 per participant, as compared with an incremental cost of $725 per enrollee for the JTPA other services strategy for adult women.[12] Earnings gains over the follow-up period more than offset program costs in all three of the low-intensity WIN programs for which three years of follow-up data were available and in one for which there was only one year of follow-up. Net social benefits in these four programs ranged from $360 to $1,900 per participant, as compared with the $3,124 net social benefit of the JTPA other services strategy. In a fifth WIN program, earnings gains in the one-year follow-up period nearly equaled program costs; in the remaining two, there were essentially no earnings gains during the one-year follow-up period. Thus, although a complete comparison is not possible, the estimated net benefits of the JTPA other services strategy for adult women appear to be substantially larger than those of the comparable WIN programs.

Program costs in the New Jersey and Maine WIN OJT demonstrations were about $900 and $2,200 per participant, respectively; the incremental cost of the JTPA OJT/JSA strategy was $827 per enrollee. In the New Jersey program, earnings gains in the second follow-up year (the only year for which estimates are available) nearly offset program costs. Earnings gains in the Maine program were approximately equal to costs over a three-year follow-up period. The $1,091 net social benefit estimated for adult women in the JTPA OJT/JSA service strategy is, then, at least as large as the net benefits found in these earlier studies.

The two moderate-intensity WIN programs in San Diego and Baltimore cost about $1,400 and $2,100 per participant, respectively. The San Diego program produced a net social benefit of $140 per participant over a two-year follow-up period, while the Baltimore program yielded net social benefits of $220 over three years. In contrast, the JTPA classroom training strategy cost society $1,639 per enrollee and resulted in a net social *cost* of −$1,027 over a two and one-half year follow-up period.

In comparing the present results with those of the earlier WIN demonstrations, two important qualifications must be borne in mind. First, the present results include all adult women enrolled in JTPA, whereas the WIN studies were restricted to AFDC recipients. As we have seen, the impacts of the JTPA OJT/JSA service strategy were substantially larger, and the impacts of the other services strategy substantially smaller, for AFDC recipients than for other women. Second, the available estimates of program costs for the WIN demonstrations do not net out the costs of any non-AFDC services received by the control group. To the extent that demonstration services displaced non-AFDC services that the treatment group would have received in the absence of the demonstration, the incremental costs of these demonstrations would be lower than the figures cited here.

Taken together, these two qualifications imply that a comparison of the net benefits of the JTPA other services strategy for AFDC recipients only with the true net benefits of the comparable WIN demonstrations (based on incremental costs) would show smaller differences in net benefits than those cited here. For the OJT/JSA subgroup, the effects of these two qualifications are offsetting, so that their combined effect on the comparison of net benefit estimates cannot be predicted.

The other two previous experimental studies of employment and training services for adult women, the AFDC Homemaker–Home Health Aide Demonstrations and the Supported Work Demonstration, tested much more intensive services than those provided by JTPA.

Both focused on women receiving AFDC. The AFCD Homemaker–Home Health Aide Demonstrations were implemented in seven states between 1982 and 1985. Volunteer participants received four to eight weeks of classroom training, followed by up to a year of subsidized employment in a regular home care agency. Across the seven states, program costs varied from $4,300 to $8,700 per participant, with an average of $6,800. Net social benefits of the program (including both participant earnings gains and the value of output produced) were positive in six of the seven states; overall, net social benefits averaged over $4,000 per enrollee.[13] Similarly, the Supported Work Demonstration, conducted in the late 1970s, provided up to 12 months of subsidized employment to long-term AFDC recipients, at an average cost of $5,300 per participant (in 1976 dollars).[14] The estimated net social benefit of the program was $8,400 per participant.

In summary, then, the net social benefits of JTPA services for adult women in the OJT/JSA and other services subgroups were larger, and those for women in the classroom training subgroup were much smaller, than those of the most nearly comparable WIN programs of the 1980s. Only the other services strategy came close to the large net benefits estimated for the much more intensive AFDC Homemaker–Home Health Aide and Supported Work Demonstrations.

Adult Men

The previous experimental evaluations of employment and training services for adult men are limited to three populations: low-income men who received or had applied for AFDC; displaced workers, who lost relatively high-paid, stable jobs because of technological change or foreign competition; and low-income men who were ex-offenders or ex-addicts. Obviously, none of these populations are directly comparable to the JTPA population.

Two of the WIN programs discussed earlier served adult male AFDC-UP recipients.[15] One provided low-intensity services such as group job search and unpaid work experience, similar to those offered in the JTPA other services strategy. The other provided moderate-intensity education and training services, similar to those in the JTPA classroom training strategy, in addition to group job search and work experience. Both cost about $1,400 per participant, as compared with net incremental training costs of $214 and $915 for adult men in the JTPA other services and classroom training strategies. The earnings gains produced by these programs in the one- to two-year follow-up period covered by their evaluations offset only a small fraction of program costs. In contrast, the JTPA other services and classroom training strategies for adult men produced net social benefits of $644 and $323, respectively.

The Texas Worker Adjustment Demonstration and the New Jersey UI Reemployment Demonstration tested a broad range of employment and training services for dislocated workers.[16] Unfortunately, neither study provided sufficient data on program costs to allow calculation of net benefits of the program.

The only other previous experimental evaluation of employment and training services for adult men was the Supported Work Demonstration, which provided up to 12 months of subsidized employment. The men served by Supported Work were ex-offenders and ex-drug addicts. Incremental program costs for ex-offenders were approximately $3,300 per participant (in 1976 dollars). This group of program participants suffered nondemonstration earnings *losses* of about −$550 and generated *increased* social costs of crime and criminal justice.[17] Although these costs were partially offset by the value of program output, on balance the program resulted in a net social *cost* of about −$3,200 per participant in this group. Ex-addicts in the Supported Work Demonstration also suffered losses of −$400 per participant in nondemonstration earnings, but the value of program output and reduced costs of criminal activity were sufficient to offset these losses and program costs of −$3,900 per participant.[18] The result was a net social benefit of $4,300 per participant.

In summary, then, only three other experimental studies have produced benefit-cost analyses of employment and training services for adult men. Two of these studies focused on AFDC-UP recipients and one on ex-offenders and ex-addicts. The only previous experimental evaluation to find positive net social benefits for adult men was the ex-addict component of the Supported Work Demonstration. In contrast, the current study found positive net benefits for adult men both for JTPA overall and for each of the three service strategy subgroups of men.

Youths

The two major prior experimental evaluations of employment and training services for youths were the Supported Work Demonstration and JOBSTART, both of which included samples of low-income youths who were high school dropouts.[19] Participants in the Supported Work youth component were primarily (88 percent) males; JOBSTART participants were about evenly divided between males and females. Over half of the Supported Work youths had an arrest record; about 30 percent of the males in the JOBSTART sample had been arrested.

Both of these demonstrations provided very intensive services. Supported Work provided up to 12 months of subsidized employment, at a cost of nearly $4,000 per participant (in 1976 dollars). The JOBSTART demonstration, begun in 1985, provided an intensive program of basic education, occupational skills training, and support services costing $4,600 per participant. Youths in Supported Work suffered losses of nondemonstration earnings of nearly −$1,000 per participant, and estimated net social benefits were −$1,465 (in 1976 dollars).[20] Male youths in JOBSTART also experienced earnings losses of −$461 over a two-year follow-up period, for a net social loss of over −$5,000 per treatment group member. Female youths experienced small earnings gains, but the net social cost of the program was still −$4,500.

The findings of previous experimental evaluations of employment and training services for out-of-school youths, then, are consistent with the present results for JTPA. All have found that male youth participants suffered earnings losses while female participants experienced only very small earnings gains and that, for both, the programs resulted in sizable net social costs.

Notes

1. This treatment of OJT wage subsidies assumes that the value of output produced by enrollees in OJT positions equals the employer's share of the enrollee's wages. This is equivalent to assuming that the OJT wage subsidy is the minimum subsidy that will induce the employer to hire the worker. If the value of output produced by the enrollee exceeds the employer's share of wages, the employer reaps a windfall benefit and social benefits would be increased by the amount of the added output. Benefits to enrollees would still be the sum of the employer's share of wages plus the OJT wage subsidy.

2. Policymakers may, of course, on equity grounds, prefer the new distribution of income, with fewer people on welfare; and both enrollees and taxpayers may derive satisfaction from enrollees' greater work effort and reduced dependence, over and above their monetary gains or losses. These benefits are considered separately below.

3. See Appendixes A and B for a detailed explanation of the estimation of the cost of services received by sample members.

4. We do not distinguish between "postprogram" earnings gains and earnings gains or losses while participating in the program, as is sometimes done in benefit-cost analyses. The measure used here is the sum of these two effects on enrollees' earnings. These two components of the program's impact cannot be reliably estimated separately and, in any case, separate estimates of the two components are not necessary for the

calculation of net benefits to either enrollees or society. As in earlier chapters, the 30-month earnings gains shown here are cumulative totals, not present discounted values.

5. These estimates are derived by subtracting average OJT wage subsidies per enrollee (including those with zero subsidies) from the estimated impact on total 30-month earnings shown in Exhibit 4.6. See Appendixes A and B for an explanation of the estimation of average OJT wage subsidies.

6. Increased taxes on earnings are estimated as 12.8 percent of earnings gains (including OJT wage subsidies). This percentage is the sum of the average effective total federal tax rate (including the Earned Income Tax Credit [EITC]) in 1988–89 for the bottom quintile of all families (9.3 percent), according to Congressional Budget Office estimates, plus the average state sales and income tax rate for poor two-parent families of four in the 16 study states (3.5 percent), according to General Accounting Office estimates (see U.S. House, 1992: 1488–90 and 1510). We used a weighted average of state tax rates in the 16 study states, with weights equal to the proportion of the 30-month earnings sample in each state.

7. This assumes no discounting of benefits; for the present discounted value of earnings gains to exceed the costs of the program, it would take somewhat longer.

8. Receipt of these services was measured from responses to the First Follow-up Survey, because only a subsample was interviewed in the Second Follow-up Survey. In the exhibits in chapter 5, receipt of OJT and work experience was measured with SDA data, on the grounds that these data were more reliable than follow-up survey data for the treatment group and that few controls would receive these services from non-JTPA sources, since in most communities they are only provided by JTPA.

9. Legally required benefits (Social Security, federal and state unemployment insurance, and workers' compensation) were 14 percent of wages and salaries for this occupational category (U.S. Department of Labor, 1993). See Bloom et al. (1993, Exhibit G.1), for mean hourly earnings of the National JTPA Study control group and estimated program impacts on hourly earnings, by target group and service strategy subgroup.

10. See Appendix B for a detailed explanation of this procedure. See Bloom et al. (1993, Appendix E), for a detailed comparison of UI and survey earnings data for this sample.

11. See Gueron and Pauly (1991) for a detailed description of these programs and their evaluations.

12. All estimates for the WIN programs cited in this section are derived from data in Gueron and Pauly (1991, Table 4.6). Program costs and net social benefits per participant were obtained by dividing the costs and earnings gains per experimental by the proportion of experimentals who participated in any service; this is equivalent to the adjustment used to calculate cost per enrollee in the current study. WIN program costs and net benefits are expressed in 1978–85 dollars; JTPA costs used in this study are program year 1988 costs.

13. See Bell and Orr (1994) for a detailed analysis of these demonstrations. The costs and net benefits cited here have been converted to a per participant basis by dividing costs and net benefits per member of the experimental group by the proportion of that group who participated in the program in each state, to make them more comparable with the estimates of JTPA costs and net benefits per enrollee.

14. See Kemper, Long, and Thornton (1981). Costs and net benefits cited here have been converted to a per participant basis by dividing costs and net benefits per member of the experimental group by the proportion of that group who participated in the program (97 percent), to make them more comparable with the estimates of JTPA costs and net benefits per enrollee.

15. See Gueron and Pauly (1991).

16. See Bloom (1990) and Corson et al. (1989).

17. This loss of nondemonstration earnings was more than offset, from the participant's perspective, by demonstration earnings of approximately $3,600. From a social perspective, however, demonstration earnings are a transfer from taxpayers to participants. See Kemper et al. (1981).

18. Participants in this group received approximately $3,800 in demonstration earnings. Thus, participants enjoyed positive net benefits despite the loss of nondemonstration earnings. From a social perspective, however, demonstration earnings are a transfer from taxpayers to participants.

19. See Kemper et al. (1981) and Cave and Doolittle (1991).

20. From the participant's perspective, these losses were more than offset by demonstration earnings of $3,550. From a social perspective, however, these earnings are a transfer from taxpayers to participants.

Chapter Seven

INTERPRETATION AND POLICY IMPLICATIONS OF THE FINDINGS

The National JTPA Study has provided answers to some of the most fundamental questions about JTPA: Does the kind of employment and training services provided by JTPA increase earnings and reduce reliance on welfare? For whom? Do some service strategies work better than others? Do the benefits of JTPA outweigh its costs? However, the answers to these questions do not translate directly into prescriptions for employment and training policy. This chapter interprets the findings in the context of national policy and discusses the steps that the government might take on the basis of these findings.

We address the following questions:

- How reliable and generalizable are these results as a guide to national policy?
- What policy issues are posed by the results for adults?
- Why didn't the program have more positive effects for youths?
- Where the program is not working, what might work better?
- How would we test new approaches?
- What should be done until we know what works better?
- What has been the government's response to these results?
- What do these results imply for the ongoing measurement of JTPA's performance?

HOW RELIABLE AND GENERALIZABLE ARE THESE RESULTS AS A GUIDE TO NATIONAL POLICY?

The National JTPA Study has, for the first time, provided estimates of the impacts of the nation's main training program for disadvantaged workers that are not subject to selection bias, the problem that has plagued most earlier evaluations of training programs. Like any other study, however, the National JTPA Study has limitations that may affect its applicability to national policy.

Perhaps most important, this study is based on a sample drawn from 16 study sites that are not a probability sample of all JTPA service delivery areas and that may not be representative of the nation. As we have shown in this volume and elsewhere, the study sites are quite similar to all SDAs nationally. In particular, the characteristics of enrollees, local levels of earnings and unemployment, industrial mix, poverty rates, barriers to employment faced by enrollees, JTPA performance standards, and program cost in the study sites were, on average, virtually identical to those of the average SDA nationally.[1]

Nevertheless, these SDAs voluntarily participated in this study when other SDAs refused to do so; thus, they may differ from other SDAs in unobservable characteristics that make them unrepresentative of the nation as a whole. Moreover, the study sites do differ from the national population of SDAs in several notable respects: they do not include any very large cities, and they tended to emphasize classroom training and job search assistance *more*, and on-the-job training and miscellaneous services *less*, than their counterparts nationally.[2] For these reasons, the most that can be claimed for this sample is that it represents a broad range of local environments and programs, serving a varied mix of participants that is very similar to that of the national JTPA population.

It is not clear what effect these differences between the study sites and SDAs nationally might have on the estimates of program impact. The principal reason that local programs refused to participate in the program was unwillingness to randomly exclude eligible applicants from the program; it is difficult to say whether such unwillingness would be positively or negatively correlated with program impacts. It might be argued that those SDAs that agreed to participate *couldn't* self-select themselves on the basis of impact, because the true impact of individual programs was unknown; the decision to participate could still, of course, be based on factors that were, by chance, correlated with impact. It is noteworthy, however, that on the one measure of performance that *was* known to local programs—the JTPA performance indicators—on average, the study sites were virtually identical to SDAs nationally.[3]

As part of our interim analysis of 18-month data, we conducted an exploratory analysis to identify local factors that might have influenced program impacts. Three types of factors were considered: (1) characteristics of the JTPA programs; (2) prevailing labor market conditions; and (3) the types of persons accepted into the programs. No clear patterns emerged from the analysis, and almost none of the factors analyzed had a statistically significant influence on earnings impacts. Our ability to detect such effects was severely limited, however, by the small samples at each site, the limited number of sites involved, and the large number of local factors that might affect the impact of the program.[4]

A further analysis of possible site effects was conducted by James Heckman and Jeffrey Smith, as part of their work on the National JTPA Study. Heckman and Smith analyzed the 18-month impact estimates for adult men and male youths (including arrestees). By dropping one site at a time from the analysis and re-estimating program impacts, they examined the sensitivity of the overall impact findings to which sites were included.[5] Because estimated impacts varied by site, the overall impact estimate varied depending on which site was excluded. This variation was appreciable for male youths, although in no case were estimates of positive impacts obtained. For adult men the variation was much less pronounced.[6] Taken together, these analyses seem to suggest that site effects are not sufficiently large to call into question the basic findings of the study—that the program had modest positive effects on the earnings of adults and no positive effect on the earnings of youth.

The estimation approach used here is, of course, only one of a number of possible approaches, but represents, in our judgment, the most straightforward, reliable way to analyze the available data. Alternative estimation approaches will produce somewhat different estimates, but all of the methods examined to date produce results that indicate that JTPA modestly increased the average earnings of adult women and men in the program at the 16 study sites, but did not increase the earnings of female or male youths.

For example, Heckman and Smith performed a series of sensitivity tests of the 18-month impact findings for adult men and male youths (including arrestees) presented in our 18-month report. They considered: (1) an alternative way to compute the standard errors of the impact estimates (developed by White, 1980); (2) different ways to handle "outliers" (unusually high values) in the earnings data (by deleting these cases); and (3) several ways to combine the estimates of earnings impacts across sites (using different sets of weights). For male youths, the specific estimates of impacts and the statistical significance of these estimates varied depending on the combination of analytic procedures used. But no combination produced estimates of positive program impacts. For adult men, the specific estimates varied much less, and were quite close to those presented in our 18-month report. The estimated statistical significance of these estimates did vary somewhat, and some results appeared to be more significant than those presented in our 18-month report.[7] Again, we conclude that the main findings of the study are not sensitive to the estimation procedures employed.

In the end, each reader must decide how much credence to place in these results as a guide to policy. We have tried to be as explicit and objective as possible about the strengths and limitations of the study so that that can be an informed decision. In making that decision, it is important to consider the alternative bases for making policy decisions. The National JTPA Study is, in fact, the *only* comprehensive national assessment of the impacts of JTPA.[8] Other than the results of this study, the only bases on which the effects of the program can be inferred are scattered local evaluations, the judgment of informed observers, and the testimonials and success stories provided by local program operators.

Several other features of this study, which affect the interpretation of the results, not their validity, should be noted. First, because program staff assigned different types of enrollees to the different service strategy subgroups, the results of one service strategy may not be applicable to enrollees in a different service strategy subgroup. This means that one cannot conclude that a subgroup with little or no earnings gains would have been better served by a different service strategy that produced larger earnings gains for a different group of enrollees. The study was designed only to measure the impact of each service strategy on the group for whom it was recommended. To do otherwise would have required a design that would have changed the way JTPA operated; this would have invalidated the study as an evaluation of the *existing* JTPA program.

Second, the study was designed to evaluate *only* the services normally provided by JTPA, not alternatives to JTPA. This means that the study is primarily *diagnostic*, not *prescriptive*. That is, although we can identify those parts of the program that have positive impacts and those that do not, we cannot say what alternative services would have worked better.

A final feature of the study that affects the interpretation of its results is that it estimated the impact of the *incremental* services provided by JTPA, relative to the level of non-JTPA services available to the control group. It did not estimate the full impact of JTPA relative to no services. Moreover, this service increment may or may not correspond to the amount by which services would be increased or reduced in the aggregate if JTPA were expanded or contracted. If, for example, JTPA were abolished, the loss of services from the standpoint of society as a whole would depend on the degree to which JTPA services substitute for services from other sources—i.e., whether non-JTPA employment and training services would adjust to offset some of the loss of JTPA services. This cannot be known a priori. What we can say with confidence is that the impacts estimated here were produced by the observed treatment-control service differential, at the costs estimated here. Thus, the impact estimates and benefit-cost analysis presented here are valid measures of the effects of the observed treatment-control service differential.

WHAT POLICY ISSUES ARE POSED BY THE RESULTS FOR ADULTS?

Overall, we found that JTPA worked reasonably well for adults. Although the program-induced gains in earnings were relatively modest—less than $900 per year in the postprogram period—the incremental cost of the program was even smaller. Thus, for every $1.00 invested by society in JTPA training for adults, the program returned approximately $1.50 in earnings gains to enrollees. This does not mean that the program could not be improved, but it does suggest that the adult program was basically sound.

The service strategy subgroup results offer some guidance as to where efforts to improve the adult program might be focused. Of the six adult service strategy subgroups analyzed, only one—classroom training for adult women—was found not to be cost-effective from the perspective of society as a whole. For this group, the highest incremental training costs of any service strategy ($1,639) combined with relatively small earnings gains ($615) to produce a net social cost. Clearly, policymakers need either to find ways to reduce the cost and/or increase the effectiveness of this service strategy or to adopt a different service approach for this subgroup of women. Later sections of this chapter discuss these options in more detail.

While all three service strategies were found to be cost-effective for adult men, total estimated earnings gains over 30 months were not significantly different from zero in any of the three. Adult men in OJT/JSA enjoyed statistically significant earnings gains in the second postprogram year, however, and the gains in that year alone ($1,125) were sufficient to offset the incremental costs of training ($1,030).

In the other two subgroups of adult men, estimated 30-month earnings gains were relatively small—$1,248 in the classroom training subgroup and $878 in the other services subgroup. Net benefits were positive in these subgroups only because the incremental cost of services was correspondingly low ($915 and $214, respectively). From a policy perspective, the issue here is whether such low-cost, low-intensity service strategies are appropriate for this group of men. If the objective of the program was to significantly upgrade the skills of these workers, then the program was not achieving that objective. If, however, the program simply sought to reemploy workers in a cost-effective manner, that objective was being achieved.

We found virtually no evidence of systematic variation in the impacts of JTPA across subgroups of adult enrollees defined by baseline characteristics.[9] Thus, there is no evidence here that the effectiveness of JTPA could be improved by changes in the targeting of services or that some subgroups of adults were being served less well than others.

In addition to its implications for JTPA policy, the study also has implications for employment and training policy in other programs, most notably those for welfare recipients. JTPA substantially increased the earnings of AFDC recipients, particularly those in the OJT/JSA service strategy. This suggests that strategies that are strongly oriented to immediate employment and skill development through work can be highly effective for at least some AFDC recipients.

In applying this finding to welfare policy, however, several qualifications must be noted. First, it is important to recognize that JTPA participants were volunteers; there is no guarantee that similar results would occur if the same services were provided on a mandatory basis. Second, the proportion of the AFDC caseload that volunteered for JTPA was quite small.[10] Finally, it should be borne in mind that the large earnings gains estimated for AFDC recipients in this study resulted in no significant reductions in AFDC receipt rates or average benefits.[11] Taken together, these considerations suggest that, although services of the type provided by JTPA may be a very cost-effective way to increase the earnings of a small subgroup of recipients, one should not necessarily expect them to result in major changes in overall AFDC costs or caseloads.

WHY DIDN'T THE PROGRAM HAVE MORE POSITIVE EFFECTS FOR YOUTHS?

JTPA did not significantly increase youths' earnings, or reduce their welfare benefits, over the 30-month follow-up period, either overall or in any of the six youth service strategy subgroups. Nor were significant positive earnings effects found for any of 39 youth subgroups formed on the basis of baseline characteristics. While these results are consistent with those of earlier studies, it is nonetheless important to ask why they occurred.

On the basis of the data available, we can be more confident in ruling out some possible explanations than in stating with any certainty why the program was ineffective for youths. For example, one hypothesis might be that participation in the program diverted enrollees from employment and that this reduction in earnings offset increases in earnings once they were out of the program. That hypothesis is not supported by the data. As shown in Exhibit 5.17, in four of the six youth service strategy subgroups, earnings impacts were no more positive in the last 12 months of the follow-up period, when virtually all sample members had left the program, than they were in the first 6 months after random assignment, when one would expect such diversion to be concentrated. Only among female youths in the classroom training subgroup did we see a clear pattern of reduced earnings during the first 6 months followed by positive impact estimates in the succeeding periods. But even for this subgroup, the estimated impacts in the latter part of the follow-up period were not statistically significant.

Nor do the data support the hypothesis that youths received no greater services than they would have had they not entered JTPA. As we saw in Exhibit 5.13, the program significantly increased the percentage of the sample receiving services by at least 50 percent in all but one of the service strategy subgroups; in the OJT/JSA subgroup of male youths, JTPA nearly tripled the proportion receiving services. Moreover, the absolute increases in service for youths were of the same order of magnitude—in fact, in many cases larger—than the corresponding service differentials for adults (see Exhibit 5.3), for whom program effects on earnings were much more positive.

The findings of positive earnings impacts for adults also argue against explaining the lack of effects for youths in terms of poor program administration or low-quality training providers, since the adult and youth programs were administered by the same organizations and relied on many of the same training providers. Given the similarity of program inputs for adults and youths, what the disparity in program impacts for the two groups does seem to imply is that the training needs of youths are very different from those of adults. Youths may need more intensive services, or at least different kinds of services, than adults for training to be effective. The next section considers a number of alternative types of services that might be more effective for youths.

The lack of *any* positive impacts on youths' earnings—either in this study or in earlier experimental studies of youth training programs—makes it extremely difficult to say with any confidence why JTPA did not have positive impacts.[12] If examples of successful training programs for youths were available, one could compare them with JTPA to see what JTPA did differently—or failed to do—that might account for its lack of success with this group. But in the absence of successful models, it is almost impossible to say which of the many program features that JTPA does or does not possess is responsible for the disappointing results for youths. Asking why JTPA did not work is in fact equivalent to asking what alternative program approach would work. We therefore turn to an examination of such alternatives, both for youths and for the service strategies that were least effective for adults, and to how they might be tested.

WHERE THE PROGRAM DID NOT WORK, WHAT MIGHT WORK BETTER?

The results of the National JTPA study have identified certain components of the adult programs that could be improved, as well as showing that the youth programs had virtually no positive effects on enrollee earnings. In the case of adults, there are examples of successful training approaches, both within and outside JTPA, that can provide models for improving the performance of those components that were not as effective as they might be. For disadvantaged youths, there are almost no examples of training programs that have been rigorously evaluated with positive results. In searching for alternatives to the services studied here, then, our only guidance comes from the few evaluations that do indicate program success, the informed judgment of employment and training professionals, and theories of youth development. This section describes some of the alternative approaches that these sources suggest. The following section discusses how these alternatives might be tested.

Incremental Reforms of JTPA

The results presented here are based on JTPA program operations during program years 1987–90. Since that time, there have been several changes in the JTPA program, intended to improve its effectiveness. Most notably, the 1992 JTPA amendments established a separate youth program (Title II-C), targeted services to those with multiple employment barriers (including school dropouts, pregnant and parenting youths, ex-offenders, and youths with low basic skills), required comprehensive assessments and individualized service strategies, reformed on-the-job training practices, mandated that SDAs address the full range of youths' service needs, encouraged longer-term services, and authorized provision of work experience, community service, and mentoring. Although these changes have probably increased the quality of services provided to youths (as measured by conventional standards), no rigorous impact analysis has been conducted since the amendments were implemented. Thus, there is no evidence that these changes improved the effectiveness of the program.

A further incremental change that might be considered is provision of post-program support services to former enrollees who have been placed in jobs. While they are in the program, enrollees receive a limited range of support services, such as counseling, child care, and transportation, as well as assistance in obtaining services from other programs. But support services and assistance end once the enrollee obtains a job and leaves the program. Without such support, many graduates may fall prey to the well-documented high turnover rate of disadvantaged workers, especially youths.[13] If so, continued support once the enrollees are employed may be critical to maintaining any gains achieved by the program until they are sufficiently well established in a job to deal with these needs on their own.

More Intensive Services

Increases in service intensity might take any of a number of forms. They might involve changes in the mix of existing services, away from low-cost services such as job search assistance and pre-employment skills training toward vocational skills training or on-the-job training. Or they might involve services that are more intensive or of longer duration than any of the services now provided. For example, rather than offering the 3–5 months of occupational skills training that was typical of JTPA, the program might enroll participants in a two-year vocational program. Alternatively, enrollees might attend more hours of training per week, or training might be more individualized, with a higher ratio of staff to trainees.

In the case of adult men in the other services subgroup—that is, those for whom neither classroom training in occupational skills nor OJT was recommended—it appears that JTPA provided little more service than individuals would have received if they had not entered JTPA. Of those in this group who enrolled in any service, over half received "miscellaneous" services—a collection of primarily low-intensity services such as assessment, job-readiness training, vocational exploration, job shadowing, and tryout employment (see Exhibit 3.17). Treatment group members received, on average, only 43 additional hours of service at an incremental cost of $181 (see Exhibit 5.3). If policymakers wish to increase the effectiveness of the program for adult men, they might consider enrolling more members of this group in more intensive services—especially the service that appears to have been the most effective for adult men, on-the-job training. There is, of course, no guarantee that this service would work as well for these men as it did for those for whom it was recommended.

While JTPA was frequently criticized for providing insufficiently intensive services for youths, there is little evidence that more-intensive services would have larger impacts for youths, much less that those impacts would be large enough to justify their added cost, both in terms of the operational costs of the program and the forgone earnings of participants. Certainly, within the range of services provided by National JTPA Study sites, the more intensive services were no more effective than the less intensive ones.

Moreover, neither of the two previous experimental evaluations of more intensive services for disadvantaged youths found positive impacts on earnings. The Supported Work Demonstration provided closely supervised subsidized employment for up to 18 months for severely disadvantaged youths, most of whom were males.[14] The JOB-START demonstration provided an intensive mix of basic education, occupational skills training, job placement assistance, and training-related support services for 17- to 21-year-old dropouts, about evenly divided between males and females.[15] In both of these demonstrations, the intensity of service, as measured by length of participation and cost, was roughly twice that of JTPA.[16] For the sample as a whole, neither study found significant impacts on earnings over follow-up periods of 27 and 48 months, respectively. (As discussed in the next subsection, there were significant impacts in one JOBSTART site.) This does not, of course, mean that some package of more intensive services would not be more effective for youths—only that the specific packages tried in these demonstrations were not.

Integrated Education and Training

JTPA tended to provide remedial education in a classroom setting, separate from occupational skills training. Education that is integrated into skills training is likely to be viewed by enrollees as more relevant and less intimidating, especially for those who have previously failed in a classroom setting. The Center for Employment Training (CET) in San Jose, California, which uses this approach, has been found to have positive impacts on earnings in two random assignment evaluations.[17] While these results strongly suggest that this approach should be examined more closely, they do not convincingly demonstrate the effectiveness of the approach. Any of a number of other attributes of the CET program could be responsible for these positive findings (e.g., their close working relationship with local employers in the design of training, instruction, and placement of graduates; their skilled, experienced staff; or the nature of the local labor market).

To attempt to determine whether the success of CET is inherent in the approach or the result of other local factors, DOL has funded replications of the CET model in more than a dozen localities across the country and has contracted for random assignment evaluations of these replication programs.[18]

Developmental Strategies

Many would argue that disadvantaged youths need more than just occupational skills or assistance in finding a job if they are to become productive members of the work force. A more holistic approach would attempt to address the whole range of developmental needs of at-risk youths, seeking to build their self-esteem, motivation, and sense of responsibility, as well as imparting vocational, academic, and social skills. Ideally, such an approach would be part of a continuing school-to-work strategy that seeks to instill socially productive attitudes and behaviors before dysfunctional traits become ingrained.

We know of no full-scale implementation of such a model, although many elements of this approach are embodied in the youth corps programs that operate in many localities across the country with funding from state and local governments and the new federal AmeriCorps program.[19] Perhaps the best known are the California Conservation Corps and City Year in Boston, although there are now youth corps in virtually every state and major city. They attempt to build positive work skills and habits, and an enhanced self-esteem and sense of social responsibility, by involving out-of-school youths in a combination of community service, remedial education, and training in vocational and life skills. Corps members participate on a full-time basis for 9 to 15 months; they receive stipends close to the minimum wage and, in some cases, postservice payments that can be applied to further education. Although these programs do not view themselves as job training programs, they incorporate many elements of a developmental approach to job training.

Dropout Prevention Programs

Early intervention to keep youths in school might be more effective than attempting to deal with their labor market problems once they have dropped out. There is some evidence that such programs can reduce the dropout rate among at-risk youths through a combination of vocational counseling, skills training, and intensive tutoring and academic assistance. For example, a random assignment evaluation of a set of five programs aimed at at-risk youths in vocational-technical high schools found 20–29 percent reductions in the dropout rate.[20] We do not know what effect these programs had on longer-term employment and earnings, however.

Another promising model for dropout prevention is the Quantum Opportunities Program, funded by the Ford Foundation in four cities.[21] This program involved intensive counseling and tutoring by highly committed youth workers, starting in the freshman year of high school and continuing for four years. Participants were paid $1.33 an hour to participate in program activities ranging from tutoring sessions to performing community service to attending cultural events, plus a $100 bonus for each 100 hours of participation; an equal amount was set aside in a college fund for the student. The average four-year cost of the program was $10,600 per participant. A random assignment evaluation of the program found that it increased basic skills and educational attainment, and lowered birth rates among the participants. These results were based on a sample of only 100 participants and 100 controls, however, and there is some question whether the program can be replicated in other sites. To address this question, and to provide a larger base of evidence, the Ford Foundation and DOL have funded additional Quantum Opportunities sites and plan to measure their impacts in a random assignment evaluation.[22]

A number of dropout prevention demonstrations were funded by the Department of Health and Human Services in the past several years; some of these incorporated random assignment evaluations, but to date no final results are available. The Department of Labor has also funded demonstrations of alternative schools in seven cities. These schools, modeled on Brooklyn's High School Redirection, are designed to meet the educational needs of youths with low reading skills who are at risk of dropping out. Random assignment evaluations are now underway in several of these cities.[23] If dropout prevention strategies prove to be effective, they could be pursued within JTPA Title II-B, which serves in-school youths, or as part of a more comprehensive school-to-work program.

School-to-Work and Apprenticeship Programs

Programs designed to help disadvantaged youths in the transition from school to work might prevent some of the labor market problems faced by disadvantaged youths. Programs such as four-year Tech-Prep and secondary-level career academies attempt to combine work-based training with academic studies to provide career-oriented schooling for non–college-bound youths. These programs are based on the theory that not only is such training more relevant to the needs of the labor market, but that by allowing students to see the relationship between what they learn, their performance, and their ability to pursue a rewarding career, they will be more motivated and more likely to stay in school. Youth apprenticeship programs take this approach one step further by establishing a direct transition into a permanent job after high school.[24] To date, there has been little rigorous evaluation of these approaches, although one such program, the career academies operating in ten sites across the country, is currently being evaluated with random assignment.[25]

Community-wide Interventions

It may be that interventions like JTPA that focus on individuals are insufficient to overcome the forces of peer pressure and lack of economic opportunity that constrain and influence the behavior of disadvantaged youths in high-poverty areas. It may be that community-wide interventions, providing a range of social and economic development services in addition to job training, are needed to create economic opportunity and change the prevailing attitudes and social mores of youths in such communities. Such a saturation program is currently being tested in the Youth Fair Chance demonstrations, funded by the Department of Labor.[26]

Mobility Programs

An alternative approach to overcoming the destructive social and economic forces that characterize high-poverty areas is to subsidize mobility out of such areas. Such a program would need to provide counseling and assistance in finding suitable housing, as well as post-move housing subsidies. In studies of mobility programs of this type in Chicago and Cincinnati, Rosenbaum (1991) and Fischer (1991) found relatively large effects on the employment rates of public housing tenants who moved from inner cities to the suburbs. These studies were based on nonexperimental comparisons of movers and non-movers, however, and may therefore be subject to selection bias. An experimental test of this approach, called Moving to Opportunity for Fair Housing, is currently being implemented in five cities by the Department of Housing and Urban Development.[27] Programs of this type would clearly not be run within JTPA, but they are a policy alternative to job training. It might well be that the resources currently devoted to training for disadvantaged youths would be more effectively used to help their families move out of high-poverty areas.

Residential Programs

Another way to remove disadvantaged youths from the deleterious effects of high-poverty environments, at least temporarily, is to provide training in a residential setting. This approach is best exemplified by the Job Corps program, which provides basic education and vocational training for severely educationally or economically disadvantaged out-of-school youths in over 100 residential centers across the country. A nonexperimental evaluation of Job Corps in the late 1970s found it to be cost-effective, despite the high costs of residential training.[28] An experimental evaluation of Job Corps is currently underway.[29]

HOW WOULD WE TEST NEW APPROACHES?

As the preceding section makes clear, there are a large number of alternatives to the type of services provided by JTPA for those subgroups of enrollees for whom JTPA was not effective. Indeed, within each of the broad strategies just sketched, there are innumerable possible variations, with potentially different effects. How can we determine which, if any, of these approaches is more effective than the existing program?

As noted, some of these approaches are already being evaluated with experimental methods. It is important that the remaining options be subjected to similar tests as soon as possible. Under JTPA Titles II-A and II-C, DOL spends approximately $1 billion a year, including over $100 million dollars on services to out-of-school youths. Until we can document that these services are effective, or replace them with services that are, we risk not only the waste of substantial budgetary resources but also the lost opportunity to improve the labor market prospects of large numbers of disadvantaged workers. This means that we cannot afford to continue the pattern of the past, in which alternative strategies were tested seriatim, with each test taking a number of years to complete. Rather, we need to minimize the time required to evaluate the entire list of candidate approaches by testing multiple strategies simultaneously. Simultaneous testing of different approaches will also help to ensure the comparability of the evaluation results.

Given limited evaluation resources, it will be important to choose carefully the approaches to be tested, to maximize the usefulness of the evaluation results for policy. Toward that end, we recommend that the models selected for testing be relatively straightforward, "generic" versions of each of the broad approaches just described. Testing of complex models or combinations of approaches will complicate and limit the interpretation of the evaluation results in several ways. First, it may be difficult to determine which components of a complex treatment led to the observed program effects. Second, the more complex the treatment, the more uncertain it will be that it can be replicated in other localities. In any case, it will be critical to include in any evaluation a process analysis designed to document the program that was implemented, so that, if successful, it can be replicated.

It is, of course, important that any tests of alternative approaches be rigorously evaluated with experimental methods. Experience has demonstrated that simply trying out alternative program strategies without rigorous evaluation is not enough. For example, a National Academy of Sciences committee that reviewed some 400 reports produced under the Youth Employment and Demonstration Projects Act (YEDPA) concluded that:

> Despite the magnitude of the resources ostensibly devoted to the objectives of research and demonstration, there is little reliable information on the effectiveness of the programs in solving youth employment problems. . . . It is evident that if random assignment had been consistently used, much more could have been learned. (Betsey et al., 1985).

The cost of our failure to learn more from the YEDPA demonstrations was not only the $4 billion spent on those projects, but also the resources that have been devoted to ineffective youth training programs in the intervening years.

Even experimental evaluations of the selected approaches may not yield reliable guidance for policy, however, unless the tests are carefully designed both to yield results that can be generalized to the larger population of interest for national policy and to be comparable to one another. As we have seen in the National JTPA Study, true generalizability is difficult to achieve in this kind of evaluation. Indeed, it would probably be impossible to induce a nationally representative sample of program operators to implement a demonstration program. It will be important, however, to test new approaches in a wide range of programmatic and labor market settings and to include a sufficient number of sites to ensure that the results are not unduly influenced by factors unique to a small number of sites. The National JTPA Study may provide a useful standard for the number and diversity of sites required, since its results have been widely accepted as reliable guides for policy, even though it was not based on a national probability sample.

Perhaps the most difficult challenge in designing a series of tests of alternative employment and training approaches will be to ensure that the results of different tests are comparable. The natural inclination of evaluation funding agencies is likely to be to mount independent tests of alternative approaches in different sites; this pattern is already evident in the tests described in the previous section. This unfortunately confounds treatment with site and participant characteristics, even when each approach is tested in multiple sites. It would be greatly preferable to test multiple approaches in the same set of sites, to control for local labor market and population characteristics and ensure that any differences in estimated impacts reflect differences in program effectiveness, not differences in the local participant population and environment.[30] We recognize that some approaches (e.g., those that rely on saturation of the community) cannot be colocated with other approaches. Wherever possible, however, colocation should be attempted. Where alternative program strategies cannot be colocated, a premium should be placed on implementing the demonstration in as many and diverse sites as possible, to "average out" the effects of local factors.

WHAT SHOULD BE DONE UNTIL WE KNOW WHAT WORKS BETTER?

Even if an agressive strategy of testing new approaches were launched immediately, it would be a number of years before evaluation results would be available to guide policy. What policy should be followed in the interim? Any of three general strategies might be adopted:

- Shift resources from those services that have been shown to be ineffective to those that are cost-effective;
- Continue to fund existing services at current levels; or
- Substantially reduce or eliminate funding for those parts of the program that have been shown to be ineffective and shift funds to demonstrations to test more promising approaches.

The first strategy is really only applicable to the adult program, since there were no cost-effective services for youths. This approach would, for example, shift the focus of training for adult women from the classroom training strategy—the one adult service strategy subgroup for whom JTPA was not cost-effective—to the OJT/JSA or other services strategies. It presumes that these strategies would be as effective for women who were not currently assigned to them as they are for those who were. While there is no guarantee that this is the case, in the absence of better information, it is not an unreasonable assumption. The differences in measurable characteristics and control group earnings between women in the classroom training subgroup and those in other subgroups were not large and, in any case, the impact of JTPA did not seem to vary systematically with enrollee characteristics. It seems preferable, then, to shift adult women from classroom training to the OJT/JSA or other services strategies, rather than continuing to provide ineffective services or simply not serving those women.

For youths, policymakers are faced with a choice between the second and third approaches. The case for the second approach would rest on the arguments that we cannot simply give up on disadvantaged youths and that the youth program has been substantially improved since the time of this study. For example, many JTPA practitioners would argue that the 1992 amendments substantially strengthened the youth component of JTPA. In the absence of a rigorous evaluation of the postamendment program, however, this argument would have to be accepted on faith if existing services are to be continued at their current levels.

The third strategy is based on the premise that we waste resources by continuing to provide ineffective services. At a minimum, proponents of this approach would argue that we should hedge our bets by substantially reducing our investment in services that are questionable at best and testing many alternative approaches. The risk of taking this approach is, of course, that we may be forgoing an opportunity to help a generation of disadvantaged youths if the reforms already instituted have been effective.

The pervasive negative evaluation findings for youths—both in this and other studies—suggest that continuing to provide the existing services is a waste of resources, both for the taxpayer and for the youths themselves. It seems unlikely to us that the changes in the program enacted in 1992 were sufficient to transform the youth program into a success. Until training approaches with proven cost-effectiveness can be identified, we would argue that the resources devoted to existing services for this group should be substantially reduced and funds devoted to a major test of new approaches.

WHAT HAS BEEN THE RESPONSE OF THE GOVERNMENT TO THESE RESULTS?

In response to the results of the National JTPA study, the Department of Labor has generally followed the approach recommended above. In its fiscal year (FY) 1996 budget request, DOL proposed a 47 percent reduction in funding for Title II-C (the program for out-of-school youth) and a modest increase in funding for Title II-A (the adult program). Congress responded to this request by applying an even larger budget reduction to the previously enacted FY 1995 appropriation for Title II-C, as part of the midyear recission package. In a year when major cuts were being made in almost all social programs, however, Congress allowed the 11 percent increase in funding for adult programs from FY 1994 to FY 1995 to remain intact.[31] Thus, both the positive and negative findings of the study appear to have had an important effect on national policy.

The study findings also prompted DOL to seek more effective training strategies for out-of-school youth. One of the department's first reactions to these results was to fund the replications of the San Jose CET program described earlier and to begin planning an experimental evaluation of its impacts. The department also sponsored a series of public meetings around the country, at which representatives of the local employment and training community suggested ways to improve services for youth, and convened a meeting of experts in youth employment and training, research and evaluation, and youth development. An outgrowth of this latter meeting was the experimental replications of the previously described Quantum Opportunities Program.

When these replication studies are added to the ongoing evaluations of youth corps, career academies, Youth Fair Chance, Moving to Opportunities, and Job Corps described earlier, an impressive array of alternative approaches to youth services will have been subjected to evaluation with random assignment. Further steps would be useful, however. As discussed earlier, the existing and planned experimental evaluations of alternative services for youth are being undertaken independently, in separate sites. This raises the danger that their results will be confounded with site-specific factors, making comparisons across approaches problematic. It would be extremely useful to mount a demonstration in which multiple training approaches were implemented in the same site. Although it probably would not be feasible to test more than two or three approaches in the same site, a design based on different pairings of programmatic approaches in overlapping sets of sites would provide a much more solid basis for comparison than one in which each approach is tested in a different set of sites. At a minimum, any approaches that are found to be effective in the current round of evaluations should be tested against each other in this way before being adopted in the ongoing program.

For adults, program policy has moved away from the approaches that were found to be most effective in the National JTPA Study. "Stand-alone" OJT and job search assistance have been abolished and emphasis shifted to classroom training, which was not cost-effective for adult women and was the least cost-effective strategy for adult men. These changes were made as part of the 1992 amendments, before the results of the National JTPA Study became available, but there has been no effort to reverse them on the basis of the study findings. In fairness to DOL, however, it must be noted that the results for adults were much less clear-cut than the results for youth.

WHAT DO THESE RESULTS IMPLY FOR THE ONGOING MEASUREMENT OF PROGRAM PERFORMANCE?

One of the most disturbing aspects of the results of the National JTPA Study is that, although JTPA had one of the most highly developed performance measurement systems of any social program, that system gave no indication that the program was not improving the earnings of youth. As shown in Exhibit 3.9, on average both the 16 study sites and all SDAs nationally exceeded the main JTPA performance standards for youth (the entered employment rate and the positive termination rate).

The system's failure to detect the lack of program impact on youths' earnings should not be surprising. The JTPA performance indicators were intended to measure the performance of each SDA *relative to other SDAs*, not against any absolute standard.[32] To determine whether *any* of the SDAs has a positive impact on earnings would require knowledge of what enrollees' earnings would have been in the absence of the program—which can be provided only by a control group. Because the JTPA performance management system relied entirely on information about the outcomes of program participants, it could not determine whether those participants were better off for having enrolled in the program; at best, it could only tell whether participants in one SDA were better off than those in others.

Our findings for youths suggest that this type of performance standards system needs to be augmented with some form of monitoring system capable of measuring performance against an absolute standard of achievement. The most obvious approach would be periodic replication of this study, perhaps with a national sample of local programs. Valuable as we believe this study has been, we do not recommend that approach. The first results from the National JTPA Study were not available until nearly six years after its initiation; an ongoing program needs more continuous feedback than such a study can provide. Because it involved random assignment of large samples in a small number of sites, the National JTPA Study was also relatively burdensome to program staff in the study sites.

We do believe, however, that only a monitoring system based on random assignment of program applicants can provide a reliable measure of the absolute performance of the program. To provide such a measure on an ongoing basis with minimal burden on program staff, we would recommend random assignment of a small fraction of program applicants to a control group in a large number of sites, on an ongoing basis. If, for example, 5 percent of all applicants were assigned to a control group in a rotating sample of 50 randomly selected sites, the resulting annual sample would have roughly the same statistical power as the sample in this study. This very low rate of assignment to the control group would substantially reduce program staff resistance to the evaluation. (We would nevertheless recommend that site participation be mandatory.) On-site automated random assignment, using standardized software, rather than the call-in system used in the National JTPA Study, would substantially reduce staff burden. Baseline data collection beyond the existing Standardized Program Information Report (SPIR) could also be eliminated to further reduce staff burden. Follow-up data on participant employment and earnings could be obtained at low cost from administrative records, such as Unemployment Insurance (UI) wage records or Internal Revenue Service earnings records (W-2 forms).

Such a system, once instituted, could produce regular annual reports on the impact of the program on the earnings of participants, at approximately the same level of disaggregation and statistical precision achieved by the National JTPA Study. Finer disaggregation or greater precision could be obtained simply by pooling across annual samples.

While ongoing random assignment of program applicants would be a departure from past performance monitoring practices, the idea is not without precedent. For example, in 1991, the Food and Nutrition Service of the U.S. Department of Agriculture proposed to adopt a performance monitoring system based on random assignment for the Food Stamp Employment and Training Program.[33]

We would view such a system as a supplement to, rather than a replacement for, the current performance standards system. The current performance standards system would still be needed to measure relative performance at the local program level; the evaluation system described previously would produce systemwide estimates of overall program impact. Only by institutionalizing such a system into the ongoing operation of the program, however, can program performance be continuously monitored in the terms that matter most for policy—impacts on the earnings of participants.

Notes

1. See Exhibits 3.2–3.9 in this volume; chapter 5 in Bloom (1991); and Appendix A in Bloom et al. (1993).

2. It should be noted, however, that two study sites, Jersey City and Oakland, are located in highly urban areas with the same kinds of social and labor market problems that characterize very large cities. Moreover, the impact estimates at the service strategy subgroup level effectively control for service mix.

3. See Exhibits 3.8 and 3.9.

4. Bloom et al. (1993) presents this analysis, which was based on estimates of impacts on earnings per assignee at 18 months.

5. Overall impact estimates were obtained by weighting the site impacts inversely proportionally to their estimated standard errors. Separate analyses were conducted based on OLS and White's (1980) estimates of the site standard errors.

6. The impact estimates for adult men ranged from $437 to $697 when sites were weighted with ordinary least squares (OLS) standard errors and from $474 to $708 when White (1980) standard errors were used. The impact estimates for male youths ranged from −$442 to −$1,246 when OLS standard errors were used and from −$310 to −$1,107 using White (1980) standard errors.

7. More specifically: (1) For both adult men and male youths, standard errors of the overall impact estimates produced by White's method were almost identical to the OLS standard errors presented in our 18-month report. (2) Impact estimates presented in the 18-month report handled outliers by editing their values on the basis of examination of the survey data from which the earnings measure was constructed (reported wage rates, hours worked per week, and the start and end dates of specific jobs). The alternative method used by Heckman and Smith was to "trim" the data by deleting the sample members with the highest values of earnings. The data editing approach produced an 18-month impact estimate of $550 ($t = 1.61$) for adult men and −$854 ($t = 1.99$) for male youths. The data trimming approach produced impact estimates for adult men that ranged from $595 ($t = 1.6$) when no outliers were excluded to $650 ($t = 2.33$) when the top 5 percent of the earners were deleted separately from the treatment group and the control group. Corresponding results for male youths were −$1,142 ($t = -2.32$) with no deletions and −$680 ($t = 1.91$) with a 5 percent exclusion. (3) Impact estimates in the 18-month report combined results across sites by pooling the samples from all of the sites; as an alternative, Heckman and Smith computed a weighted mean of the individual site impacts using weights that were inversely proportional to the estimated standard errors of the impact estimates for each site. For adult men, Heckman and Smith obtained an impact estimate of $555 ($t = 1.53$) using OLS standard errors as the basis for weights and an estimate of $591 ($t = 1.63$) using White standard errors. The corresponding results for male youths were −$720 ($t = 1.69$) using OLS standard errors and −$526 ($t = 1.24$) using White standard errors.

8. We discuss later in this chapter the JTPA performance measurement system, which measures outcomes, not impacts.

9. See the F-tests of differences among groups in Exhibits 5.8 and 5.9.

10. The rates of participation in JTPA among AFDC recipients in the National JTPA Study study sites cannot be readily computed because published data are not available on the size of the AFDC caseloads in these SDAs, which are often multicounty areas or other political jurisdictions that may not be congruent with local AFDC administrative areas. In an earlier study of a voluntary program of subsidized employment for AFDC recipients (the AFDC Homemaker–Home Health Aide Demonstrations), approximately 2 percent of those recipients who were contacted volunteered to participate.

11. The reasons for this apparent inconsistency are being investigated in a follow-up study by Abt Associates, using the National JTPA Study data.

12. Some alternative explanations of these findings are being explored in follow-up analyses conducted by Abt Associates. Using nonexperimental methods, this work will explore whether these results are attributable to ineffective training; insufficiently intensive training; training of lower quality than that received by the control group; training that benefited only certain members of the treatment group; negative effects on nonenrollees that offset positive effects for enrollees; or effects on the reservation wages of enrollees that led them to be less likely to work.

13. See Olson, Berg, and Conrad (1990).

14. See Kemper et al. (1981).

15. See Cave and Doolittle (1991).

16. See Cave and Doolittle (1991: 80).

17. See Cave et al. (1993) and Burghardt et al. (1992).

18. This evaluation began in 1995. It is being conducted by MDRC and Berkeley Planning Associates.

19. The impacts of a small subset of these programs on youths' earnings and other outcomes are being evaluated by Abt Associates, using experimental methods.

20. See Hayward and Tallmadge (1993).

21. See Hahn (1994).

22. This evaluation begin in 1995; it is being conducted by Mathematica Policy Research and Berkeley Planning Associates.

23. Both the DHHS and DOL programs are being evaluated by Mathematica Policy Research.

24. See U.S. General Accounting Office (1993) for an overview of efforts to develop comprehensive school-to-work programs in four states and a discussion of some of the obstacles faced by such initiatives. Lerman and Pouncy (1990) present the case for youth apprenticeships.

25. This evaluation is being conducted by MDRC.

26. This demonstration is being evaluated by Mathematica Policy Research; technical assistance to the demonstration sites is being provided by Brandeis University and Abt Associates.

27. This demonstration is being evaluated by Abt Associates.

28. See Mallar et al. (1980).

29. This evaluation is being conducted by Mathematica Policy Research.

30. To eliminate the effect of differences in participant characteristics across programmatic approaches, it would be necessary to randomly assign participants to different treatments. This was not done in the National JTPA Study because the objective of that study was to measure the effectiveness of JTPA as it normally operated, including assignment of participants to alternative service strategies. In a test designed to compare alternative program approaches, however, it would be appropriate to randomly assign participants to alternative treatments, to measure their effects on the same participant population.

31. As this is written, the FY 1996 job training appropriation has not been passed. The House bill would fund year-round youth programs at the FY 1995 level of $127 million, less than 20 percent of the FY 1994 budget for youth programs. The Senate bill would fund year-round youth programs at $311 million, about 50 percent of the FY 1994 level. Both houses would reduce funding for adult programs by 25–32 percent below the FY 1995 budget.

32. The degree to which the JTPA performance standards system has been successful in achieving this objective is being investigated in follow-up analyses of the National JTPA Study data by Abt Associates.

33. See "Proposed Food Stamp Regs Released" (1991).

DATA SOURCES

The data for this study are available in a public use file from the Employment and Training Administration, U.S. Department of Labor.[1] The following data sources were used:

- A random assignment telephone file compiled during the intake of the experimental sample and covering all 20,601 experimental sample members
- A Background Information Form (BIF) completed by 20,501 experimental sample members at the time of their application to JTPA
- JTPA enrollment and tracking data provided by the 16 service delivery areas (SDAs) that served as study sites
- First Follow-up Survey interviews with 17,217 members of the experimental sample
- Second Follow-up Survey interviews with 5,468 members of the experimental sample
- Earnings data from state unemployment insurance (UI) agencies for members of the experimental sample in 12 of the 16 study sites
- State AFDC and/or food stamp records for members of the experimental sample in four of the 16 study sites[2]
- JTPA expenditure records provided by the 16 SDAs
- Published data on instructional costs of high schools and colleges
- A telephone survey of vocational/technical schools named by First Follow-up Survey respondents

This appendix discusses each of these data sources, reviewing the content of the data and the construction of edited variables. The measures of outcomes, service receipt, and cost, which often relied on more than one data source, are discussed in Appendix B.

RANDOM ASSIGNMENT TELEPHONE FILE

The random assignment telephone file was compiled as JTPA applicants at the 16 study sites were randomly assigned to the treatment and control groups. Specifically, after SDA staff had determined an applicant's eligibility for the program and recommended services, a staff member would call the Manpower Demonstration Research Corporation, where a computer program would randomly assign the applicant to the treatment or control group (see Exhibit 2.2 in chapter 2). As part of this process the computer program generated a file of identifiers and basic descriptors for the 20,601 members of the full experimental sample.

Content and Collection Method

These identifiers and descriptors all came from information on the Background Information Form (BIF) that the applicant had completed at application. The SDA staff member read the following BIF data over the telephone: name, Social Security number, date of birth, gender, ethnicity, recommended services and service strategy, and SDA. The random assignment computer program then computed age at random assignment (from the current date and date of birth), date of random assignment (the current date), and treatment/control status (assigned at random).

Completeness

Because all of the identifiers and descriptors for a given program applicant had to be complete for random assignment to take place, the random assignment telephone file has no missing data.

Editing

The random assignment telephone file was merged with the BIF file (discussed in the next section) before either file was edited or used to construct analysis variables. When in conflict, values from the BIF took precedence over values from the telephone file for all variables except the date of random assignment and treatment/control status.

THE BACKGROUND INFORMATION FORM

Background Information Form responses serve as the basis for the vast majority of the baseline characteristic variables used in the impact analysis. These variables are used for several purposes: to describe the characteristics of the sample; to define the target groups, service strategy subgroups, and other key subgroups examined in the analysis; and to serve as covariates to improve the statistical precision of the impact estimates by controlling for potential random differences in baseline characteristics between the treatment and control groups.

Content and Collection Method

The BIF provides information on sample members' demographic and household characteristics: earnings, income, and income sources, including public assistance; work, education, and training histories; and other characteristics at the time of application to JTPA. A copy of the four-page form appears in Bloom (1991).

Most items on the BIF were filled out by sample members during the JTPA intake process, with help from SDA staff as needed. Three key variables were recorded directly by SDA staff, however: the SDA, the specific program services recommended, and the service strategy encompassing those recommended services.

The BIF also served as the SDA's record of the random assignment telephone call.[3] The SDA staff entered treatment/control status onto the form during the call. Completed forms were mailed to the study team for data entry and double-key-entry verification.

Completeness

We obtained from the SDAs completed BIFs for almost all experimental sample members: 20,501 of 20,601 persons, or 99.5 percent. For 55 of the 64 variables on the form, usable data were obtained for 90 percent or more of the sample.

Editing

All variables were checked for out-of-range values or violations of the form's skip patterns (that is, answers to questions that should have been skipped or skips of questions that should have been answered). Unallowed values were recoded to missing, and skip pattern violations were resolved either by inferring the correct answer to a question from other related responses or by recoding all conflicting variables to missing.

ENROLLMENT AND TRACKING DATA FROM THE 16 SDAS

For standard reporting purposes, SDAs maintain machine-readable records on all persons enrolled in JTPA under Title II. We requested enrollment and tracking data from each SDA to measure the enrollment rates of treatment and control group members; to measure the time that treatment and control group members spent in specific program services; and, in conjunction with expenditure records provided by the SDA, to calculate costs per day for specific program services. Because the expenditure records (described later in this appendix) covered program expenditures for all Title II activities in program year 1988, it was necessary to collect enrollment and tracking data for all Title II enrollments during that program year, in addition to data on the experimental sample.[4]

Content and Collection Method

Data from the SDAs' management information systems show enrollment and termination dates for spells of JTPA enrollment, as well as the start and stop dates of each specific program service received during an enrollment spell. Multiple—and sometimes overlapping—services during an enrollment spell were common, whereas multiple spells of enrollment occurred on occasion but never overlapped.

Each SDA provided a comprehensive file on all Title II enrollment spells that began during the sample intake period—November 1, 1987 to September 30, 1989—and extended as far as November 30, 1990, in most SDAs. From these files, we extracted the data on all spells for which either (1) the enrollee was an experimental sample member or (2) part or all of the spell occurred during program year 1988. The former spells were used in analyzing JTPA services received by sample members; the latter spells were used in conjunction with aggregate cost data provided by the SDA to calculate the cost per hour or day of JTPA services during program year 1988.

Completeness

By definition, the SDA data contain complete records of the formal enrollment in JTPA of all sample members in the program years covered. Hence, there are no missing records. However, there were occasionally missing or inconsistent dates in the file. The incidence of these cases and the imputations applied to them are described in the section following.

There is some evidence that JTPA services were received by sample members who were not formally enrolled. Doolittle (1993) reported the results of a survey of 307 nonenrolled treatment group members. Roughly half received some JTPA services, although these services were typically much more limited than those received by enrollees.

Editing

In the extracted files covering program year 1988 and experimental sample enrollments, 2.3 percent of the enrollment spells had missing or inconsistent dates (such as dates of service receipt that fell outside an enrollment spell or stop dates that preceded start dates). We applied a set of imputations (such as inferring the stop date of a specific service from the Title II termination date, or using the mean duration of spells with valid dates to infer a stop date) to these dates.

Codes for specific program services, which varied by SDA, were converted into the following service categories: classroom training in occupational skills; on-the-job training; job search assistance; direct placement; basic education; work experience; customized training; and other services.

FIRST AND SECOND FOLLOW-UP SURVEYS

The First and Second Follow-up Surveys queried members of the experimental sample about their activities after random assignment. Data from the follow-up surveys were used, sometimes in conjunction with other data sources, to prepare many of the outcome measures analyzed in this study. In addition, follow-up survey data were used to identify the target group of male youths who reported having been arrested before random assignment.

Content and Collection Method

The First Follow-up Survey, conducted between October 1989 and January 1991, attempted to interview the 20,501 experimental sample members for whom BIF contact data were available, and succeeded in interviewing 17,217. Survey questions focused on respondents' activities during the period between random assignment and the interview, a period of 12 to 37 months (21 months, on average).[5] This report makes use of answers to follow-up survey questions about jobs held, schools or training programs attended, welfare benefits (for respondents in certain study sites), and arrest histories.

The Second Follow-up Survey, conducted between July and December 1991, attempted to interview a random subset of the experimental sample. To achieve an adequate sample size for each target group, the sampling was stratified by target group, so that 22 percent of the adult women (1,765 persons), 26 percent of the adult men (1,766 persons), and 62 percent of the youths (3,521 persons) in the experimental sample were randomly selected for the survey. The survey succeeded in interviewing 5,468 of the persons selected. For respondents who had answered the First Follow-up, the Second Follow-up focused on the period between the two interviews. For the 472 respondents who had not answered the First Follow-up, the Second Follow-up focused on the period between random assignment and the interview. The Second Follow-up interview was conducted 20 to 48 months after random assignment (35 months, on average). This report makes use of answers to questions about jobs held, schools or training programs attended, educational attainment, welfare benefits (for respondents in certain study sites), and arrest histories.

Each follow-up interview was carried out by telephone if possible or in person if the respondent could not be interviewed by telephone. Interviewers from the National Opinion Research Center (NORC) in Chicago used contact data from the BIF (and, for the Second Follow-up Survey, contact data from the First Follow-up), as well as address checks through the post office and other sources, to locate respondents. Names and telephone numbers of friends and relatives from the BIF and First Follow-up Survey were also used for contact purposes.

Computer-assisted telephone interviewing (CATI) was used for all telephone interviews. A computer program displayed each question for the interviewer and recorded each answer as it was entered by the interviewer. CATI provided tight control over skip patterns and prompted the interviewer for corrections when out-of-range values were entered. In-person interviews were conducted in respondents' homes or other convenient locations. Responses were first recorded on paper and then keyed into the CATI program in the NORC central office.

Completeness

Among the 20,601 persons in the experimental sample, the percentages responding to the First Follow-up Survey were:

	Treatment (%)	Control (%)
Adult women	87.5	86.8
Adult men	78.8	76.8
Female youths	88.0	85.6
Male youths	82.9	79.6
All target groups	84.1	82.4

Among the 7,052 persons randomly selected for the Second Follow-up Survey, the percentages responding to the Second Follow-up were:

	Treatment (%)	Control (%)
Adult women	81.8	81.8
Adult men	73.0	71.0
Female youths	79.3	81.8
Male youths	74.8	76.6
All target groups	77.4	77.9

For the variables used in constructing the central outcome measures for this report, item-specific response rates met or exceeded 90 percent in all cases.

Construction of Edited Variables

The initial steps in survey variable construction paralleled those described earlier for the BIF—editing of out-of-range values and skip pattern violations. A much more extensive variable construction process was used to convert data on job characteristics into a set of monthly earnings and employment measures. In this process, First and Second Follow-up job spell data were used to construct monthly time series variables running from the month of random assignment to the month of the latest interview.[6]

If any dates for a job were missing or inconsistent with other job dates, all monthly earnings and employment variables were given a special missing code in all months. This missing code was used with 0.9 percent of the respondents. Where the special missing code was not used, summary measures of earnings and employment were constructed. Monthly earnings and hours worked were constructed from variables pertaining to each job: dates of employment; regular hours per week; pay per hour or per other time period; overtime hours and pay; tips, bonuses, or commissions; and weeks of unpaid absence or temporary layoff. Missing or extreme monthly values[7] were replaced with imputed values as described in Exhibit A.1. When more than one job was held within a single month, the monthly measures summed across jobs.

Exhibit A.1 IMPUTATION OF MISSING EARNINGS AND
EMPLOYMENT VARIABLES

Imputation steps	Percentage of person-months undergoing imputation in each step
First step	4.2
Where overtime hours or pay, tip and bonus earnings, and/or weeks of layoff are missing, calculate total earnings (or hours) as regular earnings (hours) times the average ratio of total to regular earnings (hours) for the rest of the sample (i.e., in months in which both are available).	
Second step	1.8
Where regular hours, pay period, or pay per pay period are missing, impute total monthly hours and/or earnings as the mean of the measure across all other months with employment for that individual.	
Third step	2.1
If hours and/or earnings are missing for all reported jobs, predict monthly hours and/or earnings from a regression equation estimated on all person-months with employment, using as regressors the respondent's baseline characteristics, characteristics of the most recent job in the follow-up period, and time since random assignment.	

EARNINGS DATA FROM STATE UNEMPLOYMENT INSURANCE AGENCIES

State agencies responsible for administering the unemployment insurance (UI) program collect quarterly data on wages and salaries for most workers. These "wage reports" are submitted by employers for individual workers, identified by their Social Security numbers (SSNs). Data obtained from these systems in 12 of the 16 sites are used in the analysis.[8]

Content and Collection Method

Not all employers file wage reports with the UI system. Notable exceptions include federal government, railroad and agricultural employers, and the self-employed. Despite these omissions, an in-depth study of UI earnings data concluded recently that "the vast majority of employers are covered in all states."[9] In most cases total earnings are reported for each covered job, including wages, salaries, tips, and bonuses.

We obtained UI earnings data through agreements with state UI administrators. Data requests were submitted to each state at regular intervals, usually every six months. Each request contained the SSNs of all experimental sample members in the site who had been randomly assigned by that time. The states used the SSNs to extract earnings data for the sample. Most data files received from the states contain five calendar quarters of data, with a response lag of one or two quarters.

Each earnings record was matched to the research database by SSN and, where possible, by name and/or date of birth. Incomplete or flawed data files were re-requested and any problems were discussed with state staff members. For each SSN, states would supply zero, one, or more records for each quarter, depending on the number of covered jobs held by the person during the quarter.

Completeness

State data files received by the study team were subjected to checks of completeness. For example, quarterly record counts were compared with expected counts based on follow-up survey data and with counts in other quarters; successive data files were compared for consistency. If a state data file was judged to have incomplete data for a particular quarter (as was often true for the last quarter covered by the file), that file's data for that quarter would not be used in the analysis. Since successive data files usually overlapped by one or two quarters, data for incomplete quarters could usually be obtained from the next data file supplied by the state.

In the 12 sites where UI earnings data were used in the analysis, the data are complete for virtually all experimental sample members, subject to the caveat that not all employment is reported to the UI system. The length of follow-up in the UI data varies by random assignment cohort; some late random assignment cohorts in Jackson and Omaha were excluded from the 30-month earnings sample because there were not enough follow-up quarters of UI data (see Appendix B).

Construction of Edited Variables

UI earnings data for individual sample members were collapsed into a set of quarterly earnings variables through a series of three steps.

First, for each data file, earnings across jobs within each quarter were summed. Second, total earnings for each quarter were extracted from the most recent data file that provided complete data for that quarter. Third, zero earnings were imputed for those quarters in which the state provided complete data on covered jobs but no record for the person in question.

STATE AFDC AND FOOD STAMP RECORDS

State welfare agencies maintain monthly records of payments to individual recipients of Aid to Families with Dependent Children (AFDC) and food stamps. State records on AFDC in four sites and food stamps in two sites were used in the analysis.

Content, Collection Method, and Completeness

As the state welfare records are maintained by the same agencies that administer the welfare benefits, they would, under ideal circumstances, contain complete and accurate information on the AFDC and food stamp benefits received by sample members. However, as explained below, only a few states were able to provide complete data.

Data on the amount of AFDC and food stamp benefits received during each calendar month were obtained through agreements with state welfare agencies. Data requests were submitted to each state at regular intervals, in most cases every three to six months. Each request contained the Social Security numbers (SSNs) of all experimental sample members in the site who had been randomly assigned by that time. The states used the SSNs to extract benefit data for the sample.

State data files received by the study team were subjected to checks of completeness. For example, monthly record counts were compared with expected counts based on Background Information Form data and with counts in other months; successive data files were compared for consistency. In some states, data files were incomplete because only data on welfare cases active in the month the file was created were retrieved. In other states, programming errors resulted in incomplete files. Although incomplete or flawed data files were re-requested and problems were discussed with state staff members, only four states (California, Colorado, Illinois, and Indiana) were able to provide complete data on AFDC, and only two states (Colorado and Indiana) were able to provide complete data on food stamps.[10]

Construction of Edited Variables

Benefits for each month were extracted from the most recent data file that provided data for that month. Zero benefits were imputed for those months in which the state provided complete data on benefits paid but no record for the person in question.

EXPENDITURE DATA FROM 16 SDAS

Data on JTPA program expenditures were requested from each SDA for use in the benefit-cost analysis. The data collected measure Title II expenditures for all program activities in the SDA during Program Year 1988 (1987 in Decatur). Appendix B explains how these data were used, in conjunction with enrollment and tracking data and cost data from other sources, in the benefit-cost analysis.

We collected data for program year 1988 because the majority of the study sample in each SDA was randomly assigned in program year 1988, with the exception of Decatur, where random assignment took place during program year 1987 and data were collected for that program year. We conducted visits to each SDA to collect expenditure data. This effort included an accounting of all expenditures funded by Title II. The primary source was the general ledger of expenditures, but we also referred to vendor contracts, vendor invoices, and summary expenditure reports prepared for state agencies.

Although all SDAs are required to record expenditures in the categories of administrative, supportive service, and training, the allocation of expenditures to specific Title II activities was not readily available from the general ledger. We collected information from SDA staff to identify specific activities associated with expenditures recorded in the general ledger and other sources. SDA fiscal staff were generally able to identify the activities associated with specific expenditures.

Allocating staff salaries to specific activities required additional efforts. In most cases, staff salaries were identified as a single entry in the general ledger. To allocate salary expenditures to specific activities, we designed a Staff Time Allocation Form (STAF) on which all SDA staff recorded the number of hours spent on each of seven Title

II activities: classroom training in occupational skills; on-the-job training; job search assistance; basic education; work experience; outreach, intake, and assessment; and the National JTPA Study. STAFs were administered during three weeks—one week in fall, one in winter, and one in spring. Using the time allocation and the salary for each staff member, we calculated the percentage of salary expenditures to be allocated to each activity.[11]

To allocate administrative and other costs not directly attributed to a specific activity, we applied the proportions of total allocable costs that were directly attributable to each activity. For example, if SDA records indicated that 15 percent of all training and supportive service expenditures were readily identified as expenditures for job search assistance (JSA), we applied this percentage to administrative and other costs to arrive at the total administrative and other costs to be allocated to JSA. Further allocation was required for some SDAs in which supportive service expenditures were not directly attributable to a specific activity; these costs were distributed based on the proportion of participants in each activity.

Another division was made between expenditures for adult and youth enrollees. The SDA expenditure ledgers generally either separated adult and youth expenditures or gave the overall proportion of costs attributable to each. We allocated costs reported by other sources according to the proportions in the ledgers.

After these allocations were made, we calculated, for adult and youth enrollees separately, site-specific measures of total Title II expenditures for program year 1988 in each of nine categories: classroom training in occupational skills; on-the-job training (OJT); job search assistance; basic education; work experience; customized training; direct placement; outreach, intake, and assessment; and the National JTPA Study.[12] In the case of OJT, we calculated the total costs of wage subsidies, as well as other costs (job development, monitoring of OJT positions) associated with OJT.

PUBLISHED SCHOOL EXPENDITURE DATA

JTPA expenditure and enrollment data cannot independently provide adequate cost measures for a social benefit—cost analysis, for two reasons. First, JTPA expenditures on basic education and classroom training in occupational skills are likely to represent less than the full resource costs of providing those services.[13] Second, the costs of non-

JTPA employment and training services received by treatment and control group members must be included in a benefit-cost analysis.

As explained in Appendix B, the benefit-cost analysis uses First Follow-up Survey data on the employment and training services received by treatment and control group members, in conjunction with JTPA expenditure and enrollment data, published school expenditure data, and a telephone survey of vocational/technical schools named by First Follow-up Survey respondents. This section describes the published school expenditure data.

Two- and Four-Year Colleges

Research Associates of Washington (n.d.) contains institution-level data collected by the National Center for Education Statistics, U.S. Department of Education, on expenditures per student at two- and four-year colleges. Estimated full instructional costs per full-time enrolled student are reported. Estimated full instructional costs equal the sum of expenditures on instruction, student services, academic and institutional support, and plant operation and maintenance, less 33.3 percent of expenditures on funded research and public service.

We used this source to obtain the full annual cost of instruction per full-time student at 119 institutions that First Follow-up Survey respondents reported attending. We converted these annual costs to costs per hour using information provided by staff at the U.S. Department of Education, regarding the typical number of hours in a full-time year at two- and four-year colleges.

High Schools

The U.S. Bureau of the Census (1991) reports annual federal, state, and local government expenditures per pupil for educational instruction, disaggregated by state or large public school system (enrollment of 15,000 or more). Only expenditures for regular elementary and secondary school students are included; special education and adult education programs were excluded from the survey. From this source, we obtained expenditures at the school district level for 9 of the 16 SDAs; at the county level for 1 SDA; and at the state level for the remaining 6 SDAs. We converted these annual expenditure figures to site-specific estimates of cost per hour, using information provided by staff at the Education Commission of the States, who provided a listing of the required number of school days in each state and information about the typical number of hours in a school day.

TELEPHONE SURVEY OF VOCATIONAL INSTITUTIONS

Published data on institution-level expenditures for vocational and technical institutes are not available. To obtain measures of per student expenditures for such institutions, we conducted a telephone survey of vocational and technical schools named by First Follow-up Survey respondents. This telephone survey was designed to collect information on the tuition charged for a full-time student, the type of course associated with the tuition, and the total number of classroom hours associated with the tuition. If various levels of tuition were charged for different types of courses, we asked for information on the various tuitions charged. We collected this information both for the 1988–89 school year and for the 1992–93 school year.

On the First Follow-up Survey, 2,782 respondents classified their most recently attended schools or training programs as business schools (vocational), technical institutes, or other vocational training. Specific names for these institutions were provided by 2,176 respondents, who named 416 different institutions. We were able to obtain cost data for 41 of these institutions from Research Associates of Washington (n.d.), discussed earlier. We targeted our tuition survey at the most frequently mentioned of the remaining 375 institutions.

To be included in our tuition survey, an institution had to be named by at least 5 percent of those First Follow-up Survey respondents in the study site who reported attending a vocational program. The 64 institutions that met this criterion were named by a total of 1,530 respondents. We received information from a total of 50 institutions, accounting for 44 percent of all First Follow-up Survey responses in the vocational categories. This, combined with the published cost data, brings the data coverage to 68 percent of all follow-up survey responses in the vocational categories. The information we collected was used to calculate institution-specific measures of cost per classroom hour.

Notes

1. Information identifying the persons in the study sample is omitted from the public use file.

2. Appendix B explains that in the impact analysis, these data were combined with follow-up survey data on sample members in other sites.

3. The form also explained the confidentiality of the data and solicited the applicant's (or the applicant's parent's or guardian's) permission to secure information on the applicant from other public agencies.

4. For Decatur, we collected expenditure and enrollment and tracking data for program year 1987 because the experimental sample in Decatur was enrolled primarily during that year.

5. Because the survey was conducted over a 16-month period, whereas random assignment occurred over a 23-month period, the scheduled length of follow-up was shorter for late random assignment cohorts than for early cohorts. The actual length of follow-up was sometimes longer than scheduled because of time lags in locating and interviewing sample members.

6. Calendar months were used to define these variables. For example, if the date of random assignment was March 9, 1989, then month 0 was defined as March 1989, month 1 as April 1989, and so on. The month of random assignment (month 0) was not included in the impact analysis.

7. Monthly values exceeding 347 hours of work were replaced, affecting 0.6 percent of all person-months. Earnings data were replaced in the 0.7 percent of person-months in which the ratio of earnings to hours worked (earnings per hour) fell below $.50 or exceeded $50 and in the person-months in which hours exceeded 347.

8. The data received from California, Montana, and New Jersey were incomplete or inaccurate; Ohio did not agree to provide data.

9. See Baj, Trott, and Stevens (1991). Note, however, that because we collected data only from the states in which study sites were located, jobs in other states are not recorded in our UI records.

10. Iowa and Mississippi provided complete data on certain response files but not others. The data from these states therefore had gaps in coverage and were not used in the analysis for this report.

11. In three sites it was not necessary to allocate salary costs in this manner. In Coosa Valley and Oakland, all training activities were provided under single-service contracts with vendors. Outreach, intake, and assessment services were also provided by a vendor. In Providence, the SDA accounting system tracked salary costs by activity.

12. While customized training and direct placement were not included as categories on the STAFs, some SDAs had expenditures for these activities recorded in their general ledgers.

13. The SDA often pays only a portion of the tuition for a JTPA enrollee to attend a course. In addition, tuition is often lower than the full resource cost, especially at public institutions.

ESTIMATION METHODS

This appendix specifies the samples analyzed; the measures of outcomes, service receipt, and cost; and the statistical methods used for this study. First, we define the target groups. We then discuss the estimation of impacts on earnings, educational attainment, AFDC and food stamp benefits, arrest rates, employment and training services received, hours of employment or training, and costs of services received. The sections on impacts on earnings and educational attainment introduce some of the methods mentioned in later sections. Appendix B of Orr et al. (1994) covers the same topics in more extensive detail.

TARGET GROUPS

This study estimates program impacts on five target groups: adult women, adult men, female youths, male youth non-arrestees, and male youth arrestees. Adults were at least 22 years old at random assignment; youths were 16 to 21 years old at random assignment. Age and gender were determined from Background Information Form data.

Male youths were classified as arrestees or non-arrestees according to First and Second Follow-up Survey data. The First Follow-up asked each youth respondent, "Between your 16th birthday and [the date of random assignment], were you ever arrested and charged with a crime or a parole violation?" Among the 2,094 male youth respondents, 483 answered yes; 1,569 answered no; and 42 did not answer the question. The Second Follow-up asked the same question of each youth respondent who had not had a First Follow-up interview. Among the 133 male youths who responded to the Second Follow-up but not the First, 34 answered yes; 93 answered no; and 6 did not answer the question.[1]

We classified as arrestees the 517 male youths who answered yes to the preceding question on either the First or Second Follow-up Survey.

The remaining 2,041 male youths in the full experimental sample, including those who did not respond to the surveys and those who did not answer the question, were classified as non-arrestees.

IMPACTS ON EARNINGS

Sample and Outcome Measure

BASIC APPROACH

For 12 of the 16 study sites (hereafter, the "UI sites"), earnings data are available from the First and Second Follow-up Surveys and unemployment insurance (UI) wage records. For the remaining four sites (Butte, Mont.; Jersey City, N.J.; Marion, Ohio; and Oakland, Calif.— hereafter, the "non-UI sites"), usable UI data were not obtained, so the follow-up surveys are the only source of earnings data.

The First Follow-up Survey attempted to interview all experimental sample members; because of cost considerations, the Second Follow-up attempted to interview only a random subsample (see Appendix A). For persons who responded to the First Follow-up but either were not sampled for or did not respond to the Second Follow-up, monthly survey earnings data are available for the first 12 to 37 months after random assignment (21 months, on average). For persons who responded to the Second Follow-up, monthly survey earnings data are available for the first 20 to 48 months after random assignment (35 months, on average). Thus, survey earnings data for the full 30-month period analyzed in this study are available for only a subset of the experimental sample, primarily Second Follow-up respondents. In the later random assignment cohorts, even Second Follow-up respondents do not typically have 30 months of survey earnings data.

In the UI sites, UI earnings data are available for virtually all experimental sample members. For about three-quarters of the experimental sample in these sites, the UI data cover all of the calendar quarters corresponding to the first 30 months after random assignment. For the later random assignment cohorts, data for the last one to three calendar quarters in this period are missing.

We conducted a comparison of the survey and UI earnings data for the subsample for which both data sources were available (including those with zero earnings in either or both data sets).[2] The main conclusions were:

- Mean survey earnings were higher than mean UI earnings for all target groups, all sites, and all follow-up quarters.
- Overall employment rates from the two data sources were similar.
- The difference between the data sources could not be explained by out-of-state employment, lags in reporting earnings to UI, or errors in Social Security numbers.
- Errors in the reporting of overtime earnings on the survey (discussed later in this section) explained some, but not all, of the difference.
- For all target groups except the male youth arrestees, the treatment and control groups had similar ratios of mean survey to mean UI earnings, so that the two data sources produced similar percentage impact estimates.
- For male youth arrestees, the survey data suggested large negative impacts, whereas the UI data showed no appreciable impact.

In the subsample for which both data sources were available, it was not possible to determine which data source was more reliable. Moreover, in the full experimental sample, each data source has its own gaps: the UI data are not available for four sites and miss jobs not covered by UI, whereas the survey data are potentially subject to recall error and nonresponse bias, and have shorter follow-up for most sample members (because only a random subsample was selected for the Second Follow-up Survey).

As a compromise between the goals of including as large a sample as possible and including as many months of follow-up as possible, we chose the largest possible sample that had earnings data for the first 30 months after random assignment and that preserved the statistical properties of a randomized experiment. The details of the sample definition and the construction of the outcome measure are provided in the subsections following. For all target groups except male youth arrestees, the basic approach was as follows. In the non-UI sites, we used survey earnings, and we included only Second Follow-up respondents. In the UI sites, we used survey earnings for those persons with 30 months of survey data. For the remainder of the sample in the UI sites, we used UI earnings, multiplied by the ratio of mean survey to mean UI earnings in the portion of the sample for which both data sources were available.

THE 30-MONTH EARNINGS SAMPLE

The analysis of impacts on earnings was based on a 15,981-person subsample of the full experimental sample of 20,601 persons. Members of the full experimental sample were excluded from the 30-month analysis sample for any of several reasons, discussed next. Exhibit 2.4 in Chapter 2 lists the number of sample members who remained at each stage of the process, by target group.

First, we excluded certain experimental sample members who were randomly assigned at a different treatment/control ratio than the majority of the sample. The standard ratio was 2/1. During the course of random assignment, however, five SDAs that had difficulty recruiting JTPA applicants were allowed to increase the treatment/control ratio temporarily to 3/1 or 6/1 for specific target groups. To keep the treatment and control groups well-matched on site and cohort, we randomly selected and excluded from the analysis one-third of those treatment group members assigned using a 3/1 ratio and two-thirds of those treatment group members assigned using a 6/1 ratio. This procedure excluded 473 "extra" treatment group members.

The 5 sample members in Oakland who were under age 22 at random assignment (according to Background Information Form data) were dropped, because youths were excluded from the experimental design in Oakland. We then excluded all remaining sample members randomly assigned after December 1988 in Jackson; April 1989 in Butte, Jersey City, and Marion; and June 1989 in Omaha. These "late cohorts," containing 1,104 persons, were excluded because they were randomly assigned too late to have 30 months of follow-up data. Next, in the four non-UI sites, we excluded the 2,672 remaining sample members who were *not* part of the random subsample that the Second Follow-up Survey attempted to interview. This exclusion was made because very few of these persons had 30 months of follow-up data. In the four non-UI sites, we also excluded the remaining 43 male youth arrestees. This was done because the survey and UI data gave contradictory results for male youth arrestees in the other 12 sites. To allow a comparison of the two data sources over a common sample for this target group, we excluded the male youth arrestees in the non-UI sites.

The preceding exclusions left the treatment and control groups well-matched because either they were applied to the two groups symmetrically or (in the case of the exclusion of the "extra" treatment group members) they restored symmetry between the two groups. The sample remaining after these "exogenous" exclusions contained 16,304 persons. From this sample, 323 persons were dropped because of missing data. Almost all of this sample loss was in the non-UI sites; in the UI sites, there was virtually no sample loss at this stage because

UI earnings records were used for survey nonrespondents. The 30-month earnings sample consists of the remaining 15,981 persons.

IMPUTATIONS APPLIED TO SURVEY DATA

Appendix A describes the monthly earnings measures that were constructed from the First and Second Follow-up Survey data. Several imputations were applied to these data before they were used in the impact analysis. The survey data typically covered only a portion of the month of the last interview. We imputed earnings for the entire month by extrapolation. For example, if the Second Follow-up interview took place on August 16, 1991, and the monthly earnings measure showed $480 for August 1–16, then we set earnings for August 1991 to $930, based on the rate of $30/day for the period observed.

Two findings suggested that the survey earnings data exaggerate overtime earnings. First, our comparison of the survey and UI earnings data found that the proportion by which survey earnings exceeded UI earnings tended to be substantially higher when overtime earnings had been reported on the survey.[3] Second, overtime earnings as a proportion of total earnings reported on the survey were implausibly high: 14.5 percent for adult women, 20.9 percent for adult men, 18.0 percent for female youths, and 21.9 percent for male youths in the fourth quarter after random assignment.[4]

The apparent exaggeration of overtime earnings may be due to the wording of the survey questions. Respondents who answered yes to "Did you work any paid overtime on this job?" were then asked "How many overtime hours did you work in an average week?" and "How much overtime pay did you usually earn in an average week before taxes and other deductions?" It was probably natural for respondents to give the average for those weeks in which they worked overtime, not the average for all weeks. Because the monthly earnings and hours measures described in Appendix A assume that the respondents' answers apply to all weeks on the job, these measures are likely to exaggerate overtime earnings and hours.

In addition, our inspection of a sample of observations with very high overtime earnings showed that overtime earnings were sometimes grossly overstated because of errors such as (a) recording total earnings instead of overtime earnings or (b) recording the hourly overtime wage rate in cents instead of weekly overtime earnings in dollars.

We edited the overtime earnings data to adjust for the averaging errors and gross errors described previously. First, we attempted to correct gross errors: for all person-months for which overtime hourly earnings were greater than three times regular hourly earnings and also greater than $10.05/hour, we reset overtime earnings to 1.5 × regular hourly earnings × overtime hours.[5] Second, we attempted to adjust for averaging errors by multiplying all overtime earnings values by a factor that was derived from a comparison of survey and UI earnings for observations with and without overtime earnings on the survey. This factor was 0.35 for adult women, 0.70 for adult men, 0.42 for female youths, 0.50 for male youth non-arrestees, and 0.76 for male youth arrestees.[6]

Finally, in the non-UI sites, we imputed earnings in the last one to three months of the 30-month period for 114 persons who had earnings data for the first 27 months but not for all 30 months. We imputed the value from the most recent month with valid earnings data.

IMPUTATIONS APPLIED TO UI DATA

A small number of observations in the UI data had unusually large earnings values. For 103 persons, earnings exceeded $10,000 in a calendar quarter. We judged the accuracy of these values by comparing them with values in adjacent quarters. We classified 51 values of quarterly UI earnings as erroneous outliers.

For quarterly UI earnings values which were either missing or erroneous outliers, we almost always imputed earnings from the nearest quarter with valid data.[7] Imputations were most common near the end of the 10 quarters of follow-up. About 6 percent of all persons with UI earnings data had imputed values in the quarter of random assignment. In each of postassignment quarters 1 through 7, only 2 to 5 percent of values were imputed. After quarter 7, the percentage of sample members with imputed values rose—to 8 percent in quarter 8, 15 percent in quarter 9, and 25 percent in quarter 10.

Next, for each target group, we computed the ratio of mean survey earnings to mean UI earnings in the sample of person-quarters that had both survey and UI data, including those with zero earnings in either or both data sets. (We computed this ratio after adjusting the survey overtime data.) This ratio was 1.22 for adult women, 1.35 for adult men, 1.34 for female youths, 1.52 for male youth non-arrestees, and 1.84 for male youth arrestees.[8] We multiplied all UI earnings values by this ratio, "scaling" the UI data for the purpose of combining UI and survey data in the analysis (as described later).

Finally, we converted the time units for the UI earnings data from calendar quarters to months and then to quarters after random assignment by assuming that earnings were distributed equally among the three months of each calendar quarter. For example, consider a sample member randomly assigned on October 22, 1988. UI earnings data are available for quarters 1988:4 (October–December), 1989:1, and so forth. In our impact analysis, however, follow-up month 1 for this person is November 1988 and follow-up quarter 1 is November 1988 through January 1989. For follow-up months 1 and 2, we set "monthly UI earnings" equal to one-third of quarter 1988:4 earnings. For follow-up month 3 (January 1989), we set monthly UI earnings equal to one-third of quarter 1989:1 earnings. We then set UI earnings for follow-up quarter 1 equal to the sum of monthly UI earnings for follow-up months 1–3.

COMBINING SURVEY AND UI DATA

For adult women, adult men, female youths, and male youth non-arrestees, we pooled survey and UI data as follows. In the non-UI sites, we used survey earnings and included only Second Follow-up Survey respondents in the 30-month earnings sample. In the UI sites, we used survey earnings for persons who were sampled for the Second Follow-up and had 30 months of survey data. For all other persons in the UI sites, we used scaled UI data (as described previously), for all 30 months of the follow-up period. Thus, for each person in these four target groups, we used a single data source for all months. This approach was adopted, rather than using survey data for all months for which they were available and scaled UI data for the remaining months, to avoid confounding changes in impact over time with differences in data sources. The mix of data sources for each target group is shown in Exhibit B.1.

For male youth arrestees, we did not combine the two data sources, because they gave divergent results. We present impact estimates from survey data and scaled UI data separately. In months 1–18, both survey and UI data are available for 416 persons. In months 19–30, UI

Exhibit B.1 NUMBER OF OBSERVATIONS FROM EACH DATA SOURCE IN 30-MONTH EARNINGS ANALYSIS

	Four Non-UI sites	Twelve UI sites		
	Survey data	Survey data	Scaled UI data	Total
Adult women	280	893	4,929	6,102
Adult men	252	797	4,053	5,102
Female youths	198	1,130	1,329	2,657
Male youth non-arrestees	115	636	953	1,704

Note: Male youth arrestees are not included in this exhibit because we did not pool survey and UI data for that target group.

Exhibit B.2 BASELINE CHARACTERISTICS USED AS COVARIATES IN
           IMPACT REGRESSIONS

Ethnicity
   Two dummies: Black, non-Hispanic; Hispanic
   (*Omitted: White, non-Hispanic; American Indian; Alaskan Native; Asian; or Pacific
   Islander*)

Education and training histories
   High school diploma (dummy)
   General educational development certificate (GED) (dummy)
   Ever received vocational or occupational training (dummy)

Work histories
   Ever employed (dummy)
   Employed at application (dummy)
   Total earnings in 12 months before application
   Weeks worked in past 12 months (two dummies; *omitted: zero*):
      1–12 weeks
      13–52 weeks

Public assistance histories
   Receiving AFDC at application (dummy)
   Ever AFDC case head (dummy)
   Years ever as AFDC case head (2 dummies; *omitted: less than 2 years*):
      2–5 years
      More than 5 years
   Receiving food stamps at application (dummy)
   Received unemployment compensation anytime in 12 months before application
      (dummy)
   Required to apply to JTPA in order to receive welfare or as part of WIN (dummy)

Household composition
   (two dummies; omitted: *No spouse or own child present*)
   Own child living at home, no spouse present
   Married, living with spouse

Number of own children age 18 or younger living at home

(continued)

---

data are available for all 416 persons, but survey data are available
through month 30 for only 217 persons, because only a random subsample was selected for the Second Follow-up Survey.

Impacts per Assignee, by Target Group or
Service Strategy Subgroup

This subsection explains the estimation of impacts per assignee as
well as treatment and control means (including quarterly earnings
trends) at the target group or service strategy subgroup levels. We use
ordinary least squares to regress earnings on a treatment group

Exhibit B.2 BASELINE CHARACTERISTICS USED AS COVARIATES IN
IMPACT REGRESSIONS (continued)

Family income in 12 months before application
   Five dummies: Less than $3,000; $3,000–$6,000; $6,001–$9,000; $9,001–$12,000;
   and $12,001–$15,000 (omitted: more than $15,000)

Living in public housing (dummy)

Car available for regular use (dummy)

Telephone at home (dummy)

Age at random assignment (dummies)
   For youths (omitted: 16–17):
      18–19 years
      20–21 years

   For adults:
      22–25 years
      26–29 years
      30–35 years
      36–44 years
      45–54 years
      (omitted—55 years of age or older):

Recommended program services
   Six dummies, not mutually exclusive. The six service categories are: classroom
   training in occupational skills; on-the-job training; job search assistance; basic
   education; work experience; and miscellaneous services.

Site
   Full set of dummies, omitting one. Number of dummies depends on target group
   and outcome measure.

Second Follow-up Sample
   Dummy indicates whether person was randomly sampled for Second Follow-up
   Survey. Because only UI earnings data were used for those not sampled for the
   Second Follow-up, whereas survey earnings data were often used for those in the
   Second Follow-up sample, this regressor may explain part of the variance of the
   outcome measure in certain time periods or subgroups.

Source: Data source for all regressors except the last is Background Information Form
file. Some regressors were omitted from regressions for certain target groups or
subgroups to avoid multicollinearity.

dummy and the baseline covariates, shown in Exhibit B.2. Where the
value of a baseline covariate is missing, we insert the target group
mean. A separate regression is estimated for each target group, for
each service strategy subgroup within each target group, and for each
period analyzed. The estimated coefficient on treatment is our estimate of the impact per assignee. We estimate the control mean by
substituting the target group or subgroup mean covariate values into

the estimated model and setting the treatment dummy to zero.[9] The estimated treatment group mean is the sum of the estimated control mean and the impact estimate.

For the male youth arrestees, we present two impact estimates, one from survey data and one from scaled UI data. The estimate from scaled UI data is computed by the method described previously. The estimate from survey data is derived by a more complicated procedure.[10] The complication arises because although survey data for months 1–18 are available for all 416 male youth arrestees in the 30-month earnings sample (hereafter, "the arrestees"), survey data for the full 30-month follow-up period are available for only 217 male youth arrestees (hereafter, "the long follow-up group"). The long follow-up group is an approximately random subsample of the arrestees, because the Second Follow-up Survey attempted to interview a random subset of the experimental sample. Therefore, if we can ignore potentially nonrandom attrition between the two follow-up surveys, a consistent impact estimate for the arrestees can be derived solely from the long follow-up group. However, efficiency would be lost by ignoring the data for months 1–18 for the short follow-up group (the 199 arrestees outside the long follow-up group).

To estimate the impact on arrestees' earnings consistently without losing the information from the short follow-up group, we adapted a "difference estimator" analyzed by Konijn (1983) and derived its standard error without Konijn's independence assumptions. To understand the approach, first consider the problem of estimating a mean. Suppose we want to use survey data to estimate mean earnings during the 30-month follow-up period for the arrestees. We could simply take mean 30-month earnings for the long follow-up group. However, a more efficient estimate can be obtained by adding (1) mean earnings during months 1–18 for the arrestees and (2) mean earnings during months 19–30 for the long follow-up group. Let x denote earnings during months 1–18 and y denote earnings during months 19–30. To derive an estimate of standard error, note that the mean of x for the arrestees can be expressed as the sum of (199/416) times the mean of x for the short follow-up group and (217/416) times the mean of x for the long follow-up group. Therefore, our estimate of mean 30-month earnings can be expressed as the sum of (1) the mean of (199/416) · x for the short follow-up group and (2) the mean of (217/416) · x + y for the long follow-up group. Under random sampling from an infinite population, the covariance of (1) and (2) is zero, so the variance of their sum is the sum of their variances.

Applying this idea to impact estimation with regression adjustment, we estimate one regression with the short follow-up group and one regression with the long follow-up group. In the short follow-up group, we regress (199/416) x on the treatment dummy and the baseline covariates shown in Exhibit B.2. In the long follow-up group, we regress (217/416) x + y on the same regressors. Our impact estimate is the sum of the treatment coefficients from the two regressions; its estimated standard error is the square root of the sum of the estimated variances. The estimated control mean is the sum of the estimated control means from the two regressions.

Tests for Changes in Impact Over Time

To assess the statistical significance of apparent changes in impact over time, we performed tests of the following null hypotheses: (1) annualized impacts in the in-program period (months 1–6) and the first postprogram year (months 7–18) were equal; and (2) impacts in the first and second postprogram years were equal.

The tests are based on the fact that the *change in impact* on earnings between two periods is equal to the *impact on the change* in earnings between the periods. So the null hypothesis of zero change in impact is equivalent to the hypothesis of zero impact on the change in earnings. We therefore regressed the change in earnings on the treatment dummy and the baseline covariates in Exhibit B.2 and performed the two-tailed *t* test on the treatment coefficient. The dependent variables corresponding to the null hypotheses in the previous paragraph were (1) earnings in postprogram year 1, minus annualized in-program earnings (i.e., earnings in months 1–6 times two); and (2) earnings in postprogram year 2, minus earnings in postprogram year 1.

Impacts per Assignee, by Study Site or Key Subgroup

Exhibits 4.5 and 4.16 present impact estimates by study site; Exhibits 5.8, 5.9, 5.19, and 5.20 present impact estimates for key subgroups of the target groups. All subgroups were defined using information from the random assignment telephone file or the Background Information Form. Persons who were missing data on a variable used to define subgroups were not included in any of the relevant subgroups.

We estimate one regression for each set of complementary subgroups (e.g., the study sites or the three ethnicity subgroups). Defining a dummy variable for membership in each subgroup, we regress 30-month earnings on the subgroup dummies, the interactions of treatment with the subgroup dummies, and the baseline covariates in Exhibit B.2. (The uninteracted treatment dummy is omitted to avoid multicollinearity. Certain baseline covariates are also omitted when necessary.) Our estimates of impact per assignee are the coefficients on the treatment × subgroup interactions.

To perform an *F* test of the null hypothesis that the true impacts on complementary subgroups are equal, we estimate an auxiliary regression in which the treatment × subgroup interactions are replaced by the uninteracted treatment dummy. This regression restricts the impacts on the subgroups to be equal. The *F* test compares the sums of squared residuals from the restricted and unrestricted regressions.

The estimated control means in Exhibits 5.8, 5.9, 5.19, and 5.20 are the unadjusted means for control group members within each subgroup.

Impacts per Enrollee

The previously specified impact estimates represent the average effect of access to JTPA on all treatment group members, whether they received JTPA services or not. Between 31 percent and 38 percent of the treatment group members in each target group did not enroll in JTPA, and 1.1 percent to 2.4 percent of the control group members did enroll. To estimate the program's effect on persons who actually enrolled, we use an adjustment proposed by Bloom (1984).[11] The adjustment relies on the following assumptions:[12] (1) Assignment to the treatment group has zero average effect on those who do not enroll in JTPA; (2) The JTPA enrollees in the control group (crossovers) would also enroll if they were assigned to the treatment group; and (3) Average outcome levels for the crossovers are the same as if they had been assigned to the treatment group.

Under these assumptions, assignment to the treatment group has zero average effect on everyone except those treatment group members who did enroll in JTPA but would not have enrolled if they had been assigned to the control group. We call this group the "non-crossover-type enrollees." The estimate of impact per assignee dilutes the program impact on the non-crossover-type enrollees by averaging it with the zero effect on all other treatment group members. To recover a consistent estimate of the impact on non-crossover-type enrollees, we divide the estimated impact per assignee by the difference between the treatment and control group enrollment rates (an estimate of the percentage of treatment group members who were non-crossover-type enrollees). Although this estimate of *impact per enrollee* pertains to non-crossover-type enrollees only, all but a small fraction of the enrollees in the study sample belong to this group.

Chapter 2 discusses the possible bias due to violations of assumption 1. Because the crossover rate is low, violations of assumptions 2 and 3 are unlikely to impart substantial bias to the estimated impacts per enrollee. Under assumptions 1–3, the null hypothesis of zero impact on non-crossover-type enrollees is equivalent to the hypothesis of zero impact per assignee. Therefore, our significance levels for impacts per enrollee are the same as those for impacts per assignee. Our estimated standard errors for impacts per enrollee are derived by treating the observed enrollment rates as fixed: we multiply the estimated standard errors for impacts per assignee by the same factors used to convert the point estimates from per assignee to per enrollee terms.[13]

Estimated impacts on earnings per enrollee are expressed in both dollar and percentage terms. The denominator for the percentage calculation is an estimate of what enrollees would have earned in the absence of the program. To estimate the latter, we subtract the estimated impact per enrollee from the unadjusted mean earnings of treatment group enrollees.

Decomposing Earnings Impacts into Impacts on Hours Worked and Impacts on Hourly Earnings

A worker's earnings can be expressed as the product of hours worked and hourly earnings. Letting y_i denote earnings and h_i hours worked, this statement is simply

$$y_i = h_i \, (y_i/h_i).$$

Analogously, the mean earnings of a group (including workers and non-workers) can be expressed as the product of two components. Let Y and H denote mean earnings and mean hours worked, respectively, with zeros included. We can express Y as the product of two components:

$$Y = H \, (Y/H).$$

When percentage impacts on the two components are small, the percentage impact on mean earnings is approximately equal to the sum of the percentage impacts on the components. The first component is mean hours worked. The second component is mean earnings divided by mean hours worked. We refer to this component as "average hourly earnings," but it is not necessarily equal to the mean of hourly earnings (y_i/h_i) for persons who worked. Rather, it is a weighted mean, with the weight on each person proportional to his or her hours worked.

To estimate the percentage impacts on mean hours worked and average hourly earnings, we first estimate the treatment and control means of hours worked. Data on hours worked are available only from the follow-up surveys, not from UI wage records.[14] Referring to Exhibit B.1, persons in the first two columns have 30 months of hours data. Persons in the third column, except survey nonrespondents, have at least 18 but less than 30 months of hours data. We estimate impact regressions separately for the UI and non-UI sites and take weighted averages with weights reflecting the sample sizes in Exhibit B.1. In the non-UI sites, we simply regress hours worked on treatment and the baseline covariates in Exhibit B.2. In the UI sites, we compute the "difference estimator" described earlier (in the discussion of impacts per assignee by target group). We then take weighted averages of the non-UI-site and UI-site estimates of the treatment and control means. Next, we re-estimate the treatment and control means of earnings, using exactly the same sample and methods used to estimate the treatment and control means of hours worked.

Finally, we derive estimates of percentage impacts on hours worked and hourly earnings from the estimated treatment and control means of hours worked ($\hat{H}^T$ and $\hat{H}^C$) and earnings ($\hat{Y}^T$ and $\hat{Y}^C$).

The estimated percentage impact on hours worked is $\dfrac{\hat{H}^T - \hat{H}^C}{\hat{H}^C}$.

The estimated percentage impact on hourly earnings is

$$\frac{(\hat{Y}^T \div \hat{H}^T) - (\hat{Y}^C \div \hat{H}^C)}{\hat{Y}^C \div \hat{H}^C}.$$

In Exhibit 4.7, the standard error estimates shown in percentage points are derived by treating the control means as fixed. For example, we divide the standard error estimate for the estimated impact on hours worked by the estimated control mean of hours worked.

IMPACTS ON ATTAINMENT OF HIGH SCHOOL DIPLOMA OR GED

Sample and Outcome Measure

Data from the Second Follow-up Survey were used to measure attainment of a high school diploma or general educational development

(GED). All respondents to this survey were asked, "Do you have a high school diploma or GED certificate?" and if so, "When did you receive it?" (month and year).[15] We used the answers to these questions, together with sample members' random assignment dates, to construct a 0/1 outcome measure indicating whether sample members had received either credential during the first 30 months after random assignment.

The *educational attainment analysis sample* consists of those members of the 30-month earnings sample who: (1) answered the preceding questions on the Second Follow-up Survey; (2) were interviewed at least 30 months after random assignment; and (3) answered no to the questions "Did you graduate from high school?" and "Do you have a GED certificate?" on the Background Information Form. This sample contains 301 adult women, 314 adult men, 605 female youths, 413 male youth non-arrestees, and 118 male youth arrestees.

Impact Estimation

Because the outcome measure is taken from the Second Follow-up Survey, the educational attainment analysis sample overrepresents the non-UI sites and underrepresents the UI sites, relative to the full 30-month earnings sample. To represent the UI and non-UI sites in the same proportions as the school dropout subgroup of the 30-month earnings sample, we estimate impacts and control means separately for the UI and non-UI sites (with OLS regressions of the outcome measure on a treatment dummy and baseline covariates) and take weighted averages.

Although the linear model can generate meaningless predicted probabilities for individual observations, the OLS estimates of the treatment and control means and impact are consistent under random assignment (assuming no survey nonresponse bias), because they converge to the unadjusted means and their difference. We use the White (1980) standard error estimator, which remains consistent under misspecification of functional form.[16]

To estimate impacts per enrollee, we first take weighted averages of the UI-site and non-UI-site enrollment rates of treatment and control group members of the educational attainment analysis sample. We divide the estimated impact per assignee by the difference between the weighted-average treatment and control group enrollment rates within the target group.

IMPACTS ON AFDC AND FOOD STAMP BENEFITS

Samples and Outcome Measures

Appendix A describes the state records of monthly AFDC benefits received by sample members in four sites (Oakland; Larimer County, Colo.; Decatur, Ill.; and Fort Wayne, Ind.) and monthly food stamp benefits received by sample members in two sites (Larimer County and Fort Wayne). In addition, First and Second Follow-up Survey data on welfare receipt are available for sample members in several sites where it was judged from the outset of the study that state records could not be obtained. Survey respondents in Butte, Mont., and Providence, R.I., who said they had received AFDC after random assignment were asked to give the months of receipt and the average monthly benefit for each spell of receipt. Similar questions about food stamps were asked of respondents in Butte, Providence, and Northwest Minnesota. Monthly time series were constructed from respondents' answers.

The state records and the survey-derived monthly data were pooled. Missing values for particular months were usually imputed from the nearest month with valid data. The imputation procedure is described in Appendix B of Orr et al. (1994). The analysis excluded those persons randomly assigned too late to have 30 months of follow-up data; the "extra" treatment group members discussed in the section on the 30-month earnings sample; those persons without Second Follow-up data in the sites where we relied on survey data; and the five youths in Oakland. The resulting *AFDC analysis sample* contains 6,206 persons in six sites (Butte, Decatur, Fort Wayne, Larimer County, Oakland, and Providence): 2,433 adult women; 2,260 adult men; 731 female youths; 580 male youth non-arrestees; and 202 male youth arrestees. The *food stamps analysis sample* contains 5,141 persons in five sites (Butte, Fort Wayne, Larimer County, Northwest Minnesota, and Providence): 1,895 adult women; 1,750 adult men; 731 female youths; 569 male youth non-arrestees; and 196 male youth arrestees.

Impact Estimation

We use ordinary least squares to regress total 30-month AFDC benefits and total 30-month food stamp benefits on a treatment dummy and a set of baseline covariates similar to that shown in Exhibit B.2. To conserve degrees of freedom, we use a shorter list of covariates with the male youth arrestee target group. To estimate impact per enrollee, we divide the estimated impact per assignee by the difference between the treatment and control group enrollment rates within the target group in the appropriate analysis sample.

IMPACTS ON ARREST RATES OF YOUTHS

The First Follow-up Survey asked each youth respondent, "Since [date of random assignment], have you ever been arrested and charged with a crime or parole violation?" The Second Follow-up Survey asked the same question for the period since the First Follow-up interview or, if the youth had not had a First Follow-up interview, the period since random assignment. (Adults were not asked these questions.) For youths in the 30-month earnings sample, the First Follow-up interview, if it occurred, took place 12 to 37 months after random assignment (21 months, on average). The Second Follow-up interview, if it occurred, took place 23 to 48 months after random assignment (36 months, on average). We report estimates of arrest rates in the 30-month earnings sample for both the *first follow-up period* (between random assignment and the First Follow-up interview) and the *full follow-up period* (between random assignment and the Second Follow-up interview).

For the first follow-up period, our outcome measure is a 0/1 indicator derived from the First Follow-up question on arrests since random assignment. We estimate impacts separately for the UI and non-UI sites (with OLS regressions of the outcome measure on a treatment dummy and baseline covariates) and take weighted averages (with weights proportional to the sample sizes in Exhibit B.1). The White (1980) standard error estimator is used. For the full follow-up period, we employ a more complicated procedure. In the UI sites, the sample with data for the full follow-up period is smaller than the sample with data for the first follow-up period, because not all members of the 30-month earnings sample in these sites were sampled for the Second Follow-up Survey. But any sample members who were arrested during the first follow-up period clearly were arrested during the full follow-up period. Thus, confining the analysis to Second Follow-up respondents would throw away information. Instead, we use the "difference estimator" described earlier in the section on "Impacts on Earnings" to estimate impacts in the UI sites. In the non-UI sites, we use a single OLS regression. We then take weighted averages of the UI-site and non-UI-site estimates.[17]

To estimate impacts per enrollee, we take weighted averages of the UI-site and non-UI-site enrollment rates and then divide the estimated impact per assignee by the difference between the weighted-average treatment and control group enrollment rates.

EMPLOYMENT AND TRAINING SERVICES RECEIVED

Sample and Measures

JTPA services were not the only employment and training services received by sample members. A number of treatment and control group members received services from non-JTPA sources. To measure the employment and training services that the treatment and control groups received from all sources, we relied on both JTPA enrollment and tracking data and First Follow-up Survey data.

We attempted to measure the hours spent by members of the 30-month earnings sample in six types of employment and training services: (1) basic education, (2) classroom training in occupational skills, (3) job search assistance, (4) on-the-job training, (5) work experience, and (6) other services. Measures of hours in all categories except on-the-job training and work experience were constructed from First Follow-up Survey spell data on schools and training programs attended, including non-JTPA programs. The categories of basic education, classroom training in occupational skills, job search assistance, and other services were formed from responses to a question about the type of program attended. The *basic education* category includes high school, GED preparation, adult basic education, special literacy programs, and English as a Second Language. The *classroom training in occupational skills* category includes vocational school and college (mostly two-year programs). The *job search assistance* category includes job search assistance and Job Club. The *other services* category includes military (non-basic) training, employer training programs, union or labor/management association apprenticeships, and programs not classified as any of the above.

Measures of hours in on-the-job training and work experience were constructed from the JTPA enrollment and tracking data. Hours were calculated from the activity enrollment dates, assuming that the enrollee spent 40 hours per week in the activity.

We summed hours across the six service categories to obtain a measure of total hours of service received. To calculate the percentage of sample members receiving each service, we took the percentage with nonzero hours in that service category. To calculate the percentage receiving any service, we took the percentage with nonzero total hours. Exhibits 4.2, 4.13, 5.3, and 5.13 show a third summary measure of services received, the mean cost. This measure is the sum of the mean "cost to society" and the mean OJT wage subsidy, both of which are discussed in the section below on "Incremental Training Costs."

The analysis sample for employment and training services consists of all First Follow-up Survey respondents in the 30-month earnings sample, except those who reported school or training spells without valid dates. This sample contains 13,283 persons: 5,253 adult women; 4,026 adult men; 2,283 female youths; 1,338 male youth non-arrestees, and 383 male youth arrestees.

Measuring the Service Increment

The estimated treatment and control levels of the percentage receiving a service, mean hours of service, and mean service cost are unadjusted means; the estimated service increment per assignee is the treatment-control difference in means. Our standard error estimate and significance test allow the treatment and control groups to have unequal variances. To estimate the service increment per enrollee, we divide the service increment per assignee by the difference between the treatment and control group enrollment rates.

IMPACTS ON HOURS OF EMPLOYMENT OR TRAINING

Our measure of hours spent in employment or training during the 30-month follow-up period (see Exhibit 5.18 and the accompanying discussion in chapter 5) is the sum of (1) hours worked during the follow-up period and (2) hours receiving employment and training services, excluding on-the-job training and work experience (to avoid double-counting hours already reported as employment). Hours worked were derived from First and Second Follow-up Survey data (see Appendix A and the previous subsection in this appendix on "Decomposing Earnings Impacts into Impacts on Hours Worked and Impacts on Hourly Earnings"). Hours receiving employment and training services were derived from First Follow-up Survey data (see section in this appendix on "Employment and Training Services Received").

The analysis sample consists of all First Follow-up Survey respondents in the 30-month earnings sample who had 30 months of data on hours worked, except those who reported school or training spells without valid dates. Relative to the 30-month earnings sample, this sample overrepresents the non-UI sites and underrepresents the UI sites. To represent the UI and non-UI sites in the same proportions as the 30-month earnings sample, we estimate impacts separately for the UI and non-UI sites and take a weighted average. To estimate impacts per enrollee, we first take weighted averages of the UI-site and non-UI-site enrollment rates of treatment and control group members in the analysis sample. We then divide the estimated impact per assignee by the difference between the weighted-average treatment and control group enrollment rates.

INCREMENTAL TRAINING COSTS

Sample and Measures

SAMPLE

The cost analysis sample is the same as the analysis sample for employment and training services: all First Follow-up Survey respondents in the 30-month earnings sample, except those who reported school or training spells without valid dates.

COST TO SAMPLE MEMBERS

A measure of training costs paid by sample members was constructed from First and Second Follow-up Survey spell data on schools and training programs attended. For each school or training program reported, respondents were asked "Did you or your family pay anything for this school or training?" and if so, "What was the total amount your family paid (in addition to funds from grants or scholarship)?" The spell data were converted into monthly time series variables by a process similar to that described for monthly earnings and employment measures in Appendix A. Because only a subsample had data for the full 30-month follow-up period, we analyzed total out-of-pocket training costs in the first 18 months after random assignment.

COST TO SOCIETY

To measure the cost to society of the employment and training services received by sample members, including non-JTPA services, we relied on the hours measures discussed in the section on "Employment and Training Services Received" above, together with estimated costs per hour derived from a variety of sources.

The section on "Employment and Training Services Received" explains that hours in on-the-job training and work experience were measured with SDA enrollment and tracking data, whereas hours in basic education, classroom training in occupational skills, job search assistance, and other services were measured with First Follow-up Survey data. For services whose hours were measured with First Follow-up Survey data, our source for the cost per hour varied with the type of program, as discussed below.

For high schools, we used the costs per hour derived from Census data as described in Appendix A, for youth respondents. For adult respondents, we adjusted these costs per hour downward using a weighting method documented in Webb, McCarthy, and Thomas (1988). This work discusses the differentiation of educational funding among different education programs and grade levels and introduces a comprehensive weighting model to convert per pupil expenditures into funding requirements for various educational programs.

For GED preparation, adult basic education, special literacy programs, or English as a Second Language, we used the same costs per hour as for adults in high schools. For colleges and vocational schools, we followed the procedure depicted in Exhibit B.3. If the follow-up survey respondent named a school whose costs were available in the published college expenditure data described in Appendix A, we used the cost per hour derived from the published data. If the school responded to the telephone survey of vocational institutions (see Appendix A) and was not a public school, we used the cost per hour derived from the tuition survey. (For public schools, we did not consider tuition a good proxy for the full resource cost.) For all other schools, we used a site-specific weighted average cost per hour of private schools responding to the tuition survey, where the weight on each school was proportional to the number of First Follow-up Survey respondents naming the school.

For job search assistance or Job Club, we used the estimated cost per day of JTPA job search assistance (discussed in next paragraph). Days in attendance were inferred from spell start and stop dates. For military training, employer training, union or labor/management association apprenticeships, or "on-the-job training" (for respondents not enrolled in JTPA on-the-job training), we used the site-specific weighted average cost per hour of private schools responding to the tuition survey. For programs classified by respondents as "other," if

Exhibit B.3 PROCESS FOR IMPUTING COST DATA FOR 2- AND 4-YEAR
COLLEGES AND VOCATIONAL/TECHNICAL INSTITUTES

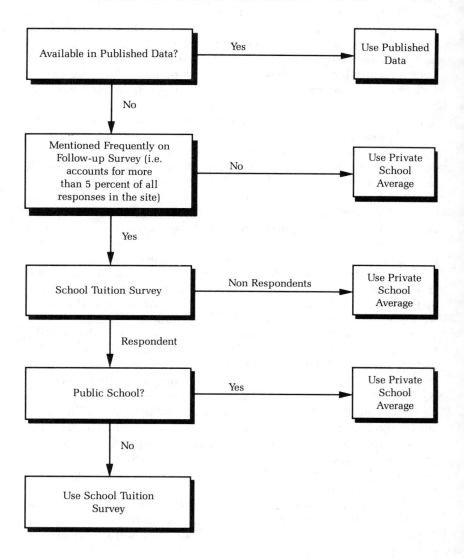

the institution named was a college listed in the published expenditure data or a private school that responded to the tuition survey, we used the cost per hour from that source. Otherwise, we used the site-specific weighted average cost per hour of private schools responding to the tuition survey.

As explained in Appendix A, we collected program year 1988 SDA expenditure and enrollment data for both the experimental sample and all program year 1988 enrollees in the study sites.[18] We used the program year 1988 data to calculate site-specific costs per day, for adult and youth enrollees separately, on-the-job training (OJT); job search assistance (JSA); and work experience. We calculated these costs per day by dividing program year 1988 expenditures in each category by the total number of person-days enrolled in that category in program year 1988. The cost per day for OJT did not include wage subsidies, which were analyzed separately.

Finally, to calculate the cost to society of employment and training services received by each sample member, we multiplied hours for each spell by cost per hour (or days by cost per day) and summed across spells.

OJT WAGE SUBSIDY

We constructed site-specific estimates of the average OJT wage subsidy per day, for adult and youth enrollees separately, by dividing program year 1988 expenditures on OJT wage subsidies by the total number of person-days enrolled in OJT in program year 1988.

To calculate the OJT wage subsidy for each sample member enrolled in OJT, we multiplied days enrolled in OJT by the estimated subsidy per day.

Measuring Incremental Cost per Enrollee

To estimate the incremental training cost or OJT wage subsidy per enrollee, we divided the treatment-control difference in means by the difference between the treatment and control group enrollment rates.

Notes

1. Among the 2,733 female youth respondents to the First Follow-up Survey, only 153 answered yes; among the 119 female youths who responded to the Second Follow-up but not the First, only 12 answered yes.

2. A comparison for the first four quarters after random assignment is given in detail in Bloom et al. (1993, Appendix E).

3. The sample for this comparison consisted of person-quarters for which each data source showed exactly one job.

4. Direct information on overtime earnings for the U.S. work force is not available. Using Current Establishment Survey data, the U.S. Department of Labor, Bureau of Labor Statistics (1991) estimated that production workers in manufacturing worked an average of 41 hours per week, including 3.8 overtime hours per week, in 1989. (Overtime hours were defined as hours for which an overtime premium was paid.) We would expect a sample of disadvantaged persons to work less overtime than the typical manufacturing worker.

5. The factor 1.5, or "time and a half," is close to the mode of the distribution of overtime hourly earnings divided by regular hourly earnings in the survey data. It also represents the most widely used method for setting overtime pay.

6. The derivation of this factor is explained in Appendix B of Orr et al. (1994).

7. The details of the imputation procedure are given in Appendix B of Orr et al. (1994).

8. Male youth arrestees were the only target group for which the treatment and control groups showed appreciably different ratios (1.72 and 2.11, respectively).

9. The equivalent procedure we used in computation was to take the mean of the dependent variable and subtract the product of the estimated impact and the mean value of the treatment dummy.

10. The conflict between the impact estimates from survey and UI data is not an artifact of this difference in estimation procedures. Bloom et al. (1993:354) presented estimates of the impact per assignee on the earnings of male youth arrestees during the first four follow-up quarters. The estimates from survey and UI data were derived using exactly the same sample and estimation method (difference in means), but the survey data gave a negative, statistically significant impact estimate of $-$1,777, whereas the UI data gave an insignificant impact estimate of $89.

11. This adjustment has been proposed independently by other researchers in the medical and social sciences. See, for example, Sommer and Zeger (1991), Dubin and Rivers (1993), and Angrist, Imbens, and Rubin (1993). When there are no covariates, the adjustment is equivalent to using assignment to the treatment group as an instrument for enrollment.

12. The informal argument given here is similar to the more precise identification result of Imbens and Angrist (1994).

13. As a check on this procedure, we used the delta method (e.g., Efron and Tibshirani, 1993:313–15), which is based on a first-order Taylor approximation, to estimate the standard error of the estimated impact per enrollee on the 30-month earnings of each target group. The delta method takes into account the variability of the enrollment rates. For each target group, the delta method standard error fell within one dollar of the standard error reported in chapter 4. Similar results were obtained by Heckman, Smith, and Taber (1994).

14. Overtime hours were deflated using the same factors applied to overtime earnings. Hours in months 16–18 and months 28–30 were sometimes imputed from values in earlier months.

15. On the First Follow-up Survey, only respondents who reported attending school or training programs for one week or more were asked whether they had a high school diploma or GED, and they were not asked when they had received the credential. In Bloom et al. (1993), attainment of a high school credential during the follow-up period was inferred by comparing baseline reports of educational attainment with responses

to this question on the First Follow-up Survey, assuming that those who did not report attending school or training had not received a high school credential during the follow-up period.

16. The White (1980) estimator is closely related to the jackknife. See, for example, Efron (1982: 19).

17. The estimation procedures are specified in detail in Appendix B of Orr et al. (1994).

18. In Decatur, where most of the experimental sample was randomly assigned during program year 1987, we used program year 1987 data.

REFERENCES

Angrist, Joshua, D. 1990. "Lifetime Earnings and the Vietnam Era Draft Lottery: Evidence from Social Security Administrative Records." *American Economic Review* 8(3): 313–336.

Angrist, Joshua D., Guido W. Imbens, and Donald B. Rubin. 1993. "Identification of Causal Effects Using Instrumental Variables." Cambridge, Mass.: Harvard University, Department of Economics, June. Photocopy. (Forthcoming in *Journal of the American Statistical Association*.)

Ashenfelter, Orley. 1978. "Estimating the Effect of Training Programs on Earnings." *Review of Economics and Statistics* 61 (February): 47–57.

Ashenfelter, Orley, and David Card. 1985. "Using the Longitudinal Structure of Earnings to Estimate the Effect of Training Programs." *Review of Economics and Statistics* 67 (November): 648–60.

Baj, John, Charles E. Trott, and David W. Stevens. 1991. *A Feasibility Study of the Use of Unemployment Insurance Wage-Record Data as an Evaluation Tool for JTPA: Report on Project's Phase I Activities*. Washington, D.C.: National Commission for Employment Policy, January.

Barnow, Burt S. 1987. "The Impact of CETA Programs on Earnings: A Review of the Literature." *Journal of Human Resources* 22 (Spring): 157–93.

Bassi, Laurie J. 1983. "The Effect of CETA on the Postprogram Earnings of Participants." *Journal of Human Resources* 18 (Fall): 539–56.

Bell, Stephen H., and Larry L. Orr. 1994. "Is Subsidized Employment Cost-Effective for Welfare Recipients? Experimental Evidence from Seven State Demonstrations," *Journal of Human Resources* 29(1): 42–61.

Bell, Stephen H., Glen G. Cain, Larry L. Orr, and John Blomquist. 1995. *Measuring Employment and Training Program Impacts with Data on Program Applicants*. Kalamazoo, Mich.: W.E. Upjohn Institute for Employment Research.

Betsey, Charles L., Robinson G. Hollister, and Mary R. Papageorgiou. 1985. *Youth Employment and Training Programs: The YEDPA Years*. Committee on Youth Employment Programs, Commission on Behavioral and Social Sciences and Education, National Research Council. Washington, D.C.: National Academy Press.

Bloom, Howard S. 1984a. "Accounting for No-Shows in Experimental Evaluation Designs." *Evaluation Review* 8 (April): 225–46.

————— 1984b. "Estimating the Effect of Job Training Programs, Using Longitudinal Data: Ashenfelter's Findings Reconsidered," *Journal of Human Resources* 19 (Fall): 544–56.

—————. 1990. *Back to Work: Testing Reemployment Services for Displaced Workers.* Kalamazoo, Mich.: W.E. Upjohn Institute for Employment Research.

—————. 1991. *The National JTPA Study: Baseline Characteristics of the Experimental Sample.* Bethesda, Md.: Abt Associates, September.

Bloom, Howard S., and Maureen S. McLaughlin. 1982. "CETA Training Programs—Do They Work for Adults?" Joint Report. Washington, D.C.: U.S. Congressional Budget Office and National Commission for Employment Policy.

Bloom, Howard S., Larry L. Orr, George Cave, Stephen H. Bell, and Fred Doolittle. 1993. *The National JTPA Study: Title II-A Impacts on Earnings and Employment at 18 Months.* Bethesda, Md.: Abt Associates, January.

Bloom, Howard S., Larry L. Orr, Fred Doolittle, V. Joseph Hotz, and Burt Barnow. 1990. *Design of the National JTPA Study.* New York and Bethesda, Md.: Manpower Demonstration Research Corporation and Abt Associates.

Bloom, Howard S., Larry L. Orr, George Cave, Stephen H. Bell, Fred Doolittle, and Winston Lin. 1994. *Overview: Impacts, Benefits, and Costs of Title II-A.* Bethesda, Md.: Abt Associates.

Burghardt, J., A. Rangarajan, A. Gordon, and J. Kisker. 1992. *Evaluation of the Minority Female Single Parent Demonstration.* New York: Rockefeller Foundation.

Burtless, Gary, and Larry L. Orr. 1986. "Are Classical Experiments Needed for Manpower Policy?" *Journal of Human Resources* 21 (Fall): 606–39.

Cave, George. 1988. "Noncompliance Bias in Evaluation Research: Assignment, Participation, and Impacts." New York: Manpower Demonstration Research Corporation.

Cave, George, and Fred Doolittle. 1991. *Assessing JOBSTART: Interim Impacts of a Program for School Dropouts.* New York: Manpower Demonstration Research Corporation.

Cave, George, Hans Bos, Fred Doolittle, and Cyril Toussaint. 1993. *JOBSTART: Final Report on a Program for Dropouts.* New York: Manpower Demonstration Research Corporation.

Cooley, Thomas F., Timothy W. McGuire, and Edward C. Prescott. 1979. "Earnings and Employment Dynamics of Manpower Trainees: An Exploratory Econometric Analysis." *Evaluating Manpower Training Programs,* ed. Farrell E. Bloch. Greenwich, Conn.: JAI Press.

Corson, Walter, Sharon K. Long, and Rebecca A. Maynard. 1985. *An Impact Evaluation of the Buffalo Dislocated Worker Demonstration Program.* Princeton, N.J.: Mathematica Policy Research.

Corson, Walter, Paul T. Decker, Shari M. Dunstan, and Anne R. Gordon. 1989. *The New Jersey Unemployment Insurance Reemployment Demonstration Project: Final Evaluation Report.* Princeton, N.J.: Mathematica Policy Research.

Couch, Kenneth A. 1992a. "Long-Term Effects of the National Supported Work Experiment, and Parametric and Nonparametric Tests of Model Specification and the Estimation of Treatment Effects." Unpublished Ph.D. dissertation, University of Wisconsin-Madison.

————. 1992b. "New Evidence on the Long-Term Effects of Employment Training Programs." *Journal of Labor Economics* 10(4): 380–88.

Dickinson, Katherine P., Terry R. Johnson, and Richard W. West. 1984. *Analysis of the Impact of CETA Programs on Participants' Earnings.* Menlo Park, Calif.: SRI International.

Doolittle, Fred. 1993. *Summary of the Design and Implementation of the National JTPA Study.* New York and Bethesda, Md.: Manpower Demonstration Research Corporation and Abt Associates, January.

Doolittle, Fred, and Linda Traeger. 1990. *Implementing the National JTPA Study.* New York: Manpower Demonstration Research Corporation, April.

Dubin, Jeffrey, and Douglas Rivers. 1993. "Experimental Estimates of the Impact of Wage Subsidies." *Journal of Econometrics* 56: 219–242.

Efron, Bradley. 1982. *The Jackknife, the Bootstrap, and Other Resampling Plans.* Philadelphia: Society for Industrial and Applied Mathematics.

Efron, Bradley, and Robert J. Tibshirani. 1993. *An Introduction to the Bootstrap.* New York: Chapman and Hall.

Enns, John H., Stephen H. Bell, and Kathleen L. Flanagan. 1987. *AFDC Homemaker–Home Health Aide Demonstrations: Trainee Employment and Earnings.* Bethesda, Md.: Abt Associates.

Fischer, Paul B. 1991. *Is Housing Mobility an Effective Anti-Poverty Strategy? An Examination of the Cincinnati Experience.* Cincinnati, Ohio: Stephen H. Wilder Foundation.

Fraker, Thomas M., and Rebecca A. Maynard. 1984. "An Assessment of Alternative Comparison Group Methodologies for Evaluating Employment and Training Programs." Princeton, N.J.: Mathematica Policy Research.

————. 1987. "The Adequacy of Comparison Group Designs for Evaluations of Employment-Related Programs." *Journal of Human Resources* 22 (Spring): 194–227.

Goldman, Barbara S. 1981. *Impacts of the Immediate Job Search Assistance Experiment.* New York: Manpower Demonstration Research Corporation.

Gueron, Judith M., and Edward Pauly. 1991. *From Welfare to Work.* New York: Russell Sage Foundation.

Hahn, Andrew. 1994. *Evaluation of the Quantum Opportunities Program*

(QOP): Did the Program Work? Waltham, Mass.: Brandeis University Center for Human Resources. June.

Hamilton, Gayle, and Daniel Friedlander. 1989. *Final Report on the Saturation Work Initiative Model in San Diego.* New York: Manpower Demonstration Research Corporation.

Haynes, R. Brian, and Renato Dantes. 1987. "Patient Compliance and the Conduct and Interpretation of Therapeutic Trials." *Controlled Clinical Trials* 8 (1, March): 12–19.

Hayward, Becky, and G. Tallmadge. 1993. *Evaluation of Dropout Prevention and Reentry Projects in Vocational Education.* Draft Final Report. Research Triangle Institute, Research Triangle Park, N.C. Photocopy.

Heckman, James, Jeffrey Smith, and Christopher Taber. 1994. "Accounting for Dropouts in Evaluations of Social Experiments." *NBER Working Paper* No. 166. Cambridge, Mass., September.

Holland, Paul W. 1986. "Statistics and Causal Inference." *Journal of the American Statistical Association* 81: 945–60.

Imbens, Guido W., and Joshua D. Angrist. 1994. "Identification and Estimation of Local Average Treatment Effects." *Econometrica* 62 (March): 467–75.

Kemper, Peter, David A. Long, and Craig Thornton. 1981. *The Supported Work Evaluation: Final Benefit-Cost Analysis.* New York: Manpower Demonstration Research Corporation.

Kiefer, Nicholas M. 1979. "Population Heterogeneity and Inference from Panel Data on the Effects of Vocational Education." *American Economic Review* 76 (September): 604–20.

Konijn, H. S. 1983. "Estimation of the Mean or Total When Measurement Protocols of Different Accuracy Are Available." In *A Festschrift for Erich L. Lehmann,* ed. Peter J. Bickel, Kjell A. Doksum, and J. L. Hodges, Jr. Belmont, Calif.: Wadsworth International Group, pp. 286–304.

LaLonde, Robert J. 1986. "Evaluating the Econometric Evaluations of Training Programs with Experimental Data." *American Economic Review* 76 (September): 604–20.

Lerman, Robert, and Hillard Pouncy. 1990. "The Compelling Case for Youth Apprenticeships," *The Public Interest* 101 (Fall): 62–77.

Mallar, C., S. Kerachsky, C. Thornton, M. Donihue, C. Jones, D. Long, E. Noggoh, and J. Schore. 1980. *Evaluation of the Economic Impact of the Job Corps Program. Second Follow-up Report.* Washington, D.C.: U.S. Department of Labor.

Manpower Demonstration Research Corporation, Board of Directors. 1980. *Summary and Findings of the National Supported Work Demonstration.* Cambridge, Mass.: Ballinger.

Olson, L., L. Berg, and A. Conrad. 1990. *High Job Turnover among the Urban Poor: The Project Match Experience.* Center for Urban Affairs and Policy Research, Northwestern University. Photocopy.

Orr, Larry L., Howard S. Bloom, Stephen H. Bell, Winston Lin, George Cave, and Fred Doolittle. 1994. *The National JTPA Study: Impacts, Benefits, and Costs of Title II-A.* Bethesda, Md.: Abt Associates.

Perry, Charles R., Bernard E. Anderson, Richard L. Rowan, and Herbert R. Northrup. 1975. *The Impact of Government Manpower Programs: In General, and on Minorities and Women.* Manpower and Human Resource Studies, no. 4. Philadelphia: Industrial Research Unit, Wharton School, University of Pennsylvania.

"Proposed Food Stamp Regs Released." 1991. *Employment and Training Reporter.* September 18, p. 27.

Research Associates of Washington. n.d. *Higher Education Revenues and Expenditures: Institutional Data, 1988–89 and 1987–88,* 2d ed. Washington, D.C.: Research Associates of Washington.

Rosenbaum, James E. 1991. *Black Pioneers—Do Their Moves to Suburbs Increase Economic Opportunities for Mothers and Children?* Evanston, Ill.: Center for Urban Affairs and Policy Research, Northwestern University.

Rosenbaum, J.E., D. Stern, S.F. Hamilton, S.E. Berryman, and R. Kazis. *Youth Apprenticeship in America: Guidelines for Building an Effective System.* Washington, D.C.: W.T. Grant Foundation Commission on Youth and America's Future.

Rubin, Donald B. 1974. "Estimating Causal Effects of Treatments in Randomized and Nonrandomized Studies." *Journal of Educational Psychology* 66: 688–701.

———. 1980. "Discussion of 'Randomization Analysis of Experimental Data: The Fisher Randomization Test,' by D. Basu." *Journal of the American Statistical Association* 75: 591–93.

Scheffé, Henry. 1959. *The Analysis of Variance.* New York: John Wiley & Sons.

Sommer, Alfred, and Scott L. Zeger. 1991. "On Estimating Efficacy from Clinical Trials." *Statistics in Medicine* 10: 45–52.

Stromsdorfer, E., H. Bloom, R. Boruch, M. Borus, J. Gueron, A. Gustman, P. Rossi, F. Scheuren, M. Smith, and F. Stafford. 1985. *Recommendations of the Job Training Longitudinal Survey Research Advisory Panel.* Washington, D.C.: Employment and Training Administration, U.S. Department of Labor.

U.S. Bureau of the Census. 1991. *Public Education Finances: 1988–1989.* Washington, D.C.: Author, April.

U.S. Department of Labor, Bureau of Labor Statistics. 1991. *Employment, Hours, and Earnings, United States, 1909–1990:* Vol. 1 (Bulletin 2370). Washington, D.C.: Author.

———. 1993. *Employment Cost Indexes and Levels, 1975–93.* Bulletin 2434. Washington, D.C.: Author.

U.S. General Accounting Office. 1989. *The Job Training Partnership Act: Services and Outcomes for Participants with Differing Needs.* GAO/HRD-89-52. Gaithersburg, Md.: U.S. General Accounting Office.

————. 1990. *The Job Training Partnership Act: Youth Participant Characteristics, Services, and Outcomes.* GAO/HRD-90-46BR. Gaithersburg, Md.: U.S. General Accounting Office.

————. 1991. *The Job Training Partnership Act: Racial and Gender Disparities in Services.* GAO/HRD-91-148. Gaithersburg, Md.: U.S. General Accounting Office.

————. 1993. *Transition from School to Work: States are Developing New Strategies to Prepare Students for Jobs.* Washington, D.C.: U.S. General Accounting Office, September.

U.S. House. Committee on Ways and Means. 1992. *Overview of Entitlement Programs: 1992 Green Book.* Washington, D.C.: U.S. Government Printing Office.

Wald, Abraham. 1940. "The Fitting of Straight Lines if Both Variables Are Subject to Error." *Annals of Mathematical Statistics* 11 (September): 284–300.

Webb, L. Dean, Martha M. McCarthy, and Stephen B. Thomas. 1988. *Financing Elementary and Secondary Education.* Columbus, Ohio: Charles E. Merrill.

Westat, Inc. 1981. *Continuous Longitudinal Manpower Survey Net Impact Report No. 1: Impact on 1977 Earnings of New FY 1976 CETA Enrollees in Selected Program Activities.* Rockville, Md.: Westat.

————. 1984a. *Continuous Longitudinal Manpower Survey: Summary of Net Impact Results.* Rockville, Md.: Westat.

————. 1984b. *Job Training Longitudinal Survey: Summary Description of JTLS Study Design.* Rockville, Md.: Westat.

White, Halbert. 1980. "A Heteroskedasticity-Consistent Covariance Matrix Estimator and a Direct Test for Heteroskedasticity." *Econometrica* 48 (May): 817–38.

LIST OF EXHIBITS

Chapter Five

ABOUT THE AUTHORS

Stephen H. Bell is a senior economist and project director at Abt Associates. His research focuses on econometric methods for public policy evaluation, including measurement of program impacts using classical experiments and nonexperimental methods. His most recent publications include "Is Subsidized Employment Cost Effective for Welfare Recipients?"; in the Winter 1994 *Journal of Human Resources*, "Design of the Project NetWork Return-to-Work Experiment for Persons with Disabilities" in the Summer 1994 *Social Security Bulletin*, and *Program Applicants as a Comparison Group in Evaluating Training Programs*, published by the Upjohn Institute Press in 1995.

Howard S. Bloom is professor of public administration at the Robert F. Wagner Graduate School of Public Service, New York University and was co-principal investigator of the National JTPA Study. Professor Bloom is an expert on evaluation research methodology and employment and training policy. He has written several books and numerous articles on program evaluation, including most recently, *Back to Work: Testing Reemployment Services for Displaced Workers* (1990, W.E. Upjohn Institute for Employment Research, Kalamazoo, MI).

George Cave is a senior research associate at the Manpower Demonstration Research Corporation (MDRC). A specialist in labor economics and econometrics, he has been principal investigator or co-principal investigator for a number of random assignment evaluations of programs for out-of-school and in-school youth, including JOBSTART, Career Beginnings, and Career Academies. In addition, Dr. Cave has been principal investigator or co-principal investigator for random-assignment studies of welfare-to-work programs in Maine, New Jersey, and Virginia. His current projects include random-assignment evaluations of New Chance, a program for teen mothers, and Parents' Fair Share, a program for noncustodial fathers of children receiving AFDC.

Before joining MDRC, Dr. Cave was Assistant Professor of Economics and Afro-American Studies at Princeton University.

Fred Doolittle is assistant director of research at MDRC in New York City. He served as project director for the implementation of the National JTPA Study. Dr. Doolittle currently directs MDRC's research on the New Hope project in Milwaukee, the Center for Employment and Training replication sites, and the Parents' Fair Share Demonstration. He is the author of "Second Chance Programs for Youth" in *Changing Populations/Changing Schools* (1995) and numerous MDRC reports and articles. He formerly was a member of the faculty at Harvard and Princeton.

Winston Lin is research associate, Manpower Demonstration Research Corporation, and former senior analyst, Abt Associates. He specializes in econometric and statistical analysis of experimental data.

Larry L. Orr is a senior economist and vice president of Abt Associates. His research interests include the analysis of public policy issues using experimental methods and the evaluation of employment and training programs; he has participated in the design of more than 20 randomized field experiments. Dr. Orr was project director for design, data collection, and analysis of the National JTPA Study. He serves on the editorial board of the journal *Evaluation and Program Planning* and from 1991–93 was a member of the National Academy of Science *Committee on Postsecondary Education and Training.* Dr. Orr is author of *Income, Employment, and Urban Residential Location,* published in the U.S. in 1975 by Academic Press and in Japan in 1979 by Keiichi Tanaka, and coauthor of *Program Applicants as a Comparison Group in Evaluating Training Programs,* published in 1995 by the W. E. Upjohn Institute. Prior to joining Abt, he directed the Office of Technical Analysis, U.S. Department of Labor, and the Office of Income Security Policy Research, U.S. Department of Health, Education, and Welfare.